Prophets With Honour
A Documentary History of Lekhotla la Bafo

Prophets With Honour

A Documentary History of Lekhotla la Bafo

Robert Edgar

Ravan Press Johannesburg

Published by Ravan Press (Pty) Ltd
P O Box 31134, Braamfontein
South Africa 2017

© Robert Edgar

Cover design: Jeff Lok
Back cover: photograph of Josiel Lefela
           shortly before his death, taken
           by Sheridan Johns
Typeset by: Opus 61

ISBN 0 86975 312 6

Printed by National Book Printers, Goodwood, Cape

To Edwin Mofutsanyana and
Edgar Motuba, men of courage

Table of Contents

Acknowledgements

While collecting the material for this volume, I have been assisted in many different ways by numerous individuals, and I would like to acknowledge my debt to them: Burns Machobane, Pule Phoofolo, Mosebi Damane and David Ambrose of the National University of Lesotho, for sharing their insights into Lesotho history and facilitating my research at every stage; J.M. Frantsi, for carrying out several key interviews after I had returned to the United States; Francina Moloi and Edward Fobo, for remaining loyal friends over many years; Bob Cummings and my colleagues in the African Studies and Research Program at Howard University, for their constant encouragement and support; my parents, Mr and Mrs Russell Edgar, for having patience with my wanderings; and David Coplan, Chris DeBroglio, Chris Goldman, Molebo Lefela, Sehleke Lefela, Maryinez Lyons, Nana Mahomo, Samuel Mohono, Ntsukunyane Mphanya, Darlene Petkovich, Sam Ramsamy, Chris and Pam Saunders, Ganie Surtie, B.K. Taoana and Brian Willan, for all their help along the way.

This study was partly funded by a grant from the office of the Vice President for Academic Affairs at Howard University.

Introduction

One of the most intriguing movements to have emerged during the colonial period was the Basotho political association, Lekhotla la Bafo (Council of Commoners). Founded after World War I, the group developed a unique political platform, blending a passionate defence of Basotho chieftainship and culture with a vigorous anti-colonial and Pan-African stance. For over four decades, they played a significant role in rallying Basotho opposition to colonial rule and in laying the foundations for modern political parties in Lesotho. What makes Lekhotla la Bafo so distinctive is not only the originality of its ideas, but that so many of its documents — letters, speeches, petitions, and articles — have been preserved. Most rural protest movements leave few historical traces. This collection of Lekhotla la Bafo's works is an exception, and therein lies a measure of its importance.[1]

Before turning to an examination of Lekhotla la Bafo, some comments should be made about the colonial environment in which the movement took shape. The British government reluctantly agreed to assume protection over Basutoland in 1868, but made it clear that it wanted little to do with the new colony by handing over administrative responsibility to the Cape Colony in 1871. Cape rule proved disastrous, however, as attempts to replace Basotho chiefs with magistrates and to disarm the Basotho brought about the *Ntoa oa Lithunya* (Gun War) in 1880-81, in which Basotho armies successfully fended off Cape colonial forces. The British had to face up to the ineptitude of Cape officials and resume formal administration in 1884, but they still defined their role in minimal terms, the governor's agent stating in 1884 that 'nothing more was to be attempted at first than the protection of life and property and the maintenance of law and order on the Border'.[2] Officials were to economize on administrative expenditures and to interfere as little as possible in the domestic affairs of the Basotho. This meant reversing the Cape policy of subverting chieftainship and, instead, giving free rein to the chiefs in maintaining their authority over commoners.

Colonial officials were clear about their role in Basutoland — as one put it, ' . . .the administration is concerned in upholding the existing hierarchy' — and they based their policy on the assumption that the chiefs would remain a force for conservatism and stability.[3] They were expected to be agents of social and economic control and, with few exceptions, they met British aims. One consequence of this relationship was that the checks Basotho commoners traditionally had on their chiefs and the redistributive mechanisms that existed in the pre-colonial period gradually dissolved. As Alan Pim observed in the 1930s, 'control from below is much less effective', and in the absence of any restraining British pressure many chiefs took advantage of the situation to parcel out land inequitably and exact fines to exploit commoners.[4] They used the authority of their courts to levy excessive fines in stock theft cases; they allocated the best and largest amounts of land for themselves; and they called out labour to work without compensation on *lira* lands. The effect of their abuses was to drive some commoners off the land and to force others on to the South African labour market.[5]

To draw chiefs into the colonial hierarchy the British established a consultative body, the Basutoland National Council. It began meeting in 1903, though only after several decades of wrangling between British officials and senior Basotho chiefs.[6] When the Cape government had taken over administration of Basutoland in 1871, the governor's agent, Colonel C.D. Griffith, had instituted a National *Pitso* in 1875 for periodically consulting with chiefs. This *pitso* had only a nominal resemblance to traditional *pitso*s at which commoners could criticize chiefs and have a genuine exchange of views. In contrast, the colonial *pitso* informed, but did not consult the Basotho about colonial policies.

In 1883, Cape officials broached the idea of replacing the National *Pitso* with a national council of chiefs and headmen, but their proposal was rejected out of hand because the Basotho questioned the motives of the Cape so soon after the Gun War. After taking over administration the following year, the British periodically floated the idea but it foundered repeatedly because neither senior chiefs nor the Paramount Chief wanted to see their privileges undermined by other contending factions. Finally, after the Anglo-Boer War, the British were able to win over Lerotholi who was anxious to hand over a stable paramountcy to his successor, and the council began meeting. In 1910, it received statutory recognition because the British needed to salve Basotho opinion, inflamed after a clause in the South Africa Act held out the prospect that the High Commission territories might one day be handed over to the Union of South Africa.

From its inception the National Council had limited authority. Proclamation 7 of 1910 stated that its purpose was 'to discuss the domestic affairs of the territory, including appropriation of money paid in taxes; to ventilate opinions and grievances, to deliberate on tribal disputes, and to confer with the administration on tribal affairs'. Its members included the Resident Commissioner, who appointed five members, and the Paramount Chief, who selected the other ninety-four chiefs and headmen. A few commoners made their way in by representing chiefs or through the Resident Commissioner's appointments, but the council was designed to do little more than bolster chiefly interests, a point that one Resident Commissioner, J.C. Sturrock, candidly admitted: 'In plain point of fact it is a body swayed by a large majority who have at bottom only one main object in view, namely the upholding of what they call their own rights and positions.'[7]

Although Lerotholi 'expressed the hope that the Council would become a law-making body', the British carefully entrenched its advisory role. Its debates covered a wide range of domestic issues and occasionally addressed controversial ones, but it must be kept in mind that in essence the council was a 'talkshop' which brought chiefs together.

British officials often portrayed themselves as disinterested caretakers (and thus at a later stage of the colonial period blamed the chiefs for Basutoland's decline), but an underlying aspect of their rule was facilitating Lesotho's continuing transformation into a labour reserve for the white-dominated South African economy.[8] What the Basotho may have gained as a result of British protection was more than offset by their being sacrificed on the altar of South Africa's labour needs. The British paid little attention to developing Lesotho until late in the colonial period, an approach that subsidized the South African economy. As Basutoland's economy declined, her people were forced to seek work outside her borders but at depressed wage levels. This relationship was not without its benefits for the British economy, a fact attested to by a Basutoland Resident Commissioner, Godfrey Lagden:

> Though for its size and population Basutoland produces a comparatively enormous amount of grain, it has an industry of great economic value to South Africa, viz., the output of native labour. It supplies the sinews of agriculture in the Orange Free State, to a large extent it keeps going railway works, coal mining, the diamond mines at Jagersfontein and Kimberley, the gold mines of the Transvaal and furnishes, in addition, a large amount of domestic services in the surrounding territories . . . . To [those] who urge higher education of the natives, it may be pointed out that to educate them above labour would be a mistake. Primarily the native labour industry supplies a dominion want and secondarily it tends to fertilise native territories with cash which is at one diffused for English goods.[9]

Immediately after the British established control, Lesotho, despite its reduced borders, had gone through a period of relative prosperity largely stimulated by the demand for grain at the Kimberley diamond mines. By the final decades of the nineteenth century grain production had been undercut by a variety of factors — the disruption of the Gun War, natural disasters, the opening of a railway from the Cape to Kimberley and the importation of cheaper foreign grains, and restrictions imposed by the Orange Free State and Transvaal on Basotho exports — and many of the features of a labour reserve economy had begun to crystallize. Soil exhaustion and erosion, overstocking and overgrazing, overpopulation, declining agricultural production, and increasing migration of labourers became the order of the day.

Before the turn of the century, Lesotho brought in more from export earnings than from the remittances of migrant workers, who still had a measure of control over when and how long they would work in South Africa. This changed dramatically as exports dropped off and more and more Basotho were forced to leave the country for longer periods. In 1911, a census recorded that nearly 25 000 men and women were annually seeking employment in South Africa; by 1936, 101 000 were going out. This was an increase from 5.8 per cent of the total *de jure* population to 15.3 per cent. Basotho agricultural production did not collapse overnight. In the best of years, farmers were able to export grain and wool, but a decline in the 1920s sounded the death knell. First, the price of wool plummeted from 10d per pound in 1928 to 2d per pound in 1932, dropping export earnings for wool from 700 000 to 120 000 pounds. Second, a severe drought in 1932-33 killed half the country's sheep and goats and stopped agricultural production in its tracks. It was in the midst of these increasing political and economic pressures that Lekhotla la Bafo came into being.

Any discussion of Lekhotla la Bafo has to begin with the two brothers from Mapoteng, Josiel and Maphutseng Lefela, who were its guiding spirits for most of its existence. They came of a commoner Bataung family from the Quthing area who moved to Thaba Bosiu during the Mfecane. Their grandfather, Lefela, became an adviser to Moshoeshoe's younger brother, Makhabane, who died in battle against the Thembu in 1835. When Makhabane's son, Lesaoana, moved to Mokunutlung in 1846, Lefela and his family went with him. Lefela's son, Isaac Molebo, became adviser to a headman and accumulated a considerable amount of land and cattle. He converted to Christianity and his children, including his third and sixth born sons, Josiel and Maphutseng, were baptized Christians.[10]

As founder and the most prominent leader of Lekhotla la Bafo,

Josiel is the better known of the two. Born around 1885, he appears to have picked up at least a Standard III education before leaving home to work for a time in the South African mines and as a policeman in Bechuanaland.[11] Returning to Lesotho, he earned a living over the years in a variety of occupations: running an eating house and a butchery in Mapoteng, hawking goods in the mountains, practising as an *ngaka* (a traditional doctor),[12] organizing circumcision schools,[13] and farming. Despite being a junior son, he was able to inherit a significant portion of his father's wealth. Although Maphutseng remained in the shadow of his brother for most of his life, he played an equally critical role in Lekhotla la Bafo as a propagandist. He was born around 1895 and was probably the best educated of Lekhotla la Bafo's members since he had gone as high as Form C at Lovedale Institution in the Eastern Cape in 1918 – 1919 and taught in Catholic schools before devoting himself to his brother's association. A well-read man, he supplied much of the intellectual firepower for the group and, as general secretary, was responsible for much of the association's correspondence, which flowed out of Mapoteng in a steady stream.[14]

Josiel's entry into national politics resulted from his service as secretary and adviser to his local chief, Peete. He was well versed in traditional law and chiefs from around Mapoteng often called on him for advice in their courts and to observe cases in the District Commissioner's court at Teyateyaneng. Chief Peete thought so highly of him that in 1916 he delegated him to take his seat on the National Council.[15]

His first few years in the council were not marked by controversy, although he did gain notice when, in September 1916, he proposed founding a company, the 'Basutoland Association to oversee the abroad Basuto invalids', for collecting funds to assist indigent and injured Basuto workers in South Africa with return train fares and debts up to £3.[16] Since he intended charging subscribers a commission for his services, he requested government supervision, but colonial officials were not anxious to have their names associated with his undertaking for even then they deemed him ' . . . to be an agitator of inconsequent thought'.[17] After being put off by two Resident Commissioners, in 1918 he brought his scheme before the National Council, which gave its approval and, in February 1919, the colonial administration issued him a certificate to start his charity. He also asked for an official letter of introduction to labour agents inside and outside Lesotho to facilitate the collection of money. This the Resident Commissioner, E.F. Garraway, refused to provide since he did not want anyone thinking the administration was authorizing Lefela's venture.[18] No further mention is made of the work of his association, and it is presumed that it died out soon after Lekhotla la Bafo was formed.

It was after World War I that Lefela began publicly levelling criticisms at the National Council, a prelude to his founding of Lekhotla la Bafo.[19] He disapproved of the unrepresentative nature of the council, contending that it served the interests of the chiefs exclusively. He shared the growing disillusionment of many commoners that since the chiefs had become prisoners in their 'political dungeon', they had distanced themselves even further from their subjects and were abusing their privileges. He proposed breaking their stranglehold on the council by establishing a second chamber, the Lekhotla la Bafo (Council of Commoners), patterned after the British House of Commons, so that commoners could take their affairs and grievances directly to Maseru and Matsieng without going through the body he called the 'graveyard'. Addressing the National Council, he elaborated on his justification for a second house:

> I wish to explain the good that will be done by the Council of Commons. There are many complaints throughout the nation. There is no mouthpiece to voice the grievances of the people. If the Council of Commons be authorized anybody will be able to voice their complaints to it, and such complaints could be sent to the secretary of the Council of Commons. The reason why there are so many complaints is that we do not meet with our chiefs.[20]

His plea fell on deaf ears since all but a handful of council members were unsympathetic to his views. Support came from one of the few other commoners on the council, Ralehlatsa Ramaisa, who remarked,

> You should see, sons of Moshesh [the chiefs], that people are becoming your enemies, they only lack assistance to fight you . . . . Those people are with you only because their houses are in this country.[21]

A few chiefs gave credence to Lefela's statements. They saw their subjects turning against them and the British gradually reining in their powers. One prominent backer was Chief Motsoene, who had his own disputes with Paramount Chief Griffith Lerotholi and whom Lefela supported in his succession dispute with the sons of Jonathan Molapo. He charged that

In Leribe people cry to me and to Jonathan but nothing is done for them
. . . . I understand Josiel who does not want the Council of Commons (if
there were an alternative), he wishes the complaints of the common
people to be attended to. Sons of chiefs 'eat up' people's stock for trifling
reasons. Commoners are also God's people, why should they not forsake
the chiefs when we hate them? . . . There are no Basuto here but
Egyptians.[22]

Lefela's proposal went nowhere in the council, and on 27 September
1919 he convened a meeting at Mapoteng at which he and his supporters
agreed to found an association, Lekhotla la Bafo, to advance their
causes (Documents 1-4).[23] Chief Peete then recommended that they put
their case for a separate council directly to Paramount Chief Griffith,
who was then on a visit to England, and, in January 1920, they decided
to approach him.

Not surprisingly, Griffith was unequivocally opposed to their idea.
The Basotho nation, he claimed, was too weak to accommodate
another council. Moreover, he was not willing to deal with Lefela and
his colleagues because they were upstarts. As Lefela recounted it, 'He
[Griffith] said we were in too great a hurry and that young pack oxen
should not be used for conveying grain at times of famine.'[24] A backer
of Griffith added in a similar vein, 'today he [Lefela] brings us a child
before we have allowed him to marry'.[25]

Griffith had wanted to dismiss Lefela from the council soon after he
founded his association, but Garraway had resisted the notion since he
did not think the Paramount Chief had sufficient justification for doing
so and because he believed councillors could only be removed at the
request of their own chief. In any event, it was not necessary to make
Lefela a martyr in the eyes of his own people since he was convinced
that if he were given enough rope, ' . . . he would give us an opportunity
for removing him before long'.[26]

That opportunity came a short time later when Lefela contributed an
article, 'How we shall do away with black races', to a Sesotho
newspaper, *Naledi*, accusing Europeans of plotting genocide against
Africans by building separate dormitories in the urban areas for
isolating African women (Document 5)[27]. As long as he limited his
criticisms to the internal affairs of Lesotho, colonial officials had not
censored him, but when he began to 'set black against white' in his
articles, he overstepped the bounds of propriety and Garraway showed
no hesitation in expelling him from the council on 1 November 1920

(Documents 6-11)[28]. At the meeting where he informed Lefela he was booting him out, Garraway said he could forgive him for his 'exceedingly wicked and bad' behaviour if it were purely concerning an issue restricted to Lesotho, but he had to punish him for 'deliberately trying to stir up hatred between black and white and doing all you can to destroy peace which should exist between the races'.[29]

It was in the first decade after its founding that Lekhotla la Bafo fashioned the ideology and tactics of protest that it adhered to for the next half century. Its ideology centred around two interrelated themes: the defence of Basotho chieftainship and sovereignty from the machinations of British colonial officials and the promotion of self-help schemes designed to preserve Basotho political, economic and cultural institutions from being eroded by the colonial system (Documents 12-19).

An understanding of Lekhotla la Bafo's attitude towards chieftainship is vital since the association came into being as a result of two conflicts between chiefs and commoners. The first, as I have discussed, was over chiefs excluding commoners from meaningful participation in the National Council. The second was the exploitative practices of chiefs. In the case of the latter, the protests of commoners had escalated dramatically after World War I over the methods chiefs utilized to squeeze additional revenues from their subjects. For instance, one abuse that Lekhotla la Bafo and another commoner group, the Progressive Association, drew attention to was the levying of exorbitant fines in chiefly courts. Another was the arbitrary transfer of lands from widows — who were not generating taxes — to younger men.

However, the issue that most concerned Lekhotla la Bafo and other groups in the coming decades was the chiefs' misuse of labour on the *tsimo ea lira* (land of the enemy) (Document 20). As this practice evolved during the reigns of Moshoeshoe and Letsie, only the king had the power to call out his regiment for *matsema* work, which could be performed only in the gardens of his senior wife. The food grown on this land was used primarily for feeding the army and in emergencies, but it could also be earmarked for entertaining guests and travellers, helping the destitute, and supporting royal family members. Subsequently Lerotholi empowered senior chiefs to call the people out for *matsema* labour; under Griffith, more and more chiefs came to regard *matsema* labour as their right as well. Moreover, the produce that was grown was not distributed to the people but sold on the market for profit. Besides calling out *matsema* labour for ploughing, hoeing and reaping, chiefs also demanded the performance of a variety of other tasks: taking messages, gathering firewood, and building dams, court houses, and the houses of chiefs' sons. In many cases labourers were not paid or fed and some were mistreated and beaten. Those who did not work were subject to a fine of one goat.

Thus, for many commoners, *matsema* labour was akin to forced labour, as they spent more and more time working the fields of chiefs without reward. Lefela described the issue in a speech before the National Council.

> The lira lands and chieftainship go hand in hand. But the chiefs now do as they like with these lira lands. The lira lands are no longer national lands. They are only benefitting the chiefs. A person who will be bold enough to suggest that these matsema be abolished will be abolishing the chieftainship, and I suggest we should sit down and examine matters carefully. We should restore the chiefs to their positions, but they should feed us, and have only one lira land. We should remember that it is one kaffir corn land, one maize land, and the chiefs now use grain from these lira lands for their own requirements and are no longer feeding the people from the lira lands.[30]

Thus, as Lekhotla la Bafo saw it, commoners were caught in a double bind. On the one hand, the British demand for taxes forced them out on to the South African labour market; on the other hand, chiefs exacting fines and labour made it extremely difficult to eke out a livelihood from the land. Lefela used the analogy of a mouse and two cats to describe their dilemma.

> If we say this is a mouse which has cats eating it, one cat eating up the head and the other eating up its back sides, it is like the modern times being on the side of the government eating us up to try and finish us. And also the old times, which is the chieftainship, they are also eating us up, and they want to finish us. And when the mouse tries to run towards its head, then the cat eats up the head; and when it pushes back then the other cat eats up the back side of the mouse. Now this mouse is the nation and the two cats appear on either side of it. The mouse has affection for the chieftainship; it has affection for the government, but both these people eat the mouse up.[31]

The vehemence of Lekhotla la Bafo's attacks on chiefly abuse has led some to place too much emphasis on that aspect of the association's platform. While there is no question that Lekhotla la Bafo opposed the excesses of individual chiefs, it did not call for an end to the old order. If anything, it sought the opposite: to restore the institution of chieftainship to its precolonial stature. Thus it did not censure chieftainship, but used it as a rallying point for organizing resistance to British colonialism. However ill-conceived their actions were, chiefs still symbolized the nation's identity and sovereignty and had to be defended in spite of themselves. 'Even if our chiefs may be ineffective or inefficient,' Lefela argued, 'instead of removing them we should try to help them, by giving them advisers.'[32] His association's position was probably an acknowledgement of the chiefs' continued dominance over the lives of commoners through their power to allocate land, but it was also a recognition that, in the midst of social and economic disintegration, chiefs remained potent symbols of cultural and national identity around which resistance could be organized. Accordingly, they had to be shielded from, not driven into the arms of the British. 'Our chieftainship is under Great Britain, but we common people are under our chieftainship. If we no longer have our chiefs then our country will be gone.'[33]

Lekhotla la Bafo's answer to the ills afflicting chieftainship was not to abolish it, but to have it conform to the precolonial ideal of chieftainship, when the maxim 'a chief is a chief by the people' — implying chiefs ruled only through the consent of the people — was still respected and honoured. They perceived the period before British rule as a golden age when the chiefs served their people fairly and in turn, '. . . were loved and popular with the people, for the true unaffected love they evinced to their people and unimpeachable honesty with which they served them'.[34]

To Lekhotla la Bafo, the virtues of chieftainship were personified by the Basotho kingdom's remarkable founder, Moshoeshoe, who is generally judged one of the most humane and intelligent rulers in African history. He was the ideal leader because of the bonds he forged with his people, a fact attested to in one of the association's songs.

> This leadership of ours
> The chieftainship of the Basotho
> The leadership that safeguards
> The rights of the nation
> It originates from Moshoeshoe
> Who, by guarding the rights
> Was respected by the nation.

Once the nation trusted him
All the rights of the nation
Were laid through him
The rights of leadership
He said belonged to the nation
The nation called them his
Through mutual trust
The rights of the nation
Moshoeshoe is the overseer.

The rights belong to the Basotho
Moshoeshoe is the servant
He does the will of the nation
In complete honesty
In this honesty
The rights of the nation
Took on the name of Moshoeshoe
Because of the trust.

Trustworthy leaders
Are guided by trust.

Moshoeshoe's benevolent rule stood in stark contrast to that of most chiefs under British colonialism and Lekhotla la Bafo would often draw out that comparison when it wanted to shame chiefs. For instance, when Lefela criticized chiefs for their laxity on brandy, he invoked the name of Moshoeshoe, who had banned the trade and sale of liquor in 1854.

If we fall through liquor, we common people will speak against you when we come to heaven and Moshesh will call upon his God to drive you away from heaven because you will have ruined his country with brandy.[35]

It was characteristic of him that even after levelling this criticism he added, 'we speak like this because we love our chiefs'.

Thus, despite the mounting evidence that many chiefs were willing collaborators who profited from colonial rule, Lekhotla la Bafo chose not to lay the burden of guilt on them but on the British. In this view, if the chiefs had misused their privileges it was only at British instigation. If the chiefs no longer heard the complaints of their people, it was because the British had usurped their authority and straitjacketed them in the National Council. '*Rex* has killed our chiefs,' declared Moshosho Sehlare. 'Before the advent of *Rex* our chiefs were very dignified persons, who were the spokesmen of the people, but today they have become insignificant because their place is taken by *Rex*.'[36]

One can also see this line of reasoning applied to an analysis of taxation. When Moshoeshoe asked for a British agent to be placed among the Basotho in 1868, he agreed to levy a ten shilling tax on his people to maintain him. After the British formally took over Basutoland in 1884, the level of taxes remained constant with revenues going to maintain colonial administration. By the 1920s, however, taxes had risen to one pound eight shillings and were proving to be a tremendous burden on Basotho peasants. Although chiefs had a stake in extracting more taxes since they were given five per cent of all they gathered, Lekhotla la Bafo placed the principal blame at the doorstep of the British. As one of its members commented, the 'money derived from our taxation is used to bribe the chiefs to induce them to abandon their interest in the affairs of the people'.[37]

Ironically, the very fact that Lekhotla la Bafo saw the salvation of the Basotho in the return to an idealized past freed them to make an uncompromising analysis of British colonialism. During the early years of its existence, its critique of colonialism centred on how Britain had abrogated its original agreement with Moshoeshoe and emasculated the institution of chieftainship, but as the decade of the 1920s wore on, it broadened its analysis to examine the role of other foreign agents and economic interests it believed had joined together in Lesotho's exploitation. It specifically targeted officials of the colonial administration — magistrates, doctors, veterinary and agricultural officers, and dipping agents — and the representatives of South African economic interests — labour recruiting agents and traders. That white South Africans comprised the majority of both these groups reinforced the suspicion of Lekhotla la Bafo that the British colonial administration worked hand in glove with the Union government.

European traders figured prominently in many of their analyses. Traders had had a presence in Lesotho since the time of Moshoeshoe, but he had carefully circumscribed their activity. Nevertheless, under his successors, they gradually extended their influence to most parts of the country and played a vital role in tying the Basotho economy into South African and international markets, a relationship that worked to the detriment of the Basotho producers and undermined indigenous industries and markets. As a leader of Lekhotla la Bafo, Lerata

Masupha, observed, traders 'had the monopoly of trade in the country. Grain, livestock and other produce of Basutoland were of no more use to them . . . .'[38]

Lekhotla la Bafo criticized the two hundred and fifty or so white traders for a variety of exploitative practices. One was freely extending credit for goods so that many people fell into debt. Another was evading the law preventing Europeans from buying land in Lesotho by making deals with chiefs to plow on the halves or by buying enough garden plots to create small farms. They sliced off even more land by constructing for their wagons roads which were off limits to the ox sleds of the Basotho. A final criticism was that trading licences were a virtual monopoly of Europeans (and a few Indians). The cost of licences was prohibitively high for all but a handful of Basotho, yet the British did not contemplate lowering fees. Most Basotho who became involved in petty trading — including Josiel Lefela — did so by hawking small items in the mountain areas, but even then they were frustrated in their attempts to obtain hawkers' licences (Document 21).[39]

To break the economic stranglehold that European traders had on Lesotho, Lekhotla la Bafo put forward various proposals. For instance, it advocated creating Basotho-controlled trading stores which would establish direct links with British firms for imported goods. Another idea was to establish a Basotho Farmers and Wool Growers Association for marketing produce and wool. Without capital these self-help schemes never got off the ground, but they signified an increasing awareness of the need to rely on one's own resources in combatting colonialism.[40]

In similar fashion, Lekhotla la Bafo questioned the motivation behind any development assistance that came from Britain. For instance, it opposed the Colonial Development and Welfare Fund, which allocated funds for Lesotho's development after the Second World War. The amount budgeted for Lesotho was modest — £830 000 to be spent over a ten year period — but Lekhotla la Bafo opposed any assistance — whether for soldier's pensions or anti-erosion schemes — over which the Basotho had no control (Document 22). It reasoned that no matter how positive a contribution development assistance might make, it was a subtle way of distracting the Basotho and paving the way for European settlement. As Josiel Lefela put it,

The British government, whenever they have paid money to a country, what followed it up? British taxpayers who are in great difficulties have a right to know where the money goes. They are starving and yet their money is being sent to us to develop our country. We don't want this money. We should send it back. Let that money go back to England to stop those debts. We want you to protect us but not to bring such matters as this which perhaps cheat us out of our country. In all respects, this country no longer belongs to us.[41]

Lekhotla la Bafo also placed European missionaries under the umbrella of imperial and commercial interests exploiting the country. An inordinate amount of its propaganda was devoted to attacking missionaries for undermining the social fabric of the Basotho nation, and for drawing the Basotho into the capitalist economy. It had a firm basis for making this charge. Missionary bodies, most notably the Paris Evangelical Missionary Society (PEMS) (1833), the Roman Catholic Church (1860s), and the Anglicans (1875), began proselytizing in Lesotho in the nineteenth century. Under Moshoeshoe they performed a variety of diplomatic and educational services but converted few Basotho. Under colonial rule, however, they began winning more adherents, who they expected to renounce their customs — polygamy, circumcision, *bohali* (bride wealth), and ancestor worship — and take up western culture which was equated with civilization and progress. By weakening the Basotho spirit of independence and identity and encouraging Basotho peasants to become involved in commodity production, selling their labour to whites, owning private property, not providing labour for chiefs, and consuming European goods, Lekhotla la Bafo charged that the missionaries were 'softening up' the Basotho and preparing them to accept the alternatives, capitalism and colonialism, being offered by their European compatriots.

One way that Lekhotla la Bafo tried to combat the 'narcotic' influence of the missionary was by supporting Basotho independent church leaders who had broken away from European led missions, especially from the PEMS. Although the Lefela brothers and other members of the organization had broken away from missions and supported a return to traditional beliefs and practices, they acknowledged how much influence Christianity had on the Basotho by not criticizing the new religion but its bearers.

We shall never hold Christ or God responsible for the commercialization of Christianity by the heartless missionaries who adopt it as the easiest means of fooling and robbing other people out of their land and country.[42]

Accordingly, Lefela sought and won support from some of the leading independent church leaders like Walter Matitta and Raymond Mohono. These men had split from European missions because leadership positions had been closed off to Africans and because they wanted to accommodate Christian beliefs to Basotho customs. Independent church leaders (and prophets) were present at most Lekhotla la Bafo meetings, and one grouping, the African Federal Church Council, even directed the association to represent its interests on a political level (Document 23).[43]

The battle for control of the Basotho mind was often waged at the level of culture, and Lekhotla la Bafo sought to preserve Basotho society from the inroads being made by the missionary-controlled educational system which, it contended, was instilling western values in their children and teaching them a distorted version of Basotho history. As a counter-measure, Lekhotla la Bafo proposed starting up schools run by the independent churches where children would learn 'patriotism and the spirit of national dignity'.[44] However, where these independent schools were already operating, they were hard-pressed to survive because they were not eligible for the educational grants that the colonial administration allocated to European-led denominations. The British had ruled that there had to be a three-mile distance between schools receiving grants, but because mission schools had been established in most areas, the independent schools could not break their monopoly. Thus, despite the fact that all adult males were required from 1927 on to pay a three-shilling tax for educational purposes, they had no control over who taught their children (Document 24).

Lekhotla la Bafo also supported founding a Basotho-controlled national technical school.[45] Believing the Basotho had been conditioned to work mines, not run them, it argued that a technical school would go far in teaching the Basotho the necessary skills to control their destiny. Lefela often recalled an experiment Lerotholi sponsored at the turn of the century in which an Afro-American representative of the African Methodist Episcopal Church, Conrad Rideout, had been invited to found an industrial school and several primary schools. Although this plan came to naught, Lefela remained hopeful that black American educators would come to Lesotho in substantial numbers and run independent schools.[46]

For an organization whose rhetoric was couched in confrontational terms, Lekhotla la Bafo was extraordinarily restrained in organizing militant action against the colonial administration. Its leaders consistently shied away from adopting radical tactics. Among the factors which account for this the most important were Lesotho's precarious political existence in the shadow of South Africa, and the historical legacy of Basotho struggles for independence in the nineteenth century. In the case of the latter, two developments were crucial. The first was the treaty signed between the British and Moshoeshoe in 1868 in which the Basotho agreed to accept British protection and a British resident. Lekhotla la Bafo regarded the colonial administration that had been erected since then as a violation of the treaty, and called for the expulsion of all but a handful of colonial officials. Only then would Moshoeshoe's original agreement be fulfilled. The second was the Basotho wars of resistance against the Boers in 1858 and 1865-68, and against Cape colonial forces in 1880-81. By focussing on the struggles that the Basotho nation had waged to preserve sovereignty and the fact that Lesotho had never lost her independence even after she had come under British protection and influence, Lekhotla la Bafo precluded the use of violence or armed struggle to achieve its aims. Instead it strove to convince Britain to live up to her original agreements with the Basotho.

Accordingly, Lekhotla la Bafo brought to bear all the legal and moral pressure it could on the British government, bombarding it at all levels with petitions and appeals. Many of these bypassed local colonial officials and went directly to the High Commissioner in Pretoria and officials in London. In the early years of the association's existence, local officials took at least cursory notice of the letters but as their hostility towards it grew, they refused to acknowledge letters unless they were sent through the proper channels. The few responses elicited were patronizing and did not address the central concerns raised. A note on the margin of one letter characterized Lefela as 'a public agitator' who was 'setting a trap for someone' and gave instructions to 'just acknowledge receipt without comment excepting to say they should mind their own business . . . .'[47]

During the 1920s British officials regarded Lekhotla la Bafo as more of a nuisance than a subversive threat, and as long as it did not stray from its non-violent tactics, they were reticent to ban its meetings, especially since officials and chiefs were invited to attend and take notes at all its gatherings (Document 25).[48] Even so, some advocated issuing a proclamation empowering the resident commissioner, J.R. Sturrock, to prohibit meetings.[49] He stopped short of proscribing Lekhotla la Bafo, although at one point he issued instructions preventing funds from being collected at its meetings.[50] Lesser officials did not act with the same restraint, and there is evidence that some district commissioners and many chiefs issued orders in the late 1920s prohibiting Lekhotla la Bafo meetings.[51] Although officials in Maseru countermanded these orders, Lekhotla la Bafo members were convinced that behind the scenes top British officials continued to encourage their subordinates and chiefs and headmen to disrupt its activities (Documents 26-27).[52]

Thus, the colonial administration and Lekhotla la Bafo confronted each other in an atmosphere of mutual suspicion and mistrust, but the closest the organization came to initiating a confrontation was in the late 1920s when it threatened to wage a campaign of passive resistance against increased taxation and the dipping of sheep (Document 28). Dipping had been a pressing issue for the Basotho since 1924 when the colonial administration had begun waging a dipping campaign to eradicate animal diseases, especially scab among sheep. Basotho farmers regarded it not only as an intrusion on their daily lives — they had to pay a fee for the dip and it took time to drive their herds to dipping pools — but as part of a white plot to kill off their flocks since a certain percentage of animals died from the dip. A speaker at one of their meetings invoked this widely-held belief when he observed:

> Just now we see some police here collecting tax from poor people who are so poverty-stricken that they have pieces of sacks on their shoulders for blankets and who have been driven into this poverty by the government through the eradication of their flocks by dipping.[53]

His view was seconded by Maphutseng Lefela, who sarcastically asked, 'Why was so much anxiety . . . shown by the government for your sheep, while your health is neglected'.[54]

By the late 1920s, acts of individual protest against dipping were common. Many Basotho simply refused to send their sheep to the tanks, and a few even assaulted dipping agents, but there was no co-ordinated resistance. Since this was a time when the plummeting price of wool (from 14*d* a pound in 1928 to 2*d* in 1932) was placing an additional burden on Basotho peasants, Lekhotla la Bafo probably could have harnessed their resentment and dissatisfaction into a rebellion like that in neighbouring Griqualand East a decade earlier.[55] Instead its leaders planned a campaign of civil disobedience built around the slogan 'Hands off our flocks. Away with the Principal Veterinary Surgeon with his lieutenants.' Proceeding on the assumption that the government would not be able to arrest a large, unified group of resisters, their strategy was to ask two to three hundred men from each district to defy the £10 fine for evading dipping and withhold their sheep from the dip.[56] However, even in this moment of defiance, Lekhotla la Bafo softened the impact of its attack by offering to attach a Union Jack to its own flag as a gesture of good will.[57] Like so many other plans this group devised, the talk of passive resistance was not translated into action.

Lekhotla la Bafo's conservative tactics, as I have noted, were in part shaped by its reading of the circumstances of Basotho 'independence', but another compelling factor that entered into its thinking was the prospect that the British might hand over the High Commission territories to the Union of South Africa (Document 29).[58] That threat had been a preoccupation of all Basotho groups since a clause in the 1909 South Africa Act had held out the possibility that Britain might transfer the protectorates to South Africa at some future time. Despite the fact that the clause stipulated that Britain should consult African opinion before any such move was made, the Basotho remembered only too well that colonial officials had not conferred with them before handing them over to the Cape Colony in 1871.[59] Another disquieting fact was that every South African Prime Minister periodically called for the incorporation to take place, and while the British ultimately did not sell out the territories, at no time did they try to assuage African apprehensions by issuing an unequivocal statement spelling out their intentions. Given this uncertainty, militant Lekhotla la Bafo tactics making Lesotho a political liability for the British would have been self-defeating.

Accordingly, Lekhotla la Bafo lobbied for greater British sensitivity to Basotho viewpoints. For instance, it was concerned that since the High Commissioner resided in Pretoria (even after the offices of High Commissioner and Governor-General were separated), the South African government, not the subjects he was supposed to represent, had constant access to him. When a new High Commissioner, Herbert Stanley, was installed in 1930, Lekhotla la Bafo made clear its opposition to his being based in Pretoria.

it is where he is advised to issue dangerous proclamations to the interests of the people living in the protectorates because there is nothing more pleasing to General Hertzog and the Boers than the issue of repressive and oppressive proclamations to Basotho people.[60]

Its solution was for Stanley to establish an office in the protectorates.[61]

The perception that South Africa was unduly influencing British decisions on the protectorates led Lekhotla la Bafo to take the innovative step of proposing that the people of Basutoland, Bechuanaland Protectorate and Swaziland band together to establish a League of Protectorates with an office in London to make representations to the British on issues of common concern like incorporation (Documents 30-32).[62] A lack of finances and a ban against Lekhotla la Bafo representatives entering Swaziland and Bechuanaland prevented the 'Parliament of Protectorates' from getting off the ground, but the idea of African states in Southern Africa jointly cooperating against South African expansionism and domination can be viewed as an early prototype for the Front Line states and the Southern African Development Coordinating Council.

Because Lesotho's survival depended on Britain's continued protection, Lekhotla la Bafo directed much of its propaganda efforts to winning friends and advocates in the international community. It contacted anyone it thought could bring additional pressure to bear on the British government. It developed a remarkable set of contacts, ranging from governments throughout the world to organizations such as Marcus Garvey's black nationalist Universal Negro Improvement Association, the left-oriented League Against Imperialism, and the philanthropic Aborigines' Protection Society (Documents 33-34).[63] If it had had adequate financial resources at its command, Lekhotla la Bafo would have played a more active role internationally. Its leaders regularly appealed at meetings for donations from chiefs and commoners to fund projects and trips: sending Lekhotla la Bafo delegates to London to lay their grievances (one of which was that Griffith refused to recognize Lekhotla la Bafo) before the King-in-Council, hiring lawyers to challenge colonial proclamations, buying and establishing a press, sending officials or representatives like J.T. Gumede to international conferences, and establishing an office in London for the League of Protectorates.[64]

Lesotho's vulnerability in relation to South Africa propelled

Lekhotla la Bafo not only to take a strong internationalist posture, but also to seek linkages with African political groups in South Africa, whose activities they followed closely. A president of Lekhotla la Bafo, Libenyane Jobo, expressing his admiration for the African National Congress (ANC) and the Industrial and Commercial Workers' Union (ICU), called them organizations 'burning with power'.[65] Lekhotla la Bafo members occasionally ventured to their meetings in South Africa, but by 1926, despite the fact that Lekhotla la Bafo announced a plan to 'associate ourselves with the African National Congress . . . as the organ under which we may be able to put our matters before the authorities', the relationship had not gelled and Lekhotla la Bafo apparently was not even able to publish news about its activities in the Congress newspaper, *Abantu-Batho*.[66]

The South African political organization with which Lekhotla la Bafo did develop a sustained relationship was the South African Communist Party (Document 35). The linkage was mutually profitable. At a time when leftists were being purged from the ANC and the ICU and the Party was beginning to organize in the rural areas, the Communists thus established connections with a militant African nationalist movement with a solid rural base, while Lekhotla la Bafo gained entry to the extensive international network of Communist associations through which it could press its case, obtained legal assistance when it was harassed by the British, and, perhaps most importantly, found access to the Party newspapers for disseminating its propaganda and news.

It was a Communist initiative that brought the two groups together in the first place. Jack and Ray Simons have related that T.W. Thibedi, one of the first African Communists and a pioneer of trade union organizing, initiated contact with Lekhotla la Bafo in 1928.[67] However, Edwin Mofutsanyana, another early African Party member, recollects that Jacob Majoro, a native of Lesotho (and later general secretary of the African Mine Workers Union), was aware of Lekhotla la Bafo's activities and proposed making an approach.[68] Whoever was responsible, the Communist Party made an overture to Lekhotla la Bafo offering it space in their newspaper, *The South African Worker*. Because Lekhotla la Bafo had been virtually shut out by both black and white newspapers in South Africa and Lesotho, it quickly snapped up the invitation and began publishing its news and opinions — using the byline 'Molomo oa Bafo' (Voice of the Commoners) — on a regular basis. This arrangement lasted for over two decades as *The South African Worker* and its successors, *Umsebenzi* and *Inkululeko*, ran Lekhotla la Bafo columns (most often written by Maphutseng Lefela) and gave coverage to its meetings and clashes with the colonial administration and Paramount Chief Griffith.

Communist Party leaders were regularly invited guests at Lekhotla la Bafo's annual meetings. The first visit came about as the result of a controversy over an invitation to Josiah Gumede, president of the ANC. Although not a Communist himself, Gumede had become a sympathizer after visiting the Soviet Union in 1928 and had put the ANC on a more radical course. When Lekhotla la Bafo invited him to speak to a meeting in May 1929, colonial officials took a dim view of his visiting Lesotho, most especially for a Lekhotla la Bafo meeting and, in February 1929, they prohibited him from entering.[69] Lekhotla la Bafo apparently had it in mind to force a confrontation with the British for it invited him again in July 1929 and May 1930 in defiance of a colonial official's threat to imprison for up to two years anyone aiding Gumede to come in.[70]

Gumede was more reluctant to defy the British than Lekhotla la Bafo and Albert Nzula, representing the Non-European Federation of Trade Unions, came in his place.[71] If Lekhotla la Bafo members were expecting him to challenge the British, they were surely disappointed for he advised them — in words that a colonial official termed 'sensible' — to state their case to the British in a respectful manner and not to alienate them. He was not impressed by the hyperbole of Lekhotla la Bafo's leaders and he was surprised that they were prepared to be arrested with Gumede. He pointed out that Gumede did not want them to court arrest, any more than he wanted to be arrested himself in a foreign territory.[72]

Nzula was the first in a stream of Communist figures like S.P. Bunting, Jacob Tjelele and J.B. Marks who attended Lekhotla la Bafo meetings over the years (Documents 36-37). The Party leader who developed the longest and closest association with the group was Edwin Mofutsanyana who, as an editor of *Inkululeko*, travelled to Lesotho often and developed a firm friendship with the Lefelas. Indeed, after he fled South Africa in 1959, he settled in Lesotho and worked closely with Josiel Lefela in drafting petitions to the United Nations.[73]

The Party assisted Lekhotla la Bafo in developing links internationally with such Communist front organizations as the Farmers and Workers of the World Unite, a Moscow-based 'organ to unite revolutionary peasant organizations in all parts of the world', the League for the Defence of the Negro Race, a Berlin-headquartered group whose members were primarily from former German colonies, and the League against Imperialism, founded in the 1920s by the Comintern as a result of pressure by delegates from colonial territories on metropolitan Communist parties to become more involved in anti-imperialist struggles. The British branch of the League was instructed to establish contact with Lekhotla la Bafo, which paid a £2 subscription fee to join the League in October 1929. In return, the League periodically passed on press clippings, some of which Lekhotla la Bafo used to update itself about South African attempts to incorporate Lesotho.[74]

In the course of its relationship with the South African Communist Party, Lekhotla la Bafo developed a sympathetic view of the Soviet Union. A column in the *South African Worker* in late 1928 on the workings of the Basutoland National Council typified this image.

> If you compare this system in Basutoland with that of the Soviets in free Russia, you will find a great difference; there people have joined to gather [*sic*] and are working only in a praiseworthy way which helps the people.
>   Under this system when the land is full of teachers of agriculture, taxes are levied according to the wish of the majority of the people, and there is cooperation of the farmers in order to get enough food for all the people together with other things of progress and good conditions of life.[75]

This particular statement may have been prompted by the gratitude of Lekhotla la Bafo to the Communist Party for giving it space in the party's newspaper, but in the years ahead, Lekhotla la Bafo continued to regard the Soviet Union as its salvation, as one power which could be relied on to apply pressure on the British in international forums. Indeed, after World War II, some Lekhotla la Bafo petitions to the United Nations were channelled through the Soviet government (Document 38).

Despite the close connections between Lekhotla la Bafo and the South African Communist Party, it is inaccurate to suggest that the latter dominated the former. Although party publications gave Lekhotla la Bafo a militant image by translating its name as the 'League of the Poor' and leftist rhetoric was liberally sprinkled throughout its writings (largely because Maphutseng Lefela had become a party member), there is no question that it remained at heart a nationalist movement centred around a defence of the Basotho nation and culture. Lekhotla la Bafo never felt its independence threatened by the party and kept up a healthy working relationship. Even when the British and the Roman Catholic Church exploited this relationship to portray Lekhotla la Bafo as a Communist front group, it never distanced itself from its ally.

Lekhotla la Bafo was not the only commoners' movement to emerge during the colonial period. Another was the Basutoland Progressive Association (*Kopano ea Tsoelopele*), established in 1907 to cater to the interests of the small educated Basotho elite.[76] In 1919, the Resident Commissioner had granted it a seat on the National Council and it had set itself the modest goal of winning the right to have several more seats. When Lefela founded his association, he did not garner any support from the Progressive Association leader, Simon Phamotse, who contended there was no need to set up another council exclusively for commoners. He believed that one had to work with the chiefs, despite their lethargy and avarice, and that this could only be done within the National Council. New groups diluted the resolve of commoners to work together, and he recommended that Lefela's group should merge with his own 'to liberate the commons from the slavery they have been put into by the sons of Moshesh'.[77] This did not accord with Lefela's approach, in which commoners taking up more seats in the national council were undercutting the power of chiefs by diminishing their representation.

Whatever their initial differences, the two organizations were not so far apart as to prevent them from discussing a merger from time to time. A halting attempt was made in 1922 when Lekhotla la Bafo wrote to the Progressive Association calling for the two to work together. Nothing came of it except the suggestion of a cumbersome title for the merged associations — Lekhotla la Bafo ea Tsoelopele ea Lesotho. Documentation does not reveal if they continued discussions on a regular basis, but a further, more serious attempt at cooperative action was made in March 1932; this initiative also involved a third commoners' group, Lekhotla la Toka (Council of Justice). What brought them together was the issue that had been hotly debated for the previous decade, excessive fines in the courts of chiefs. Even on this subject they were not in complete accord. Lekhotla la Toka and the Progressive Association thought that the colonial administration's proposals of 1929, which curtailed the independence of chiefs, should be accepted, while Lekhotla la Bafo opposed any measure designed, in its view, to abolish chieftainship.[78] Nevertheless, all three agreed that there was injustice in the courts and decided to send a joint delegation to Griffith to voice their grievances.[79] Like all the other delegations that these and other groups dispatched to Matsieng, this one was rebuffed, although not before Lefela called on Griffith to sign a 'Magna Carta'. Lekhotla la Bafo and the Progressive Association did hold at least one other joint meeting at Hermon in July 1933, but there does not appear to be any evidence to suggest they found enough common ground to justify ignoring their substantial differences.[80]

One of the reasons why the two never came close to merging was that their followings were drawn in the main from dissimilar social backgrounds. The Progressive Association drew its membership largely from Basotho educated by the Paris Evangelical Mission Society — teachers, clerks, ministers, journalists, and traders — who sought modernizing changes in the country.[81] While a number of Lekhotla la Bafo leaders and rank and file members were also products of PEMS schools, a significant number had rejected the mission's religious and educational authority and had joined or supported independent churches and schools. The organization claimed that its membership also embraced traders, labour agents and runners, teachers, independent church ministers, policemen, chief's clerks, shop clerks, and dip supervisors, and while it addressed issues of concern and interest to these people, its membership was largely small farmers and peasants and its chief aim was to articulate their interests.[82]

The difference between the two groups was most pronounced when it came to the issue of chieftainship. Their orientations, as indicated above, were distinct. While both vented their ire against the excesses of chiefs, the Progressive Association supported reforms that would circumscribe their power and Lekhotla la Bafo advocated policies that would restore traditional authority and institutions to their original vigour.

To underscore their support for chieftainship, Lekhotla la Bafo selected minor chiefs as presidents of the association. Prominent chiefs like Peete, Boshoane, and Motsoene gave some encouragement behind the scenes, but most chiefs, fearing reprisals from Maseru and Matsieng, did not openly declare their allegiance. Accordingly, the association intentionally nominated junior sons of chiefs as its presidents. Little is known about the first president, Eleazar W.

Lerata Masupha, beyond the fact that he was a junior son of Masupha, a senior son of Moshoeshoe.[83] The symbolism of selecting a son of Masupha was pertinent since Masupha had been one of the great figures of resistance to colonial rule in Lesotho. Masupha's successor was Libenyane Jobo, who took over in 1930 and served until his death around 1965. The son of Jobo, a younger brother of Moshoeshoe, Libenyane was a Paris Evangelical Mission Society member until he joined Walter Matitta's church. That was in line with other Lekhotla la Bafo members, and according to his son, he became a 'Bishop' (chaplain) of the association in charge of its religious affairs.[84] Both Masupha and Jobo came from the Thaba Bosiu area, Moshoeshoe's home base.

Lekhotla la Bafo's approach to chieftainship was not without critics from within its own ranks. Not all of Lefela's followers shared his dogged devotion to the chiefs. One dissident was another Mapoteng member, Justinus Ratsiu, who broke away from Lefela around 1925 to found Lekhotla la Toka because of disagreements over several fundamental issues.[85] For instance, Lefela supported expelling all British officials with the exception of the Resident Commissioner to conform with the original wishes of Moshoeshoe, while Ratsiu wanted all colonial officials to remain and the chieftainship to be abolished. Moreover, Ratsiu supported the work of the mission societies, a position that Lefela staunchly opposed. Because its attacks on chieftainship struck a responsive chord among many people, Lekhotla la Toka did achieve a fleeting popularity, but it did not have the general appeal or staying power of its rival and it died out sometime after World War II.[86]

While Lefela and his supporters ardently defended the institution of chieftainship, they had no reservation in criticizing individual chiefs they regarded as sellouts. Singled out for special opprobrium was Paramount Chief Griffith who, in their eyes, was a British stooge and a violator of Basotho tradition. His major transgression was that he had flaunted the rules of succession when he usurped the throne at Matsieng after his brother, Letsie II, died in 1913. The traditional practice was for the first-born son of Letsie's first wife to succeed him, but her son, Tau, died mysteriously shortly after Letsie. A son, Makhaola, was born to Letsie's second wife four years after his death, but rather than serve as a regent until an heir came of age (or beget a son of one of Letsie's wives), Griffith moved to assume the paramountcy, saying he would sit on his father's throne with both buttocks rather than one.[87] At the time of his accession, despite there being little public criticism of his action, questions were raised behind the scene and later attacks on him were based in part on the fact that Mahali, the senior wife of Letsie, was a daughter of Lefela's chief Peete. Other chiefs in his area such as Goliath Mahabane and Boshoane reportedly supported this line too. For Lekhotla la Bafo, Mahali's son, Makhaola, was the legitimate claimant to the throne, and, on numerous occasions, it proposed that Chieftainess Mahali serve as regent until he came of age.[88] Accordingly, when Griffith died in 1939, it put forward his name as his successor.[89]

Equally contemptible in Lekhotla la Bafo's view was Griffith's justification of his power grab by the argument that his Roman Catholic faith forbade him to serve as a regent or observe the custom of *kenelo*, producing an heir through the wife of Letsie. Since Lekhotla la Bafo had a deep-rooted animosity towards mission Christianity for distorting Basotho culture, it is not surprising that it charged him with being an agent of 'Romanism' — 'the most powerful and irreconcilable enemy of our freedom and our scared institutions'.[90]

The Catholic Church had not been a major factor in Basotho politics until the twentieth century. The Catholic order, the Oblates of Mary Immaculate (OMI) had been latecomers into the Lesotho mission field, arriving almost three decades later than their main rival, the French Protestant PEMS. During those early years, these two streams of Christianity had followed different strategies of conversion: the Protestants, working from the ground up, proselytized primarily among educated commoners, while the Catholics, following a trickle-down theory, concentrated their efforts on converting chiefs, who, for the most part, were taking an antagonistic stance towards the Protestants who they correctly believed were allied with Cape Colonial officials in undermining their authority. This pattern of conversion was carried over to the twentieth century, and it came to be reflected in the politics of nationalist groups such as the Progressive Association and Lekhotla la Bafo which drew their adherents largely from Protestants (and former Protestants), while factions loyal to the chiefs turned to the Catholics for support.

Griffith converted to Catholicism in 1912, and after he became the Paramount, the Catholic Church enjoyed a period of sharp, sustained growth. Whereas, in 1890, the Catholics had 3 000 adherents and in 1910, 10 000, by 1930 they had 51 000 and in 1937, 143 000. In the area of education, where state subsidies were based on student enrolment and competition with Protestants for students was extremely fierce, they had similar successes. From 1901, when they had twelve schools with 600 pupils, their numbers shot up to 130 schools with 11 775 pupils in 1933.[91] Having a sympathetic figure on the throne in Matsieng may have been a boon to the Catholics in winning converts and students, but opponents like Lekhotla la Bafo went even further by accusing Griffith of ceding to the Catholics extensive tracts of land for their mission enterprises. No evidence has turned up that Griffith gave away significant amounts of land to any mission group, but in a land-starved country like Lesotho, any grant of land would be magnified in the eyes of the ordinary moSotho, and thus fuel Lekhotla la Bafo's resistance to any moves to hand over land to foreign church bodies, Catholic or Protestant.

Griffith deeply resented Lekhotla la Bafo's attacks, and he would have banned it if the British had not restrained him. In 1937, he was presented with a chance to gain a measure of revenge when he had Lekhotla la Bafo's chairman, H.M.D. Tsoene, arrested for defaming him in an *Umsebenzi* article in which the latter had raised the issue of Griffith's illegal accession and accused him of selling Lesotho to Europeans for private gain.[92] Tsoene's trial and conviction did not intimidate the paramount chief's opponents who in the following year proposed that a special court be set up to try Griffith for his offences. British judges were to be barred from participating; instead, a major chief from Swaziland or Botswana and two senior Basotho chiefs would consider the verdict. Lekhotla la Bafo reasoned that just as Pontius Pilate had tried Jesus Christ under Jewish and not Roman law, so Griffith had to be judged under Basotho and not British law.[93]

When Griffith died in 1939, his successor, Seeiso Griffith, followed his lead in calling for an end to the restraints on interfering with the activities of Lekhotla la Bafo. This time the British, observing the association's influence growing around the country, were more willing to intervene and, on 2 February 1940, the Resident Commissioner, E.C. Richards, ordered officials to monitor all its meetings with the intent of obtaining evidence that would allow the colonial administration to suppress it.[94] The pretext for removing it from the scene came shortly thereafter through the controversy over the recruitment of Basotho soldiers for the British war effort.

As in World War I, France and Great Britain had found it necessary to prevail on their African subjects to fuel the allied war machine as labourers.[95] However, when the call went out to the High Commission Territories for the first batch of recruits to join the South African

Defence Force, many Basotho were so opposed to serving in the ranks of the white-led South African army that the British were eventually forced in July 1941 to set up the African Auxiliary Pioneer Corps for recruits from the High Commission Territories.[96] Despite being paid half the pay of Africans in the South African army, the Basotho came forth in impressive numbers. A point of comparison is that while less than 1 500 Basotho served in France with the South African Native Labour Contingent during World War I, over 21 000 ultimately saw service in North Africa, Italy, and the Middle East during World War II.[97]

This massive turnout did not necessarily reflect heightened Basotho devotion to imperial defence, but the ability of colonial officials and loyal chiefs to turn the screws on Basotho men and coerce them into signing up. Almost 12 000 men were netted in the first six months of recruitment, not coincidentally the period when the strongest opposition to recruitment surfaced.

Men could take several options in evading the recruitment net. Some escaped by going to work on the South African mines and farms. Others hid in the mountains. Still others deserted.[98] In November 1941, a mass desertion of 1 300 new recruits from Butha Buthe district took place shortly after their arrival in a Maseru training camp. After being rounded up, some were jailed, but most were disciplined and sent back to camp. The British explained that particular incident away by observing that 'men from that district have always been rather truculent'.[99]

Many men who refused to serve did so because they saw no compelling reason for going off to war, but rumour also played a part in turning people against conscription. For instance, in Leribe district in January 1942, stories circulated that 2 000 Basotho had already died in a torpedoed ship; that letters from wives were opened before they reached their husbands; and that soldiers' wives were being taken off to Johannesburg for active service.[100]

The British preferred to attribute resistance to three major influences: chiefs in Leribe district who wished to get at the newly installed Paramount Chieftainess 'Mantsebo by misrepresenting the terms of enlistment to their people,[101] French Canadian Catholic priests who were anti-British,[102] and Lekhotla la Bafo.

From the beginning of the war, Lekhotla la Bafo had not opposed the war effort *per se*, but that African soldiers were expected to serve as labourers without being trained to defend themselves (Document

39). As in the previous war, the British had respected the sensitivity of the South African government to Africans being armed and sent into combat situations. Accordingly, Lekhotla la Bafo's principal demand was that African soldiers be trained in all facets of modern warfare and weaponry. Otherwise, conscription was a subterfuge for exterminating Basotho and paving the way for a South African takeover of their country. Josiel Lefela called it a conspiracy '. . . of a Council of clever people who have planned that these countries must fight so that the low class people will deceitfully be taken into the war',[103] while Rabase Sekike saw it as the 'final solution' for the African people. The British, he wrote, were going to murder the Basotho 'in the same manner as the Europeans in North America exterminated the Red Indians and Tasmanians in Australia' and it would

> pave the way for the final usurpation and defraudment of our country and rights for Europeans to settle and exploit the Country while Basuto people will further be put under worse forms of slavery.[104]

He claimed that English children were already being sent to Lesotho under the pretext of giving them shelter from the war. As a way of avoiding certain death, he recommended that Basotho soldiers should consider surrendering to the Germans.[105] Otherwise, when they got overseas, the Basotho would

> . . . be placed under cruel dutchmen who will torture and strike them under the butts of their guns. The intention of the white man is to get us all finished so that Basutoland will be turned into farms.[106]

Lekhotla la Bafo also levelled other accusations at the British: that they were bribing chiefs by paying them bounties for recruits, that they were reneging on their promise to deduct £1 a month from the wages of soldiers and pay it directly to their wives, and that they were not exempting soldiers from hut taxes while they were on active service.[107]

When Josiel Lefela made similar statements at a meeting in Leribe district on 9 November 1941, the British, using war-time emergency regulations, moved the same month to arrest him and two of his followers, Hlakane Mokhithi and Rapoho Nthanyane.[108] They were tried and convicted on charges of sedition the following September.[109] Mokhothi and Nthanyane were given light sentences and were let out in February 1943, while Josiel Lefela was interned for a much longer period since the British thought he would stir up trouble again if he were released too soon.[110] He was finally freed on Christmas Eve 1943, after giving an undertaking that he would not participate in subversive activities or attend any political meetings (though he was not excluded from engaging in political activities).[111]

The British did not limit themselves to muzzling Josiel Lefela. In January 1942, they prohibited Lekhotla la Bafo from holding meetings for the duration of the war. Lekhotla la Bafo honoured this prohibition, but as an alternative, its leaders recommended that its members join sympathetic organizations like the Communist Party, the United Front, and the Friends of the Soviet Union. They could then hold meetings of these groups.[112] The association's leaders also regularly appealed to the British to lift the ban on their meetings and the proscription on Josiel Lefela's activities. The British ignored their requests until Lekhotla la Bafo sent a letter, in June 1946, asking the newly formed United Nations to intercede on its behalf (Documents 38, 40-41).[113] The British quickly responded not so much because they were concerned that the United Nations would assume jurisdiction over the issue — it did not — but because they were worried lest their enemies manipulate the issue in international forums.[114] Thus in October 1946, a year after the war ended, they lifted the ban on Lekhotla la Bafo.[115]

Ironically, Lekhotla la Bafo was already participating in post-war politics through its involvement in the newly established District Council system. During the war the British had begun thinking about the post-war colonial order. They intended to circumscribe chiefly authority yet further, and to inject an element of democracy into the National Council. The possibility of a huge group of 'dilutees' (returning veterans) coming home discontented with the 'mediaeval' society they had left behind was a prospect they wished to avoid.

> Many . . . will return with new ideas; perhaps with the hopes, the theories and the slogans of the apostles of the 'brave new world'. It is therefore incredible that the mass of the Basuto should continue for long to be content with the present state of affairs. The need for change is great.[116]

If alternatives were not provided, then organizations like Lekhotla la Bafo would be likely to find fertile ground for winning support. One measure that colonial officials and the National Council set in place was the District Council, which was designed to add an element of popular participation to the governing structure by allowing village meetings to elect two representatives for three-year terms. Then each of the nine District Councils sent two members to the National Council. While these elections opened up District Councils and, to a lesser degree, the National Council to more commoners, many of the new members tended to be younger brothers of chiefs.[117]

Lekhotla la Bafo wasted no time in competing in the first village elections. Although hindered by the continuing ban on meetings, its lack of organization, and the general lack of support for it outside the northern districts, Lekhotla la Bafo still scored modest successes in the Leribe and Teyateyaneng districts. In the latter district in 1946, ten of its members out of forty-six delegates were elected.

District commissioners presided over sessions of the local councils. Although their function was to discuss purely local problems and draft resolutions for consideration by the National Council, Lekhotla la Bafo members used the councils as a forum for addressing a wide range of issues, including national and international ones. Nothing fell outside their purview. Thus the resolutions of the Teyateyaneng District Council that were sent on to Maseru tended to be much more militant and wider-reaching than those from other districts. Even before the ban on Lekhotla la Bafo was lifted, one of the first measures the Teyateyaneng Council sent forward was a request that Lekhotla la Bafo be allowed to hold public meetings again and to nominate its members to the District Council and the National Council; permission was also sought for Josiel Lefela to resume membership of his association.[118] The National Council passed these resolutions with little or no opposition (Document 42).

The British did not want to grant Lekhotla la Bafo any more legitimacy than it had to, and they scrupulously avoided giving it one of the seats on the National Council reserved for professional and semi-professional associations.[119] But since the District Councils were empowered to send two delegates each to the National Council, it was through this route that the Teyateyaneng District Council returned Josiel Lefela to the National Council after a twenty-five year absence.[120]

The British move to 'democratize' the National Council was but one element in a package of reforms that they had been implementing over the previous decade aimed at bringing chiefs more directly under their supervision. Britain and South Africa had profited for many decades from chiefly rule but as an increasing number of chiefs became autocratic and abusive, and economic conditions deteriorated, colonial officials realized that if they were to contain mounting internal dissent, they had to impose a tighter administrative rein over the chiefs.

The controversy over abuses in the chief's courts after World War I had done much to alert the British to the need for change, and various proposals were advanced to make chiefs an integral part of administration. But, in 1928, when two draft proclamations defining and regulating the powers of the chiefs and the Native Courts were placed before the National Council, they generated so much opposition from chiefs that they were shelved for almost another decade. Why the British were successful at a later stage in implementing the measures is not clear, but in 1937, Proclamations 61 and 62 were enacted (Documents 43-44).

The first dealt with the overabundance of chiefs in the country. Historically, senior chiefs had placed junior sons and relations around their jurisdictions to consolidate their control. So long as land was plentiful and the population did not strain the country's resources, the system worked well, but as Colin Murray has noted,

> the placing system was consistent only with an expanding polity. When there were no new areas to settle, a new placing could only be made at the expense of existing placings. In the first decades of this century, under conditions of increasingly acute land shortage, the continuing proliferation of chiefs and sub-chiefs reached absurd proportions. A member of the National Council remarked in the early 1930s that 'there are now as many chiefs in Basutoland as there are stars in the heavens'.[121]

Proclamation 61 restructured 'native' administration so that the Paramount Chief was recognized as the chief 'native authority' and listed 1 330 chiefs, sub-chiefs, and headmen as subordinate to him. Moreover, it stipulated that the colonial administration and the Paramount Chief had to approve any future placings.

Proclamation 62 stipulated that only 'gazetted' chiefs could hold courts, thus curtailing a major source of revenue for those not recognized. In 1946, the number of courts was again sharply reduced — from 1 340 to 121 — and a National Treasury established in Matsieng. In order to compensate chiefs for the loss of revenues from

fines and *matsema* labour, the Treasury paid salaries to the Paramount Chief and 23 senior chiefs and parcelled out a block grant to
the rest of the chiefs.

In overhauling native administration, colonial officials did not want
to be perceived as undermining the institution of chieftainship, but
that was what they accomplished. Many Basotho saw the reforms as a
reversion to the much maligned Cape colonial policies that had led to
rebellion in 1880. This time the Basotho response was not so dramatic
— perhaps because senior chiefs were given increased authority — but
the changes did usher in a period of insecurity and uncertainty
especially amongst lesser chiefs who were most likely to lose
autonomy, revenue and even their positions. There is no question that
the reforms were a significant catalyst in the upswing of *liretlo* or
ritual murders that occurred in the post-war period, as chiefs sought
refuge in medicinal solutions. While it was difficult to prove who was
instigating or carrying out these murders, the police directed their in-
vestigations at chiefs, and indeed, two senior chiefs, Bereng Seeiso
and Gabashane Masupha, were convicted and hanged in 1949 for their
complicity in several murders.

Despite its continuing feud with Matsieng, Lekhotla la Bafo did not
hesitate in entering the fray on the side of the chiefs since it believed
the British were manipulating the *liretlo* controversy to discredit the
chiefs. It did not deny that murders were taking place, but it claimed
the police were bribing and torturing witnesses into perjuring
themselves at trials, with the intent of getting rid of uncooperative
senior chiefs and paving the way for Basotuland's incorporation into
South Africa (Documents 45-46). As Josiel Lefela charged,

> We know there has been a plan that in the end Basutoland must go from
> the black people and that can only be achieved if all the chiefs are gone.
> We want to know if the investigations that are directed at people who
> committed the crime, or whether they are so general as to do away with
> the chieftainship, and in the end we will find that we no longer have any
> chiefs.[122]

Many Basotho agreed with his allegations, and it is no coincidence
that during this period Lekhotla la Bafo found itself riding a wave of
support. A number of chiefs encouraged Lefela behind the scenes
because he was one of the few people who was not afraid to challenge
the British in public.

The groundswell of support for Lekhotla la Bafo alarmed colonial officials who renewed their efforts to suppress the association.[123] The pretext for doing so came on 30 August 1947, when a fire broke out at 1.00 a.m. in a student dormitory at the Roman Catholic college at Roma, killing three students.[124] The churches' anti-communist crusade after World War II had exacerbated the long standing feud with Lekhotla la Bafo, so it is not surprising that the authorities believed the arson was a plot hatched in Mapoteng (Documents 47-50).

On 15 May 1948, police arrested a Lekhotla la Bafo member, Mokeka Monyamane, as an accomplice in the crime. A month later, they jailed another member, Harold Velaphe.[125] The latter — under duress, he claimed — gave a statement to the police that a week before the fire he had attended a meeting of his group at which the plot to burn the college had been laid. Josiel Lefela had been a prime mover of the action and he had directed two groups to proceed. Razak and Mahomed Surtie, the sons of an Indian trader, Tayab Surtie, were alleged to have supplied petrol and transportation. Kelebone Rametse was supposed to have led the group which burned the dormitory. Velaphe and Monyamane were in the second group — which included Razak Surtie (driving his own truck), Rabase Sekike, Roma 'Neko, Pakalitha Mokhethea, Mentsel Konka, and Lebina Hlakane.[126] When they arrived at Roma, they saw the flames and turned back. Later they met the first group who told them they had been successful.

After signing the confession implicating his compatriots and fearing that he was going to be poisoned by the police, Velaphe escaped from jail on 27 June 1948, and made his way to Mapoteng to warn his colleagues of what was developing. He was rearrested on 2 July and several weeks later, Josiel Lefela and the others were arrested for setting the fire. However, the proof against the men was so flimsy that on 21 August all except Velaphe were set free.[127] For instance, the Surties were able to prove that their truck, which was supposed to have carried the arsonists, was being repaired in Ficksburg when the Roma fire took place. Velaphe was less fortunate. Despite the fact that he was the scapegoat and probably coerced to sign a confession, he was convicted and given a four-year sentence.[128]

This was not the end of the affair. A few months later, Maphutseng Lefela was charged with contempt of court for publishing an article in *Inkululeko* (August 1948) stating that Velaphe had signed a confession after being kept in a cold cell with no food for three days.[129] He was sentenced to a one-year term but won his appeal in November 1949, the higher court finding that there was no proof he had written the article and that when the article was written Velaphe had not been charged with any crime.[130]

The last legal chapter of the controversy was written in 1955 when Josiel Lefela made a speech in Mafeteng district alleging that the police had tortured a crown witness in 1948 to force him to give perjured testimony in the ritual murder case of Chiefs Bereng and Gabashane and that the government's doctors had murdered the Paramount Chief Seeiso in 1940 for their own ritual murder purposes.[131] The colonial administration charged him with sedition, but before his trial in May in Mafeteng he was injured in a bus accident near Ficksburg and prevented from appearing in court on time. He was subsequently arrested for contempt of court at Thaba Chitja, but this charge was dropped when doctors confirmed that he could not have completed his journey to Mafeteng.[132] Not trusting European doctors to treat him, he was allowed to return home where it was reported '. . . he hopes to have a cure effected by means of prayer'.[133]

Josiel Lefela was convicted on 29 June, but only after putting up a spirited defence. Representing himself, he opened the trial by demanding thet the presiding judge be an Indian or a Jew, not a 'Dutchman' or an Englishman since they would be prejudiced against him. He was ignored and eventually sentenced to a one-year term.[134] He appealed to the United Nations to have his case taken before the International Court at Geneva and that a United Nations commission be sent to Lesotho to investigate police abuses of witnesses.[135] He was released in March 1956. By then, he had been expelled from the District and National Councils. Nevertheless, when a meeting of ratepayers was called at Mapoteng to elect a successor (or 'bootlicker' as Lefela termed him), Lefela's name was put up for nomination and accepted overwhelmingly despite the opposition of two prominent local chiefs.[136] Although the government designated a successor, the people of Mapoteng continued to put up his name until he died in 1965.[137]

By the end of Lefela's second jail term, his association's prominence had been eclipsed by the Basutoland African Congress (later renamed the Basutoland Congress Party) founded in 1952. But this new political movement owed its impetus in no small measure to the close association of one of its leaders, Ntsu Mokhehle, with Lefela. Mokhehle was born in a village less than 20 kilometres from Mapoteng and probably learned of Lekhotla la Bafo as a young man.[138] However, his direct tutelage under Lefela began during World War II, when he was expelled for several years from Fort Hare College after student protests there, and moved to Mapoteng. At first Lekhotla la Bafo members were suspicious of him because of their deep distrust of educated people, but he eventually became a trusted supporter and for a time served as secretary for the movement.

Lefela's influence in shaping Mokhehle's views in politics can be seen in his writings in *Mohlabani*, the Congress journal. His columns on the institution of chieftainship, the historical relationship of the Basotho nation with Britain, the ritual murder controversy, and the threat of incorporation into South Africa all bear the distinctive marks of Lefela's thinking.

Mokhehle was part of a younger generation of Basotho who were beginning to assert themselves in post-war politics. Before he and others founded the Congress, they considered taking over and revitalizing a declining Lekhotla la Bafo, but they decided not to do so for a variety of reasons. Foremost was their respect for Lefela's contribution to the Basotho struggle for freedom. To them, he was the 'Moses of the Basotho', and since he showed no sign of stepping down as leader, they decided not to challenge his authority. Another factor was that Lekhotla la Bafo remained hostile to educated young people. Although it set up night schools for educating young people in politics, its leadership resisted the idea of allowing younger men to rise to leadership roles. If it had been more receptive to the younger men, the Congress may not have been established. A final reason for the establishment of Congress as a distinct entity was that Lekhotla la Bafo remained a loosely organized association without a disciplined, action-oriented programme. The Congress leadership, on the other hand, was comprised of individuals who had been active in the African National Congress Youth League in South Africa and was oriented towards organizing a mass party.

The formation of the Congress probably staved off a split in Lekhotla la Bafo since some of its members had grown dissatisfied with Lefela's personalized leadership and questioned his use of the association's finances. These dissidents backed down, however, when the Congress was formed and they gave their support to both organizations.

Although the two bodies remained distinct, on most issues they were in accord. For instance, when the Moore Commission took testimony on proposals for reforming colonial administration, both groups submitted statements opposing any move '. . . to abolish the hereditary chieftainship and replace it by appointed chieftainship' as the British were proposing.[139] Nevertheless, a critical area of disagreement did surface in their view of the future political development of Lesotho. Lekhotla la Bafo called on the British to restore the traditional system of rule, while Congress recommended that they extend more powers of self-rule to the Basotho.

The peak of cooperation between the two groups came in 1957 when, at a meeting at Thaba Bosiu, Lekhotla la Bafo passed on the torch of struggle to Congress (Document 51). But after that the disagreement over the question of how to win independence was to become more pronounced. Lekhotla la Bafo stubbornly stuck to the position it had staked out for decades — that since the Basotho had never lost their independence but had been hoodwinked by the British, who had not honoured their agreement with Moshoeshoe, the proper course was to appeal to international organizations like the United Nations to force Britain to live up to its original promises. As Josiel Lefela put it, a 'man does not request that which is his, but demands it'.[140] Congress took a more pragmatic stance — that even if Lekhotla la Bafo's reading of history was correct, the Basotho could only win independence using the framework for decolonization set forth by the British.

As a first step in that direction, Mokhehle took part in the London talks which led to Responsible Government in Lesotho, and, in 1960, he and his party successfully participated in the first elections for the Legislative Council, winning 30 of the 40 elected seats. One source maintains that Lekhotla la Bafo, which did not contest the elections, was so opposed to the Congress strategy that it threw its support behind a rival party, the Marema Tlou Party.

Lekhotla la Bafo's disillusionment with Mokhehle became complete over the issue of a memorandum it asked him to present to the United Nations. Lefela's dream of going to New York himself had always been frustrated by his group's chronic lack of funds. When Mokhehle was presented with an opportunity to appear before a committee of the United Nations in 1962, Lekhotla la Bafo deputed him to deliver their case. Some Lekhotla la Bafo members claim that Mokhehle had consented to do this, but unknown people (British liberals are most often mentioned) steered him in another direction and the memorandum was not presented in spite of the General Assembly's interest in Lekhotla la Bafo's argument.

Although by the 1960s Lekhotla la Bafo had become less and less of a factor in the drive for Lesotho's independence, Josiel Lefela and a few associates continued to draft appeals to the international community and advance proposals to reduce conflict among Basotho political factions (Document 52). After Josiel died in 1965, his sons and a dwindling band of devoted followers have tried to carry his banner forward, despite the banning of the association from holding public meetings as a result of the state of emergency declared in 1970.[141]

In assessing Lekhotla la Bafo's contribution to Lesotho's political history, one cannot measure it solely in terms of the political battles it won or lost. Concrete victories were few and far between. One cannot overlook the fact that this was partly due to organizational weaknesses and the lack of an action-oriented programme, but at the same time, it has to be kept in mind that Lekhotla la Bafo was operating in a hostile political environment in which the odds were heavily against its even making a dent in colonial structures. Lekhotla la Bafo had an alternative — to play by British rules (and there was a likelihood of being coopted if one followed that path), but that was an option that it never remotely considered.

Lekhotla la Bafo's legacy has to be seen in the light of its courageous political and social commitments and the framework of analysis it set out for the people of Lesotho. First, it stressed that in order for Lesotho to survive and keep its national identity intact, her people had to rely on their own resources and not on outside interests for cultural, educational and economic sustenance. Its leaders were 'progressive traditionalists', caught between their devotion to the precolonial past and their recognition of the far-reaching changes wrought by colonialism.[142] But however much they may have experimented with radical prescriptions, they did not stray far from their position that Lesotho's future depended on remaining faithful to the foundations of the past.

Second, Lekhotla la Bafo did not support the privileged classes in either Basotho or colonial society. Although it doggedly defended the institution of chieftainship, it did not hesitate to challenge established authority and criticize those who abused positions of power. When Josiel Lefela declared in the National Council that 'I will associate myself with the poor people', he was allying his association with the dispossessed in his society.[143] It was an attitude that Lekhotla la Bafo adhered to throughout its existence.

Finally, by situating Lesotho within the context of South African and international systems of imperialism, Lekhotla la Bafo could argue that Lesotho's leaders had to use every possible avenue to challenge external domination. In this regard, Lekhotla la Bafo's leaders remained committed nationalists, but they had the self-confidence to solicit support from different camps, including socialist countries, without fearing they were selling their souls.

As Lesotho enters her third decade of 'independence', the degree to which Lekhotla la Bafo's approaches retain their currency is remarkable.

Notes

1. This study was originally inspired by the brief mentions of Lekhotla la Bafo in Edward Roux's *Time Longer Than Rope* (Madison, 1964), and H.J. and R.E. Simons' *Class and Colour in South Africa 1850-1950* (Baltimore, 1969). These works remain essential reading for understanding African protest movements in South Africa. A more recent look at examples of rural resistance is Belinda Bozzoli (ed)., *Town and Countryside in the Transvaal* (Johannesburg, 1983). See especially her introduction, pp.1-47.

2. Godfrey Lagden, *The Basuto* (London, 1909), p.560.

3. B.E. Clifford to J.C. Sturrock, 8 October 1928. S 3/22/2/1 (Lesotho National Archives (LNA), Maseru).

4. Alan Pim, Financial and Economic Position of Basutoland Cmd. 4097 (London, 1935).

5. For a more detailed discussion of internal differentiation within Basotho society, see Roger Leys, 'Some observations on class differentiation and class conflict within the labour reserve of Basutoland', Collected Seminar Papers, no.27 (Institute of Commonwealth Studies, London), pp.87-95; Judy Kimble, ' "Clinging to the Chiefs": some contradictions of colonial rule in Basutoland, c.1890-1930', in Henry Bernstein and Bonnie Campbell (eds)., *Contradictions of Accumulation in Africa* (Beverley Hills, 1985), pp.25-69.

6. J.M. Mohapeloa, 'Indirect rule and progress towards self-rule and independence: the case of Lesotho', unpublished paper presented to the conference on Southern African History, National University of Lesotho, August 1977.

7. Sturrock's views are found in his essay on problems of colonial administration in Basutoland, July 1934, DO (Dominions Office) 35/478 20967/7 (Public Record Office (PRO), London).

8. Colin Murray, 'From granary to labour reserve', *South African Labour Bulletin*, VI, 4 (1980), pp.3-20; Judy Kimble, 'Labour migration in Basutoland, c.1870-1885', in Shula Marks and Richard Rathbone (eds)., *Industrialisation and Social Change in South Africa* (London, 1982), pp.119-141.

9. Murray, *op.cit.*, pp.13, 15.

10. Information on the Lefela family history was supplied by branches of the Lefela family at Mapoteng and Koalabata. Informants gave conflicting information as to which church Josiel belonged to — African Methodist Episcopal, Roman Catholic or Paris Evangelical Mission Society.

11. Gordon Haliburton, 'Walter Matitta and Josiel Lefela: a prophet and a politician in Lesotho', *Journal of Religion in Africa*, VII, 2 (1975), p.126. According to Haliburton, Lefela had contact with Clements Kadalie, the leader of the Industrial and Commercial Workers' Union, while he was in South Africa. This seems doubtful, since Lefela's stint on the mines most likely took place long before Kadalie came to South Africa from Malawi.

12. One of Josiel's sons, Mohakanyane, continues in this profession. Lefela married four wives: Mothepane, Anna (daughter, Hlekoa): MaMohakanyane (Mohakanyane, Dipampiri, Lefela, Mokolua, Sekhoma, Ntswaki) and MaLetsie (Letsie, Lesaoana, Story, Thuso, and Lerato).

13. Ironically, Lefela was not circumcised himself.

14. Letter from Mike Berning, Cory Library, Rhodes University, 3 June 1981; Interview, J.J. Jingoes, July 1981.

15. Interview, Chief Dyke Peete, 29 April 1980.

16. S 3/5/8/3.

17. E.H. Cole, Assistant Commissioner, Berea, to Government Secretary, Maseru, 7 October 1916, S 3/5/8/3.

18. *Ibid.*, H.M.D. Tsoene to Secretary of State for Dominion Affairs, 15 December 1937, DO 35/912 Y168/3. H.M.D. Tsoene to Aborigines Protection Society, 11 October 1932 (Papers of Anti-Slavery Society, Rhodes House, Oxford University). In 1921, the Resident Commissioner claimed that the National Council had not supported Lefela's scheme. He was hesitant to get involved because the manager of a similar association, the Paballo Society, in Mafeteng, had been jailed for misusing funds. In 1922, Garraway contended the certificate issued to Lefela was no longer valid because of his expulsion from the National Council and that he should return it.

19. For an excellent presentation of these views, see H.M.D. Tsoene to Prince Arthur Frederick, 25 May 1923, S 3/22/2/1. Some writers believe Lekhotla la Bafo was launched as early as 1913, but this is not borne out

by Lekhotla la Bafo's own records.

20. Proceedings of Basutoland National Council (BNC), Session of 1920, p.17, PRO, CO (Colonial Office) 646/3.
21. *Ibid.*, p.6.
22. *Ibid.*, p.4.
23. Tsoene to Prince Arthur, *op. cit.*
24. BNC (1920), p.13. See also Griffith Lerotholi to Resident Commissioner, 4 May 1920, S 7/4/14.
25. BNC (1920), p.14.
26. Garraway to High Commissioner, South Africa, 7 October 1920, PRO, CO 417/646; see also Garraway to Acting D.R.C., 21 June 1920, S 3/5/8/3.
27. *Naledi*, 3 September 1920, S 3/29/7/2.
28. Garraway to High Commissioner, 7 October 1920, CO 417/646.
29. S 3/5/8/3; Garraway to High Commissioner, 2 November 1921, CO 417/646. It was several months after the article was written before Lefela was suspended because the High Commissioner had to consult legal opinion as to whether Lefela could be suspended while the National Council was not in session. The legal brief affirmed that he could be expelled.
30. BNC, 43rd Session (1947), II, p.469. (Proceedings of the BNC after 1945 are found in the archive of the National University of Lesotho library).
31. BNC, 44th Session (1948), II, pp.270-71.
32. BNC, Special Session (22-30 March 1955), p.185.
33. BNC, 44th Session (1948), I, p.32.
34. J. Lefela to Dag Hammarskjoeld, 18 December 1957 (United Nations Archive/United Nations Secretariat Registries; RAG 3/11 — Central Registries 1954, TR 330, July 1956 – December 1959).
35. BNC (1920), p.6.
36. Meeting of Lekhotla la Bafo at Hlotse, 22 February 1931, S 3/22/2/1.
37. Meeting at Kennan Kethisa's, Leribe, 26-27 December 1931, S 3/22/2/1.
38. Meeting at Matsieng, 26 December 1928, S 3/22/2/3.
39. See the meeting at Maseru, 11 August 1929; H.M.D. Tsoene to Lord Passfield, 29 April 1930; H.M.D. Tsoene to Herbert Stanley, 18 April 1931, S 3/22/2/6. For a useful survey of trading activity, see Bridget Selwyn, 'A survey of the role of white traders in Lesotho from the times of Moshoeshoe to the 1950s', unpublished B.A. thesis, Department of History, National University of Lesotho, 1980.
40. Meeting of Kennan Kethisa's; Tsoene to Passfield, *op. cit.*
41. BNC, 43rd Session (1947), I, p.15.
42. Presidential Address, Matsieng, 26 December 1928, S 3/22/2/3.

43. Meeting of Lekhotla la Bafo, 11 May 1931, S 3/22/2/6.
44. Meeting at Kennan Kethisa's.
45. *Ibid.*
46. BNC, 43rd Session (1947), II, p.438. More details on Rideout are found in Carol Page, 'Black America in white South Africa: church and state reaction to the A.M.E. Church in Cape Colony and Transvaal, 1896-1910', Ph.D. Thesis, Edinburgh University, 1978, pp.193-97, 316-20, 363-73.
47. Richard Weisfelder, 'Early voices of protest in Basutoland: the Progressive Association and Lekhotla la Bafo', *African Studies Review*, XII, 4 (1969), p.402.
48. B.E. Clifford to Sturrock, 8 October 1928, S 3/22/2/2. The British were more arbitrary when it came to dealing with African 'agitators' from South Africa. Josiah Gumede and Keable 'Mote (See Document 36) were two who were not allowed to enter Lesotho on political grounds. A native of Lesotho and a leader of the ICU (*Kopano ea Basebetsi ba Khoebo* in seSotho) in the Orange Free State, 'Mote had been anathema to authorities in Lesotho ever since he had delivered a speech in Kroonstad in 1927 accusing Chief Griffith of selling his subjects to the mine owners at £1 a head. He proposed opening an ICU branch at Hlotse, but he ran up against an obdurate Resident Commissioner, who believed that 'it was undesirable from every point of view to let our natives become in any way connected with Labour Unions outside the Territory', S 3/19/62.
49. B.E. Clifford to J.C. Sturrock, 9 September 1929, S 3/22/2/3.
50. Resident Commissioner to Clifford, 28 September 1928, S 3/22/2/4.
51. High Commissioner to Paramount Chief, 24 September 1928; Clifford to Sturrock, 24 September 1928; A. Bond to Chief Boshoane Peete, 4 October 1928, S 3/22/2/2.
52. H.M.D. Tsoene to Aborigines Protection Society, 21 January 1933 (APS Papers).
53. Report of the meeting at Mapoteng, 14 December 1930, S 3/22/2/6.
54. Meeting at Kennan Khethisa's.
55. Colin Bundy, 'Dissidents, detectives and the dipping revolt: social control and collaboration in East Griqualand in 1914', *Southern African Research in Progress* (York University), V, pp.1-15.
56. H.M.D. Tsoene to J.C. Sturrock, 8 September 1929, S 3/22/2/3.
57. *Ibid.*
58. In opposing incorporation, Lekhotla la Bafo found itself in the unusual position of siding with the chiefs who were actively engaged in lobbying the British over this issue. Lekhotla la Bafo was concerned that the British would win over Basotho chiefs to the system of rural reserves that had been created in South Africa. For instance, it questioned why

the British sent representatives of the paramount chiefs of Basutoland and Swaziland in 1938 to the Transkei '. . . to learn the beauties of how the Union Government through the instrumentality of the Transkian [*sic*] Bhunga rules the natives . . . .' H.M.D. Tsoene to the Secretary of State for the Colonies, 11 May 1938, 1/33 1937-1946 (Matsieng Archives (MA)).

59. The British further promised that the Basotho would not be subject to Cape laws. This was added since resentment over Cape administration had fuelled the Gun War in 1880.

60. Requests to be submitted before British Government in regard to establishment of new post of High Commissioner, 14 December 1930, S 3/22/2/6.

61. H.M.D. Tsoene to Herbert Stanley, 18 April 1931, S 3/22/2/6.

62. *Umsebenzi*, 30 September 1929; E.L.D. Masupha to Sobhuza II, 10 July 1926, S 3/22/2/2; H.M.D. Tsoene to Chief Tshekedi Khama, 12 April 1930, S 3/22/2/6.

63. For instance, in appealing against Hertzog's moves to incorporate the High Commission Territories, Lekhotla la Bafo sent off letters of protest to France, Turkey, Japan, Afghanistan, Greece and the Soviet Union. On other occasions they threatened to take their case before the League of Nations and the International Court of Justice.

64. Report of the Meeting at Matsieng, 26 December 1928; Meeting at Maseru, 11 August 1929; Meeting of Lekhotla la Bafo at Motlatsi Ramahimane's Village, Baking, 7 December 1930, S 3/22/2/6. Josiel Lefela thought his group would gain immunity from government harassment by being financially independent. His notion may have been undermined if he had known more about the plight of the organizations he wished to emulate. 'The Communist Party and the Negro Universal Association have carried on their activities in defiance of the Governments of the countries in which they work, and no harm has come to them, because they have money'.

65. *Mochochonono*, 23 August 1933.

66. E.W.L.D. Masupha to Earl of Athlone, 26 December 1925, S 3/22/2/1. An exception was the Congress newspaper, *Ikwezi le Afrika*, edited by Pixley Seme. See the issues of 9 May, 16 May, 23 May 1931 and 25 July 1931.

67. H.J. Simons and R.E. Simons, *Class and Colour*, p.212.

68. Interview, Edwin Mofutsanyana, July 1980; July 1981.

69. B.E. Clifford to Sturrock, 8 October 1928, S 3/22/2/4; Clifford to Sturrock, 9 September 1929, S 3/22/2/3; Athlone to Resident Commissioner, 19 February 1929, DO 9/13. Before instituting the prohibition on Gumede, Athlone consulted with the South African Police for a detailed report on his background in exchange for details on any

Communist activites in Basutoland (Office of the Divisional C.I.D. Officer, Kimberley to Deputy Commissioner, South African Police, Kimberley, 29 January 1929; Commissioner, South African Police to High Commissioner, 8 February 1929, DO 9/13).

70. Report on Lekhotla la Bafo, Mapoteng, 21 May 1929; A.W. Bond to W.D.L. Masupha, 21 May 1929, S 3/22/2/3; *South African Worker*, 31 July 1929.
71. Clifford to Sturrock, 9 September 1929, S 3/22/2/3.
72. Report on Lekhotla la Bafo meeting, 21 May 1929, S 3/22/2/3.
73. Report of meeting at Thaba Bosiu, 12-14 March 1930, S 3/22/2/4; *Umsebenzi*, 27 March 1937; Interview, Edwin Mofutsanyana.
74. Presidential Address, Mapoteng, 1 January 1930; S 3/22/2/4; League Against Imperialism to H.M.D. Tsoene, 13 November 1929, S 3/22/2/4. Lefela claimed that Lekhotla la Bafo's affiliation to the League Against Imperialism was precipitated because the colonial administration failed to investigate the case of a moSotho labourer who was shot by a white farmer near Ficksburg after he demanded his wages. No charges were pressed, the British did not look any further into the matter, and Lekhotla la Bafo sought satisfaction through the League Against Imperialism.
75. *South African Worker*, 30 November 1928.
76. Weisfelder, *op. cit*.
77. BNC (1920), p.12. Simon Phamotse to *Mochochonono*, 13 July 1921, S 3/22/1/2. Simon Majakathata Phamotse (1879-1928) is a figure due greater recognition. Educated at Lovedale, he served as a postmaster in Leribe district before moving to the Transvaal with Godfrey Lagden after the Anglo-Boer War to work as an interpreter. He took up the editorship of *Naledi* in 1907 and carved out a considerable reputation for himself as a journalist (see his columns on Lesotho in *Umteteli wa Bantu* during the 1920s). He was also the dominant figure in the Progressive Association (Communications from Michael Berning and Andrew Reed).
78. *Mochochonono*, 30 March 1932.
79. *Ibid*.
80. *Mochochonono*, 23 August 1933.
81. Weisfelder, *op.cit*, p.398.
82. H.M.D. Tsoene to Secretary, Aborigines Protection Society, 21 January 1933 (APS Papers).
83. Interview, Rabase Sekike, Mokunutlung, 20 July 1980. An extensive set of interviews has subsequently been done with Sekike. See Lesoetsa Phephetho, 'Lekhotla la Bafo: resistance to British colonial rule, the chiefly abuse of power, and missionary activity — a participant's perspective', B.A. thesis, Department of History, National University

of Lesotho, 1984.

84. Interview, Lebohong Jobo, Thaba Bosiu, 16 July 1980. Jobo is seSotho for Job. Jobo was one of the first chiefs to convert to Christianity. Serving under the presidents were commoners who carried out most of the day-to-day business. The first chairman was Samuel Mapeshane, the second, Josias Tsoene, and the last, Rabase Sekike. Josiel Lefela never held a formal office. His followers reasoned that he would be made a target if the British moved against the association's officials. That he was not an officer, however, did not prevent the British from jailing him on three different occasions. Maphutseng served as general secretary until he died in 1955.

85. Lekhotla la Toka was also referred to as the 'National Council to support government justice against Basuto chiefs' tyranny.'

86. *Mochochonono*, 27 July 1932; 20 July 1932; Interview, Ntsukunyane Mphanya, July 1980. He is the son of Ratsiu.

87. Makhaola could have succeeded to the throne since, according to Basotho custom, a child is born of the cattle, not the father. His father was said to be Goliath Malebanye, the son of a sister of Letsie II.

88. Interview, George Bereng, Maseru, 7 May 1980.

89. H.M.D. Tsoene to Aborigines Protection Society, 21 January, 1933; Rabase Sekike to 'Matsaba Seeiso Griffith, 2 February 1941, MA 1/33 1937-1946.

90. *Ibid.*; *Inkululeko*, March 1942.

91. *Moeletsi oa Basotho*, 23 June 1937 (*Moeletsi* is the Catholic newspaper). Therese Blanchet-Cohen, 'The corporate structure of the Catholic Church in Lesotho, 1930-1966' unpublished thesis, University College, London, 1976, p.180.

92. *Umsebenzi*, 24 July 1937.

93. Rabase Sekike to High Commissioner, 7 August 1938, DO 35/912 Y 168/7.

94. DO 35/912 Y 168/2; Y 168/12. When Seeiso unexpectedly died in 1940, Lekhotla la Bafo supported Bereng Griffith as his successor. R. Sekike to High Commissioner, 1 January 1941, DO 35/912 Y 162/55.

95. For a detailed discussion of the problems of recruiting during World War I, see my 'Lesotho and the First World War: recruiting, resistance and the South African Native Labour Contingent', *Mohlomi*, III (1981), pp.1-15. On recruiting in Bechuanaland during World War II, see D. Kiyaga-Mulindwa, 'The Bechuanaland Protectorate and the Second World War', *Journal of Imperial and Commonwealth Studies*, XII, 3 (1984), pp.33-53.

96. The word 'Auxiliary' was dropped from the Corps' name in late 1944 so that African recruits would not be led to believe they were playing a secondary role.

97. Brian Gray, *Basuto Soldiers in Hitler's War* (Maseru, 1953).

98. Captured deserters were usually sent to Matsieng for a royal lecture or physical punishment and then sent back to their units.

99. DO 35/900 Y1/72. Visit of High Commissioner, Lord Harlech, to Basutoland, November-December 1941.

100. DO 35/912 Y 168/14.

101. DO 35/945 Y 658/4.

102. DO 35/943 Y 636/4. One official surmised that OMI priests, who were dependent on voluntary labour for running their missions, did not support recruitment for fear of losing labourers. It was verified that some Roman Catholic priests had stirred up anxiety amongst women by telling them their men would not return from war. The women would then write letters to their men, which may have encouraged desertions. The Roman Catholic hierarchy agreed to put a stop to such anti-war propaganda where it existed.

103. Meeting of Lekhotla la Bafo, Mapoteng, 26 October 1941, DO 35/912 Y 168/13.

104. Rabase Sekike to 'Matsaba Seeiso Griffith, 8 February 1942, DO 35/192 Y 168/13.

105. Rabase Sekike to Chief Boshoane Peete, Koma Koma, 31 August 1941, MA 1/33 1937-1946.

106. Meeting of Lekhotla la Bafo, Chaka's Village, 9 November 1941, DO 35/912, Y 168/13.

107. C.R. Atlee to A. Creech Jones, 6 November 1942 (Fabian Colonial Bureau papers, Rhodes House, Oxford University).

108. *Inkululeko*, January 1942; March 1942.

109. While in jail the prisoners' families were given two shillings a day for support and the prisoners one shilling a day to buy 'comforts'. Lefela was eventually transferred from Leribe to Teyateyaneng. Rivers Thompson, who was District Commissioner at the time, recalled that he supplied Lefela with government publications and proclamation books, which he consumed with great passion (Interview, Rivers Thompson, July 1980).

110. DO 35/912 Y 168/16.

111. DO 35/1177 Y 836/3. Rabase Sekike and Maphutseng Lefela also served jail sentences in late 1942 and early 1943 for sending an article to *Inkululeko* calling for the Communist Party newspaper to resume circulation in Basutoland. It had been banned in Basutoland as an anti-war journal. Ironically, although by then Germany had invaded the Soviet Union and *Inkululeko* had begun to support the war effort, and despite the fact that their article never reached Johannesburg, Sekike and Lefela were still convicted. The ban on *Inkululeko* was not lifted until after the war. Sekike's recollections of the war are found in Phephetho,

'Lekhotla la Bafo', pp.45-48.

112. Sekike to 'Matsaba Griffith, *op.cit*. Sekike also appealed to the Soviet Union to send judges to serve as assessors in cases where Lekhotla la Bafo meetings were banned and members arrested (Sekike to V.M. Molotov, Foreign Affairs Commissar, Moscow, 29 June 1941, DO 35/912 Y 168/3).

113. Rabase Sekike to Trygve Lie, United Nations, 2 June 1946, DO 35/912 Y 836/3. Although Lekhotla la Bafo placed great faith in the United Nations, UN officials were reluctant to intervene in spheres controlled by the British.

114. DO 35/1177 Y 836/3.

115. Lekhotla la Bafo was allowed to hold meetings so long as they were of a religious nature and if they had the prior permission of the District Commissioner and the chief of the area where it was to be held. Lefela was not released from his undertaking not to get involved in subversive activities or attend political meetings. DO 35/1177 Y 836/3.

116. Report of Evelyn Baring, November 1944, DO 35/1172 Y 701/1/10.

117. After he returned to the Council, Lefela focussed on the fact that the popularly elected District Councils sent but a few delegates to the Council, and he proposed that they should have parity in seats with the appointed chiefs. '. . . [A]t present there are only nine members representing the people, and you can't vote with nine people. It is clear that if you have filled a big four gallon paraffin tin with tea and then put a teaspoon of sugar into that, it is clear that you cannot taste any sugar there, and out of 100 members of council nine members only represent the people. Therefore if the people ask that more sugar should be put into the tin, they would not be wrong. It is that prayer we have that more sugar should be put in'. (BNC, 43rd Session (1947) II, p.693.)

118. BNC, 42nd Session (1946), 23 October 1946, pp.302-305.

119. Groups representing teachers, ex-servicemen, farmers, and even lepers were allotted seats on the Council. The British claimed that Lekhotla la Bafo had neither sufficient membership nor a constitution so it did not warrant a seat. The latter charge was untrue. Lekhotla la Bafo claimed a membership of 2 700 which was only slightly less than that of the Basutoland Progressive Association.

120. Lefela could not resist tweaking the nose of the British at every opportunity. In 1951, claiming that he had been suspended but not dismissed from the National Council in 1920, he asked the British to give him £465 back pay for the twenty-four years he had been excluded from the Council (Josiel Lefela to Acting Resident Commissioner, 15 August 1951, LNA file 3201/3).

121. Colin Murray and William Lye, *Transformations on the Highveld: The Tswana and Southern Sotho* (1980), pp.91-2. Details of the reform

controversy are found in L.B. Machobane, 'The political dilemma of chieftaincy in colonial Lesotho with reference to the administration and courts reforms of 1938', ISAS Occasional Paper, No.1 (1986), University of Lesotho.

122. BNC, 44th Session (1948), I, p.29. See also Michael Scott, *A Time to Speak* (London, 1958), pp.194-207.

123. Lefela's behaviour in the National Council contributed to British efforts to rid themselves of him. During debates he often spoke out of turn or talked at length on subjects not relevant to the debate. He also carried on a running battle with the Resident Commissioner, who was the Council's presiding officer. His exchanges with several Resident Commissioners became so acrimonious that he was twice expelled from the Council's chambers. On one occasion he provoked A.D. Forsyth-Thompson into declaring that 'it has rarely been my misfortune to meet anybody who so deliberately tries to sow the seeds of suspicion and distrust as does the speaker [Lefela] who is speaking now', while C.N. Arden-Clarke took him to task because 'you just go along until you find some words you do not like and you start on that. You are like a mouse that digs holes in bags of mealies at night'. (BNC, 46th Session (1950), p.273; 42nd Session (1946), I, p.59.)

124. The fire also destroyed classrooms and a library housed in the dormitory. The loss was put at £10 000. (*Basutoland News*, 14 September 1948; *Moeletsi oa Basotho*, 9 September 1947.)

125. *Inkululeko*, August 1948.

126. *Ibid.*; *Basutoland News*, 14 September 1948. The last three were members of the Communist Party who had been sent to Lesotho to help with the costs of the legal defence in the Roma fire case (Interview, Edwin Mofutsanyana, 4 July 1981).

127. *Inkululeko*, September 1948. Even then the police tried to get one of the accused to commit perjury so that Lefela at least would be convicted.

128. *Guardian*, 17 February 1949; Scott, *op.cit.*,, p.204.

129. *Basutoland News*, 30 November 1948.

130. *Guardian*, 17, 24 February 1949; 10 November 1949; *Inkululeko*, 19 November 1949. The editors of *Inkululeko*, Edwin Mofutsanyana and M.S. Diphuto, were also cited on the same charge but they ignored the summons to appear in court.

131. *Basutoland News*, 12 July 1955; Regina vs Josiel Lefela, criminal appeal 29 of 1955. (I thank Rivers Thompson for supplying me with a copy.) According to the government, Seeiso was admitted to the hospital in December 1940 with an acutely inflamed gall bladder. His condition deteriorated and two days after an operation he died of heart failure.

132. *New Age*, 19 May 1955.

133. *Mohlabani*, April-May 1955.

134. Regina vs. Lefela.
135. J. Lefela to D. Hammarskjoeld, 18 December 1957, *op.cit.*
136. *New Age*, 26 June 1956.
137. The Resident Commissioner nominated Konyama Cheba to take his place. See BNC, 52nd Session (1956), II, pp.1-7.
138. Bernard Leeman, *Lesotho and the Struggle for Azania* (University of Azania, 1985), pp.64-66.
139. Isobel Edwards, *Basutoland Enquiry* (Africa Bureau, 1955), p.15.
140. B.M. Khaketla, *Lesotho 1970* (London, 1971), p.39.
141. On his instructions, Lefela was buried close to his homestead since he feared ritual murderers would exhume his body if he were buried in a public cemetery. His funeral was paid for by the BCP. (*Basutoland News*, 9 March 1965; *Moeletsi oa Basotho*, 20 March 1965.)
142. This phrase was coined by Prime Minister Leabua Jonathan to describe Josiel Lefela. (Interview, Prime Minister Leabua Jonathan, Maseru, 6 May 1980.)
143. BNC, 47th Session (1951), II, p.555.

Maphutseng Lefela (original in Inkululeko)

Josiel Lefela, 1948 (original at Lefela homestead, Mapoteng)

Walter Matitta (original in possession of Samuel Mohono)

Edwin Mofutsanyana, 1980

Group photographs of Lekhotla la Bafo (originals at Lefela homestead, Mapoteng)

Josiel Lefela is on the far right (original in possession of Mosebi Damane)

Rabase Sekike, Edwin Mofutsanyana and Josiel Lefela at a meeting in Mapoteng, Lesotho, 4 July 1947

Documents

Introductory Note

The documents appearing in this volume are drawn from a variety of sources, a fact which reflects the extraordinary number of associations that Lekhotla la Bafo had with individuals, organizations, newspapers, and governments in Southern Africa and around the world. A great deal of documentation is found in archives containing colonial records. Lekhotla la Bafo, hoping to convince the British that it was not a subversive organization, went to unusual lengths to give copies of its speeches, petitions, and appeals to British officials. (As well as handing over copies of correspondence to local officials, Lekhotla la Bafo leaders often arranged for the originals to be sent to London beforehand, through members and sympathizers in the Union of South Africa.) Their efforts did little to alter the British perception of them, but were successful in ensuring that many of the association's documents are available in the Public Record Office (PRO) in London, the Lesotho National Archives (LNA) in Maseru, the Archive of the Paramount Chief at Matsieng (MA), the United Nations, the Anti-Slavery and Aborigines Protection Society, and various newspapers. Details on the movement would be even richer if the responses from external organizations had been located and if the papers kept by the Lefela family in Mapoteng had survived Lesotho's political turmoil of the last decade. It is said that most of the documents stored in Mapoteng were seized and burnt by government forces in a general sweep after an abortive coup in 1974. The zeal of the government in destroying what it labelled anti-government material may have been responsible for the loss of a considerable number of documents relating to the political history of twentieth-century Lesotho.

For the most part, I have not tampered with the English of the authors of these documents, but where the meaning of sentences has been unclear, I have made editorial changes.

Lekhotla la Bafo carried on voluminous correspondence with British officials at all levels in the hope that some at least would look with favour on their appeals. The exchange of letters was one-sided for while Lekhotla la Bafo letters were numerous and lengthy, the British responses (if they chose to respond at all) were cursory or terse. Indeed, because Lekhotla la Bafo regularly circumvented British officials in Basutoland, the British decided that their letters to upper echelon officials first had to go through the Resident Commissioner in

Maseru before proceeding any further.

In the following document, Lekhotla la Bafo spells out the reasons why it came into existence, and what its objectives were.

1.

H.M.D. Tsoene to Prince Arthur Frederick, High Commissioner, 25 August 1923, LNA S 3/22/2/1

We, your subjects through the Paramount Chief of Basutoland known as the 'Lekhotla la Bafo' in Basutoland most humbly and respectfully forward our grievance to you on behalf of Basuto nation as a whole.

Your Royal Highness, as you are the representative of His Majesty King George V to protect Basuto through the Resident Commissioner in the same way with which the late Chief Moshesh requested the late Queen Victoria to accept him, we forward our grievance to you on behalf of Basuto nation as a whole.

Your Royal Highness, it is with profound respect that we mention here that the late Chief Moshesh, creator and collector of Basuto nation, had established an institution through which his people had to vent their grievances in connection with their government. He had a National Council known as 'Pitso'. In this national gathering every member of Basuto nation was free to expatiate upon all matters brought before the nation in the Council; moreover the people were free to lay their grievances before their Chief; so that he might remedy them. After the death of Moshesh, the late Chief Letsie I, the successor of Moshesh, in conformity with this procedure, carried on this Pitso.

It was for this great love for this pitso that in 1884 at the disarmament peace agreement Basuto were unable to accept the advice of the late Queen Victoria's government that Basuto people should establish a Council of about 60 or 70 chiefs and headmen to be termed an Advisory Council, and that that Council had to have power to legislate. The Pitso gave them such satisfaction that they were unable to accept that advice, and furthermore they entreated the government to let them conduct their affairs with this Pitso in their relation with government. The government of the late Queen Victoria did let Basuto go on with it. The place where national gathering used to be held was

Thota ea Moli; it was at this place of Thota ea Moli where the government used to lay before the national pitso through the Paramount Chief its wishes in relation with Basuto government.[1] This mode of Council satisfied Basuto until the Chief Letsie I died. Then Chief Lerothodi, the successor of the late chief Letsie I, carried it on until 1903.

In 1903, Basuto nation was deprived of this pitso which was used to be held at Thota ea Moli. There was established the present National Council instead of Basuto Council of 'Pitso'.[2] Basuto nation was given a verbal promise that the National Council would follow the customs and laws of the late Chief Moshesh in its legislative capacity towards the people in order to satisfy them. Your Royal Highness, we regret to mention here that the nation found itself in the wilderness where there is no mode or manner of making its grievance reach the attention of its chiefs or even to give thanks for its good government in some cases. The National Council has practically become something like a very steep kloof surrounded with precipitous cliffs without passes by which the nation should get to the chiefs to lay its grievances before them for redress. When the time approaches for the National Council to meet, the notice of time when the Council meets is given only to the members of the Council. The nation is left ignorant of it, and furthermore it is not asked to say what it would like to say in relation with its government. When the Council closes, the nation is not given to know of what was being done in the Council. It will only learn from the operation of new laws made during the latest session. We may assure his Royal Highness that this act is the source of great grievance in the nation and it is this complaint that made people murmur and seek for another way of making their grievance again reach the attention of their chiefs in the Council.

In 1907, the Progressive Association came into existence and the government granted it a seat in the Council. Its aim is to gain more seats in the Council and this is the point upon which Lekhotla la Bafo is at variance with it. Lekhotla la Bafo has carefully noticed that the National Council is exclusively for the Chiefs and headmen nominated by their Chiefs in accordance with Proclamation No. 7 of 1910, section 2, subsection 4. Then the wish for more seats in the Council is equal to the wish for people to depose chiefs and replace them. Owing to the divergence upon this matter and others, on the 27th of September 1919, a meeting was held in Mapoteng, P.O. Tejatejaneng [Teyateyaneng] in which it was decided that it was necessary that there should be established some means with which the Basuto nation should make its grievances, complaints, requests and advices reach the attention of the chiefs. It was further decided that that association should be called 'Lekhotla la Bafo' to distinguish it from other associations.

It was further decided that the late Chief Peete should be given to know the resolutions of association as the association had met in his ward and furthermore that he had to be given the desire of the association was to petition the Paramount Chief to grant the nation the Commons' Council in which the nation should voice its grievances before the Paramount Chief for redress. Then it would be for him to see which of them he could lay before the government because the late Chief Moshesh in his overtures to the government said that the government should govern him, and he should govern his people. The petition wished the Paramount Chief to give the Commons a separate Council from the National Council. This was agreed upon. The late Chief Peete was formally informed and agreed with us upon this matter and wrote a letter to the Paramount Chief introducing the messengers of the petitioners and also backing up our petition. The Paramount Chief's reply was in this form: that we want to get to live in the habits of more civilised and advanced nations while we are yet backward. He further said that he could not work together with young men such as the petitioners [on] the affairs of this territory, and added that he had not even accepted the Progressive Association until that day. He advised us not to hold any more meetings . . . .

Your Royal Highness, as we see that Paramount Chief and His Honour the Resident Commissioner do not take care of this matter, although we had followed their advice given us in 1920 [and] although the Proclamation No.7 of 1910 empowers the Councillors to take care of the interests and opinions of the nation, we find ourselves justified to appeal to you with great respect and humbleness to request you be kind with us and give this nation the way of making its grievances reach the attention of those holding reins of its Government. We do not appeal to you with a charge against the Paramount and his Honour the Resident Commissioner, but we appeal to you to show you this difficulty under which this nation groans as there is no legal manner in which this nation can make its grievances reach the ears of its rulers. We pray Your Royal Highness and lay this matter before your attention that Your Royal Highness may be pleased to consult your subordinates the Resident Commissioner and the Paramount Chief and establish under your authority an institution through which this nation should be enabled to put its grievances before the rulers, and not that this nation should be like a nation without anyone to look after its interest or sympathize.

May it please Your Royal Highness we most humbly request you to be kind to give this nation the Commons' Council, which its members would be elected by the nation and which would be presided over by the government officer and that of the Paramount Chief. The matters that were considered in it would pass on to the National Council for consideration there . . . . Your Royal Highness, before we come to the conclusion, we wish to explain why we say that this Council should be presided over by Government Officer and that of the Paramount Chief . . . . We thought over this matter very carefully and have noticed that if we could say that this Council should be presided over by the Paramount Chief through his representatives alone some would perhaps think that we have some intrigue against the Government while your subjects have nothing of that kind at all. All that we wish to get is the manner in which we would be able to lay our grievances before the authorities for redress . . . .

Your Royal Highness, we suppose in the History of South Africa you are the first High Commissioner and Governor General of South Africa as the representative of gracious Royal blood of England. Furthermore, we suppose we would not be wrong to say that you are the first High Commissioner who declared in your first public speech at Cape Town that you have come to advance and protect black races of South Africa which disappointed some portion of the white community. We rejoiced in that speech and gave cheers for it because a flash of hope penetrated us that if our rulers do not give us the Council we requested, we would appeal to you, you whose ears are sharp to hear the far distant cry of your black subjects. Therefore, Your Royal Highness, we beseech you to have mercy upon us and give this nation the Council of Commons apart from the National Council which its members would be elected by the nation and the motions considered in it would next be considered in the National Council, so that you may leave an everlasting memory planted deep in the heart of the Basuto nation for generations to come.

Justine Ratsiu was an early leader of Lekhotla la Bafo, although he
later broke away in the 1920s to form his own association, Lekhotla la
Toka (League of Justice). In the following excerpt, he discusses some
of the difficulties in organising the initial meetings of Lekhotla la
Bafo.

2.

Justine Ratsiu, 'Council of Commons', *Naledi*, no date. LNA S 3/22/2/1

Allow me a space in the people's newspaper. I wish to write shortly on
the council of the above name, which assembled at Mapoteng on the
1st January 1920.

The meeting was well attended, people from all parts of Basutoland
attending. There were excuses from those unable to attend. All those
who attended enlisted in the book as members and were gladly received.
On that occasion rumours had stopped some who had wished to attend,
it being said that the 7/6 subscription was intending for building the
Ethiopian Church here. This was the bad advice which those who
dislike the council spread. It was also spread by the white people at
our place to frighten the people. The ignorant and those easily persuaded believed and turned back. Some spoke great lies by which they
tried to fight against this Council. This matter of lies is very bad.
These men who ridiculed and fought against this council did not
attend, whereas it were better they attended to listen for themselves
and not speak from far to lead away those who understand. The . . .
council received letters from other parts written by educated men
fighting this scheme. Some had promised to attend but scorned from
the outset when they heard the aim of this council by reading from
newspapers, they were afraid to come. We know the names of these
'balotsana' (wicked persons). They become councillors through us,
they backbite us to the chiefs, traders and the missionaries, they tell
lies to our missionaries by saying that we are looking for a way out
from them to Ethiopia for which we pay 7/6 . . . . Fellow men, I end
by saying that I state the truth, we are not entering the matter of the
churches by forming the council. The subscription imposed is for
managing the council, as there is no other means of finding paper and
paying   for   the   advertisement   of   the   council's   notices   in   the

newspapers. The door is open to all and you know 'enter' beware of those who tell you falsehood by saying that we are building an Ethiopian church, whereas we are building the Council of Commons and enabling our delegates to have food, what would they eat?

The constitution of Lekhotla la Bafo was written in the 1920s with the assistance of a white Johannesburg lawyer. Although copies of the constitution are found in the files of the colonial administration, the British later gave as one of their reasons for denying Lekhotla la Bafo a seat in the Basutoland National Council the fact that it did not have a written constitution.

The first sentence of the constitution is critical since several writers have placed the word 'not' between 'did' and 'satisfy', thus giving a significantly different reading to Lekhotla la Bafo's platform.[3]

3.

Constitution of Lekhotla la Bafo, PRO DO 9/12

Preamble

Whereas the later Chief Moshesh and his successor in office did satisfy the people in their government by the establishment and sustenance of a national assembly known as 'Pitso' and held at Thuta-Ea-Moli.

And whereas the said Pitso was in the year 1903 abolished and the present Basutoland National Council constituted composed of the chiefs and their advisers,

And whereas the present composition of the National Council is not in the best interests and good government of the territory by reason of the exclusion from membership of persons and associations other than the chiefs and their advisers,

It is resolved:
(a) To form an association to safeguard, promote and protect the best interests and welfare of its members and persons other than the chiefs and their advisers.
(b) To seek official recognition of said association and adequate representation in the Basutoland National Council.

(c) To uphold the principles and to insist upon the revision of the constitution of the Basutoland National Council.

(d) To encourage and insist upon the strict observance by members of law and order and to maintain loyalty to government and the chiefs.

(e) To give moral as well as active support to the missionaries and to encourage members to strive towards the attainment of higher education and all that counts for progress.

Constitution

1. The Commoners' Association will be known by the name of *Lekhotla la Bafo*.

2. This Association will establish branches throughout Basutoland and in the neighbouring countries where Basuto have gone for several purposes.

3. Lekhotla la Bafo will select two places where the headquarters will be established in Basutoland and in the Union.

   a) In Basutoland the headquarters will be established at Mapoteng and the headquarters in the Union will be under the head office at Mapoteng.

4. The Lekhotla la Bafo will hold a general meeting at least once a year to which all the branches will send delegates with the resolutions duly passed at branch meetings for consideration by the general meeting, and the resolutions passed by the general meeting will either be sent to the National Council through the Association's representatives or the members of the National Council; other resolutions which at the discretion of the meeting are not able to be sent to the National Council will either be sent to The Paramount Chief and the chiefs in their respective capacities or to be sent to His Honour the Resident Commissioner and the Assistant Commissioner in their respective capacities.

5. The general meeting of the Lekhotla la Bafo will be presided over by the President-General or Vice-President-General in the absence of the President-General.

   a) The meetings of the district branches will be presided over by the presidents or vice-presidents in the absence of the presidents.

   b) The Lekhotla la Bafo will have a general secretary and an assistant general secretary.

   c) The branches of the district will have a secretary.

d) The Lekhotla la Bafo will have a general treasurer and vice-general treasurer.

e) The district branches will each have a treasurer and assistant treasurer.

f) The Lekhotla la Bafo will have a general organiser and organisers who have passed the examination of the History of Lekhotla la Bafo, and these organisers will carry out preaching the dogmas of the Lekhotla la Bafo and these organisers will be elected for their work after having been examined by the general organiser and confirmed by the general meeting.

g) In the meetings under the President-General and the Presidents, the chairman of the Convention will manage the proceedings.

h) The General Meeting of the Lekhotla la Bafo will elect auditors for the books and accounts of the Lekhotla la Bafo.

i) The Lekhotla la Bafo will have a solicitor to act as a legal advisor to it.

j) In the absence of the office bearers the acting officers will be elected.

6. The Lekhotla la Bafo will invest its money in a Savings Bank.

7. The Laws of the Constitution of the Lekhotla la Bafo will be enacted, amended, altered or repealed by the General Meeting of the Lekhotla la Bafo in a yearly General Convention into which will come all the office bearers and delegates from the branches and which will be presided over by the President-General.

8. The Lekhotla la Bafo will have a certain number of men to form an Executive Committee which will look after the interests of the Lekhotla la Bafo. The district branches will have their committees.

a) The Executive Committee may meet several times to attend to matters which require attention prior to the General Meeting of the Lekhotla la Bafo; it may give replies to the letters of the Lekhotla la Bafo; it may appoint a time for the special meeting of the Lekhotla la Bafo if there be any matter requiring the special attention of the Lekhotla la Bafo in the opinion of the Executive Committee.

b) The General Convention will elect a Secretary and Chairman of the Executive Committee.

[Clauses 9 – 13 deal with bookkeeping procedures.]

14.The Lekhotla la Bafo will start and run businesses to increase the fund of the Lekhotla la Bafo in the places approved of by the General Convention.

15. The members will pay 2/6 for enrolment fee and pay another 2/6 for correspondence and £1 (one pound) for the fund of the Lekhotla la Bafo to enable the Lekhotla la Bafo to send out delegates to make constitutional representations before the authorities against repressive laws made for the people.

   a) The members will pay yearly 2/6 for the renewal of their names as members and another 2/6 for correspondence.

16. Lekhotla la Bafo will pay those officers who prosecute the schemes of the Lekhotla la Bafo into execution, but those members who assist with advice only without being obliged to put into execution the schemes and plans of the Lekhotla la Bafo will not be liable for payment by the Lekhotla.

   a) General Convention of the Lekhotla la Bafo will determine the amount to be paid to all the presidents, secretaries and organisers etc. if they are faithful in the performance of their duties which will be explained to all of them, one by one, in their respective duties.[4]

17. The Lekhotla la Bafo will propagate its ideals and doctrines by preaching on the platforms and in the newspapers and by other possible methods.

18. The General Convention will elect new office bearers or re-elect the office bearers within a period of three years. Through the pressure of certain unavoidable emergencies the election may be made before the lapse of three years if one officer or more office-bearers' behaviour demands such a change.

19. The Meetings of the General Convention and of the district branches will be opened and closed with prayer by the religious chaplains elected by the General Convention and the district meetings. In the absence of the chaplains the Convention may appoint acting chaplains to do the service on behalf of those chaplains.

20. [This clause deals with the handling of correspondence in the absence of officers.]

21. The members of Lekhotla or any persons confronted with disabilities or any persons whose matters are neglected by the chiefs and the government or any persons who are unable to receive advice on their respective matters or any persons who receive the advice from the chiefs and the government which makes them hopeless on account of their inconsistence to one another upon the same matter, will send their requests for advice

to the Head Office together with their reports of disabilities to put the Lekhotla la Bafo into touch with the unsatisfactory management of the matters of the people by the chiefs and the government so that Lekhotla la Bafo may be able to put the request, advice, complaint and grievances of the nation with full knowledge before the government, chiefs and the National Council.

4.

Maphutseng Lefela, 'A Manifesto of the Lekhotla la Bafo', *Umsebenzi*, 31 August 1929

Lekhotla la Bafo in its general meeting, held on the 3rd, 4th and 5th August 1929, adopted suggestions and proposals put forward before the people of Basutoland as a nation to supplant the new regulations issued by the Resident Commissioner of Basutoland to abolish hereditary chieftainship under the guise of restoring justice to Basuto courts of law.[5] The adopted suggestions and proposals serve as the constitution drawn on the principles and conditions under which Basutoland under Moshesh came under the protection of England.

The preamble of the constitution exposes, for general information, the hypocrisy, perfidy, treachery, corruptive and delusive tactics of the Government officers applied on the chiefs to be the real cause of all the disaffection manifesting itself in the people of Basutoland against their chiefs. Taught and encouraged by the Government officers through missionaries in churches and schools, this spirit has been engineered to provide an excuse for the agents of Imperialism — to speak plainly the Resident Commissioner and the High Commissioner for Basutoland — with weapons to blot out the political existence of Basutoland, to open it for the complete foreign domination of Imperialism in the interests of foreign capitalism.

The constitution provides that the eradication of all the causes of the grievances and hatred and disaffection of the people against their chiefs, and the debauchery and corruption of the chiefs with resultant bribery now at its worst in the chief's courts shall only be carried into effect by the chiefs and their people coming together in a national assembly to determine their own destinies and to enact laws which shall be directed against the causes of the grievances. For this reason the new constitution of the Lekhotla provides for the resuscitation of the Basutoland national assembly, formerly known as 'Pitso', in which chiefs and the people, including organisations of all different types of opinion and interests, shall enjoy equal rights of expression of opinion in all national matters put forward for consideration and discussion.

Under the new constitution a national newspaper shall be established for the purpose of moulding public opinion and championing the interest and welfare of Basutoland. Also a national school shall be established for the purpose of creating a new type of intelligentsia with new national aspirations and ambitions. The school shall be conducted on academic and technical lines. Another newspaper shall be established in London with a representative of Basutoland responsible to the Basuto nation for the correction of the wrong impressions and misrepresentations created by the agents of our enemy on English public opinion to antagonise our political existence.

The chiefs of Basutoland after the first conference of chiefs and people before the Paramount Chief in the presence of the Government shall sign the new constitution as a pledge to do nothing contrary to the requirements of the constitution, and the Paramount Chief shall sign all laws enacted by the Basutoland national assembly, and he shall bring all national affairs with the advice of his Executive Council, composed of principal chiefs, which shall be assisted by the Executive Council of the National Assembly.

The new constitution will be put before the people in the conference, to be held in Maseru on the first Sunday of the commencement of the session of the National Council in October next, and on the following day the delegates of the Lekhotla la Bafo will put it before the Paramount Chief and His Honour the Resident Commissioner to put the same before the Council for consideration as a substitute of the new regulations issued by the Resident Commissioner.

Now as we know for certain that the Resident Commissioner, working under the instructions from his Excellency the High Commissioner, whom we asked to make room for delegates to interpret our constitution before the members of the National Council, shall refuse to accept the constitution giving expression to the desires and wishes of the people of Basutoland and shall forthwith force his new regulations for the abolition of Basutoland hereditary chieftainship upon us as the people of Basutoland, we declare and make known throughout the world that we shall not accept these conditions. Hence, to give expression to our uncompromising attitude to reject holus bolus the new regulations forced upon us as a nation, we shall be obliged to take legal proceedings against both the High Commissioner and the Resident Commissioner before the courts of law.

Sooner or later, owing to the unlawful and unconstitutional oppressive steps taken by the powers that be, Basutoland will be a seen [sic] of unpleasant happenings because if both His Excellency the High Commissioner and His Honour the Resident Commissioner are not prepared to govern us in accordance with our desires and Moshesh's express wishes, we are prepared to meet any form of civilised barbarities, and welter in the prison cells in resistance against the conditions of slavery and expropriation of our country under the guise of restoring justice to Basuto courts of law.

Naledi ea Lesotho (Star of Lesotho) began publication in 1904. Founded by Solomon Monne and Abimael S. Tlale and published in Mafeteng, it was the only African-controlled newspaper in Basutoland.[6] Few issues of *Naledi* are extant, so we do not know how many articles Josiel Lefela contributed to it, but we are fortunate that when Lekhotla la Bafo was founded in 1919, the colonial administration began collecting and translating some of his articles for their files.[7] Some of these appear in the following section.

At the same time that the Resident Commissioner called in Lefela to dismiss him from the Basutoland National Council, he also called in Edwin Tlale, the editor of *Naledi*, to chastise him and warn him against printing more articles such as the one of 25 September, 'How shall we do away with the black race'?[8] He counselled Tlale that in the future he should be more careful and consult him before printing articles of questionable content. 'I have power to do more than talk to you in this matter, but I do this because I want you to realise that I am not your enemy but one who wishes to help and befriend you by pointing out to you where you have done such grievous wrong.'[9] At the meeting, despite the arbitrary manner of the Resident Commissioner, Tlale had kept his thoughts to himself, but he later wrote a sharp letter to him. He resented the manner in which the Resident Commissioner had tried to 'bully' him like a mining compound foreman in front of staff officers and a representative of Griffith. He would not allow the freedom of the press to be tampered with, but he thought it would be more difficult now that the chiefs thought he could be gagged.[10]

Tlale also took up Lefela's defence. He recognized that Lefela's dismissal had long been sought by the chiefs, but his peccadilloes were minor when compared to the crimes of other counsellors whose offences had been proved in court. 'Can this discrimination be because Lefela's remarks extended to white people, and that the property stolen by other Councillors was native property?'[11]

Lefela continued to submit articles to *Naledi* for a short time after his dismissal, but a second attempt by Garraway to pressure Tlale to censor Lefela was more successful. Garraway feared that his 'foolish articles' might be picked up by South African newspapers 'where they might be the cause of misunderstanding and give reason for suspicions of the loyalty of the Basotho'.[12] Because Garraway thought bringing Lefela to court would only elevate him to martyrdom, he did not bring a court case against him (an equally likely motive for his restraint was that his case was too weak) but he proposed to see Tlale again and warn him not to give an outlet to Lefela; this attempt was more successful as Lekhotla la Bafo was virtually shut out of the Basotho press for the rest of its existence.

5.

Josiel Lefela, 'How shall we do away with the black race?', *Naledi*, 3 September 1920, LNA S 3/29/7/2.[13]

For a long time the Europeans in South Africa have been considering and asking themselves how they can stop the increase of the blacks who are increasing while the Bushmen, owners of the land have disappeared; many plans for the ending of the black man in South Africa have been thought of; of those that have been tried many have come to grief on the way and have not reached maturity. Today a deep scheme has been found, which to anyone who does not look into it clearly seems to be kindness, rather than the destruction of the whole black race in South Africa. With deep design the missionaries have been instructed to encourage everywhere the founding of Young Women's Associations. These Y.W.C.A. are to be encouraged everywhere, especially to protect against those customs which they say are sinful. Today in those associations women and girls are encouraged to collect money for building a home for Christian whores, young and old, to whore in. That is the way that our people will be put an end to.

The life in the home which will be built for whores will be made attractive, the life will be pleasanter than in their own homes and in this way our girls who are annoyed will say on the slightest provocation 'I will take myself off to Johannesburg'.

Those who inquired into the reason why the black races increased, found that it was because black men kept to their own kind, so that if the Europeans wished to reduce the number of blacks the wise plan would be to encourage half-castes, so that in ten years time the black races would diminish and the half-castes increase. The Government would give these half-castes the same rights as Europeans and these rights would make the half-castes despise the blacks though they themselves were born of our own daughters.

When we first heard of this rumour we understood that a plan was being prepared and considered by which we should be deprived of the mould in which God moulds us, in order to mould Europeans. Finally it was discovered that the best means of depriving us of this mould was by making use of Women's and Girl's Associations where women and girls meet for the purpose of religion. Thus, while the men were thinking that they were being instructed, the women and girls would be shown and become acquainted with the place to which they could run away if they were to be bound by cattle-marriage or if they were ill-treated by their husbands or if they were ordered to make beer, or in any of those other ways which the missionaries say are sinful. Now in all parts of South Africa, in the name of God, women and girls are being recruited. In the European churches, they are recruited to go whoring in Johannesburg, where a house is being built for women and girls to whore in. Wake up, black man, open your eyes, rise from your sleep. Have European whores ever had houses built for them? Why this great kindness to our women and girls? When will they do it for their own kind?

African, do you understand what you are reading? To-day you Christians of the white man's churches take notice that this arrangement is a plan to diminish and to destroy before our faces the women and girls who will go there and give birth to half-castes. Men of Basutoland, a Mosuto said, 'Those who go to Mahlatsi must go carefully'. Moshesh the giver of this advice used to say only one foot should be put into religion as many tribes had been destroyed by missionaries; many governments in difficulties have had their path made easy by missions.

I will prepare myself to write an account of the Portuguese and how they came to take our people. Their plan was to come and soften the hearts of our black brethren by teaching them the word of God, and when they had softened them, they sold these people and made slaves of them. They did so that they might become the owners of these people's lands. That is not the only occasion that governments have obtained an entry by means of missionaries of their own race. Today a way of finishing the black people has been spied out by the missionaries; they give out that women and girls should be encouraged to join associations — associations in which they will be encouraged to their (spiritual?) comfort. At one, men, take your women and girls out of these associations, see that it is a danger to give these people the right to plan schemes in places where men are not present. The scheme of these people is a deep-laid one. It is spoken of earnestly and with the help of God. See, our tribe will soon come to an end and while we listen open-mouthed to' what the missionary is saying as if there were no danger in it. Wake up Basuto, and all black people, suspect this crafty plot. Lay down the law for your women and girls.

6.

Translation of an extract of an article by Josiel Lefela, *Naledi*, 30 September 1921, PRO CO 417/665.

Whilst you read this you may ask yourself where this sending about of the Basuto leads to. The Government of England only does away with Basutoland. You should remember why the Government of England went out to fight Germany and why Germany has been deprived of her colonies, and what England published as the reason for her fight, or did she fight meaning to take small nations back to bondage and deprive them of their rights? If she did not fight for that, why these fears in Basutoland, in which it appears we are being deprived by a secret plan, of our right, we the small nation that was put by Moshesh under protection. Does the protection of the Government of England mean deprivation of the rights of the small nation and the swallowing-

up of it? Should we be afraid to make our claim in England because of
some of the pledges which we see violated by the Government . . .
England recently fought with the German nation because of not
respecting pledges to protect the rights of small governments. Read
[the] history of the Government of England changing now and again
in a manner unbecoming her fame as a Christian Government, the
Government that is so famous.

7.

Extract from an article by Josiel Lefela
in *Naledi*, 18 November 1921, PRO CO 417/665.

The black man who is misled by Europeans to hate the coming of
American Negroes should throw away the idea. Let us natives strive to
welcome the American negroes with joy, for we have been told by the
respectable Mr J. Mingay Gibbins that no nation can be educated
unless it accepts immigrants from educated countries, who bring
education into countries. For that reason let us look forward to His
Excellency Marcus Garvey the President of Africa, and the
Americans, with anxious anticipation.

8.

Extract from an article by Josiel Lefela
in *Naledi*, 25 November 1921, PRO CO 417/665.

In 1836 the Dutch entered native provinces . . . . When Moshesh
spoke with him about the doings of those servants of his the Governor
Sir George Napier said, 'the Boers went out without knowledge or
consultation with the Government . . . beyond the jurisdiction of
Cape Law' . . . . This advice that Moshesh should ask to be protected
by the Government was given him by the missionaries. When Sir
George Napier heard of this application, before he sent it to the

Secretary of State, he made the following proclamation in September: 'The Queen's Government shall view with disapproval any attempt of Her Subjects to molest or loot or hurt in any way any native tribe . . . if there should be such an attempt the offending parties shall be deprived of what they dispute' . . . . This law exists up to this day although it has been slightly altered in wording . . . Moshesh was not aware of this trap. Sir George Napier, before receiving a reply from the Secretary of State, made a treaty by which he cut off Moshesh's country for the Boers, he making Moshesh a detective, policeman and magistrate, as the treaty is, and promising him a niggardly sum of £75 a year — he could take money or arms.[14] Moshesh was made to feel strong in case the Boers provoked him, and try to fight so that he might be deprived of the disputed country. Moshesh foresaw the plan and did not take offence . . . .

Members of Lekhotla la Bafo were kept well informed about the independence struggle in India through an India trader, Tayab Surtie, who had one of his stores in Mapoteng. Surtie, who had come to Lesotho in the late nineteenth century and married a moSotho woman, was an admirer of Gandhi and supplied the Lefelas with Indian newspapers and political tracts. In return, Lekhotla la Bafo never attacked the Indian community. After the Second World War, Josiel Lefela even suggested that his group should unite with Indian and other Non-European political organizations at work in the Union of South Africa.[15]

9.

Extracts from an article by Josiel Lefela, *Naledi*, 25 November 1921, LNA S 3/22/2/1.

. . . and you will agree that if England is kind and trustworthy, its kindness and trustworthiness we should see shown to our senior brothers the Indians, a black people that owe allegiance to England. And with regard to civilisation about which England boasts, that it has come to impart to nations so that they may be advanced to be able

to support themselves well, we may go and satisfy ourselves by looking at the condition of the Indians ever since they became united with
England. That is where we shall learn the aim of England with regard
to the nations united with it and whom it tells about protection, peace,
kindness and justice, and others like them. I am sorry that nice promises given to the Indians all ended by bringing them misery and heart
rending so much so that some of the promises have resulted in the
shooting of Indians with cannons, and they have died in thousands in
the town of Punjab.[16] They were killed in cold blood when they
reminded the Government of its promises the time they called them to
fight their brothers, the Turks, which their Mohomedan religion is
against. But that promise (Khalifat) as the Indians call it, has produced
for the Indians the law called the Rowlatt Act which law the Indians
could not agree to. The law says that Indians are not to object to
anything ordered by the Government through its servants. It has
appeared therefore that the law stops all complaints so that they may
not be able to make their claims. When the Indians dispute about this
law that it is bad and should be repealed, those people under the kind
Government, cannons and aeroplanes killed them while they had no
means of protecting themselves, for they had been promised protection by England like we have been, they were stripped of their
arms . . . .

Because of the misery in which the Indians are, do listen to an
Indian whose cry touches the heart — from the newspaper "The Indian
Views" of 25 March 1921, on the subject under the heading "Daring
Hell to Comparison". He says: 'If the educated man who had studied
human life, who had been misinformed and who was responsible for
calling our country a nice place wherein to dwell, were alive and saw
our life which is like that of dogs and which is led by sons of India today, surely the educated man would be seized with terrible fright when
he thought of his idea that India was a good country to dwell. Stand
up, arise you Bharta Ancestors who passed away with your glory and
royalty, and look around . . . . Behold evil days . . . ! Pray let us
look with great carefulness by the help of a magnifying glass which
has been given the power of magnifying small things, let it be a 'triple
thousand power multi microscope', and see if we are still the heirs of
India once brave and more exalted than the highest mountain, Mount
Everest. Judge, if you sons of Bharta — we are slaves of India, we are
called 'natives' in England, and with contempt we are called 'coolies'
in South Africa . . . we whom Almighty created and made for a certain

purpose of His, of helping the fathers of all heads in the world with the mat whereon to clean their dirty boots; we who are unfortunate and hated and scorned by the world. We have become property in the hands of our owners. We have been 'covered' with the saying that we are alive since the days of our forefathers of childish ignorance . . . as they did not at all know of the wisdom of the devils of other countries. That wisdom opened the doors of our nice country, they opened it to a foreign European to dirty its purity and ill-treat it for many years. When these sons of advanced people had come into India . . . they pretended to be people who stood for the doing of good for us, the devil hid himself and pretended in the garb of the priest, and told us of his kindness, he assured us about his standing for education, advance- ment and up-lifting of the Indians. We poor heathens were greatly convinced and felt called upon and with great zeal we blessed the stranger for his work of helping us for nothing and without gain. And it is well we have paid him with our tears. To go back to Satan himself, he then began to show himself well, he took his own way, he rolled himself down on our cursed country and succeeded in driving away everything, with cruelty with cannon which can't be stopped and which sound like thunder. His evil shadow passes everywhere from one end of India to another and has withered everything which comes into contact with it. And now the country is so full that there is no place to keep him. Now he gladly sings a song of his wish, rapacity and hatred. Satan continued in this way, he went with great fame showing great wisdom in sports of amusements and others which came his way. His getting high means our India getting low. As soon as we have got under his cutting sjambok we have lost our nationality and become an unfortunate starving crowd which is naked and prostrate with slavery. Poverty has forced many of us to leave their homeland and cross the sea looking for some food. But alas, all dirty corners which scornfully laugh at us are already full of them.'

Here is a pitiful cry, this is the kindness of England, this is the educating of England, this is the way that has been taken to satisfy all nations. Now before I return to our matters I shall remind you that these Indians who have been ousted from their home by hunger and want of clothing which were caused by the English and all white nations of Europe by depriving the Indians — today England agrees that Indians may be ordered away from the countries to which they fled because of hunger and want of clothing, and it was by promise that Indians could go anywhere in the British Kingdom — it was in

1858 when England softened the hearts of Indians lest they feared, so that it might prepare for the time to change its 'head' (mind) when there would be no prating, when it would stop its ears against being reminded of its promises and pledges and when it could think that its advice has crippled the nation that listened to it, and on that day it will kill the nation mercilessly.

10.

Josiel Lefela, letter of December 1921, PRO CO 417/665.[17]

Proclaim, sentinel of the Basuto, sound the warning to the Basuto; let the strength of your voice awaken all the black tribes, because destruction is not coming to the Basuto only, it is coming to all black people everywhere in Africa. The first thing is to see that the minds of the Basuto and the blacks are not filled with the intention of abandoning the protection of England by anything you may say. Yours should be a warning to those who are being hood-winked and told that there is peace: the scheme is to give the white people an opportunity to prepare so that when the time comes the black people may be finished completely in a moment and our land be forever an inheritance for the children and grandchildren of the whites. Man! Sympathise with your fellow tribesmen; leave off wanting the praise of men; wear sackcloth; fast; that the proclamation of your word may be helped by God in that you have shown that you have obeyed the command 'Love your neighbour as yourself'. 'What you wish that others should do to you, do that to them'. Only tell the people that there is no intention of going back on England . . . . If we see that England does not care for us, let us go to all the nations of the earth, to Europe, to America, even to Asia and India and ask them to beg England to free us from the slavery we are in and the plot against our lives. For that reason, tell the Basuto and all black races that death is approaching them, but that they are being deceived into believing there is peace.

Proclaim that the blacks in the churches of the white people should leave them.

Tell those Christians that the Christ they speak of is true, but the ways in which Christ has been brought to them are bad, in that they make all tribes to which Christianity is brought by the white people change their natural customs, though these customs agree with the Bible. The missionaries say that these customs are heathen; because they know that, if they can get tribes to change their customs, there will be no obstacle left to prevent all black tribes becoming the spoil of the whites . . . .

Now you know that iron instrument called the wedge with which, when several are used, trees and other solid bodies are split. The whites are a wedge to split the blacks. But if a wedge is not sharp it will be turned off and it will effect nothing. The churches of the whites are the thin end of the wedge. Where they enter, those tribes are compelled to give up their customs. When they had done this, up come the trader and the doctor brothers of the missionary, and it is made out that the things they sell are holy things. Read the 4th Sesuto Reading Book which says, 'Now Livingstone decided to search for the new countries in the interior of Africa, so that he might open for the Missions and trade a road into the interior of Africa. He was pioneer of the whites in the interior of Africa.'

Now all black people who read history will agree with me that there is no way for the whites to expand unless they follow the missionaries. Everywhere the missionaries have been pioneers, and they are followed by the trader, then comes the Government to protect the trader. The missionaries are the thin end of the wedge, the traders are the body of the wedge, and the Government is the head of the wedge that splits the tribes. If we wish to avoid their destruction which will split us to pieces, we must beware of the missionary. Not that we must drop Christianity, if we are to be a real tribe and one that England can protect, we must take out the thin end of the wedge and the wedge will cease to split our tribes . . . .

Now the warning which we must send out to the people is that God and Jesus are the sheepskin, but that those who wear it are ravening wolves . . . .

The missionaries say that God rules in heaven and on earth and that if all tribes were converted they would come together and praise the Lord. People would beat their spears into ploughshares . . . . But if our tribes really did beat their spears into ploughshares, I am sorry to say that the missions encourage their people to make bullets and murderous weapons, aeroplanes, cannons and ships of war travelling above and below the water.

Where the gospel came from one would expect them to practice it; where they should have wrought ploughshares is just where they are making weapons most vigorously. What truth is there in the missionary? What confidence can one have in him? Today be as wise as snakes in taking the advice of the missionaries, but without malice, like a turtle dove.

They have taken from us the clothing which we used to wear, but they refuse to teach us to make the garments which they have accustomed us to. These have to be brought to us ready-made, so that we may be of profit to their home-people and that their trader brothers shall not lose their market, because the things came to us ready-made. Why do they not teach us to make these things ourselves?

Today you hear that General Smuts, the whites and the missionaries have decided that the day has come for the black races to be left to live after their own custom and not to be brought up after the fashion of the whites. It is because the missionaries have found that we no longer know the style of life of our ancestors, which the missionaries have stripped us of. My countrymen, is it not the limit!

After having been taken by the missionary from our old customs with the idea of being brought into the light of progress, it is very difficult for us to return — especially as the habits and customs of the missionaries have made us ashamed to return to our old ways. It is now that these clever people think that it is the right time for us to become a mockery (neither one thing nor another).

My countrymen see that the destruction of the tribes is in the hands of the missionaries, to trust to their advice is to go to our death with our eyes open. Know that in the things we are warning you of you are being put to sleep by the churches. Fear the advice of those who are the ruin of the black people, who seem to be alive but who are deadly poison.

On certain subjects Josiel Lefela would circulate his views to the public by printing up handbills in seSotho.[18] In the following one, he discusses the problems that were created by European missionaries, who attacked the Basuto custom of *lenyalo la likhomo* (cattle paid by the bridegroom to his wife's father on the occasion of marriage).

11.

Josiel Lefela, 'Advice. Proclamation. *Lenyalo la Likhomo*. Laws should be translated into seSotho', published about 1921, LNA S 3/5/8/3.

The disapproval of *lenyalo la likhomo* by the Paris Evangelical Mission Society church is undignified for the Basotho nation at its present stage of Christian development. This disapproval is not discussed secretly by the church of God known as the P.E.M.S., mother and father of Lesotho, in the light and knowledge of God and Jesus Christ the saviour who died for the nations so that those who believe in him should be saved through him.

Lenyalo la likhomo is considered a sin, a sin which results in excommunication from the church of God, even if the father pays *lenyalo la likhomo* because of his son falling in love with a girl whose father demands *lenyalo la likhomo*. Chiefs are the servants of God who lead the nation to goodness, and this marriage troubles one section of the nation of Lesotho which is the Christians of P.E.M.S. who have born sons who are not attracted by Christian girls. So then the National Council together with the honourable father missionaries are here to investigate the wrong which is considered a sin in traditional marriage since it is disgraceful for one nation to have two types of marriages. What is there to prevent a joint meeting to come up with one type of marriage since priests are the servants of Jesus Christ son of God to teach the nation the correctness of the laws, and the chiefs are servants of God to lead the nation to goodness. Is it not proper that discussions be held jointly where deliberations of such a committee will peacefully and harmoniously resolve a uniform approach to marriage. So that where priests identify a sin in *lenyalo la likhomo* the National Council should take note and the National Council should explain its interpretation of *lenyalo la likhomo*. Marriage should be made uniform by eliminating issues which may be understood to be dirtying this gift which is given to the girl's father by the boy's father according to SeSotho custom. Marriage is the purification of the birth of every human being — so that he is born in a manner which is not unacceptable before God, and children born out of *lenyalo la likhomo* — since that marriage is unacceptable to the P.E.M.S. church — have inherited a blemish of a sinful marriage. Marriage is the chief thing among all things that ought to be put right, and striving for an agreement on one kind of marriage will be pleasing to the nation. Even Christians of the P.E.M.S. will be glad for one kind of marriage since their souls are endangered as Christians by their sons who prevent them from praying to God with clear and peaceful minds. I put this explanation before the honourable President and P.C. [Paramount Chief] that this will be one of the matters which I will present before the secretary of the Council during discussions of the next Council.

The second matter is that the books of the laws of Proclamations be translated into seSotho, because it is a custom of the Basotho to ask the chiefs about laws concerning a matter they complain about . . . . The Basotho chiefs do not know the laws of Proclamations, but these laws which the chiefs and the Basotho nation do not know but are known by those who have learned English are used if matters go to the Courts of the Assistant Commissioners, especially if they concern a white person. The majority of the people can only read seSotho, not English. It would be well, as lawyers are not allowed to come into Basutoland, if these laws were translated into seSotho by a sworn translator so that laws which affect and work among the Basotho may be known by the chiefs that they may help the people, and that those who know seSotho only may read for themselves as they will buy the books. It is a painful thing to the people not to know the laws which must work among them.

12.

Presidential Address, Matsieng, 26 December 1928, LNA S 3/22/2/3.

Chiefs, members of Lekhotla la Bafo, my fellow countrymen and women, I greet you in the name and on behalf of Lekhotla la Bafo. You all have been bold and courageous to stem the storm of ridicule, the most destructive weapon of those in power upon the weak and irresolute people, by coming to this meeting held under the auspices of Lekhotla la Bafo.

The . . . matter which requires the most serious attention and a scientific probing and treatment . . . is the abolition of chieftainship, the death knell of which has been sounded by the circulation of new draft laws to the members of the National Council by His Honour the Resident Commissioner of Basutoland which will be considered in April 1929.[19]

In the analysis of the symptoms and causes of the abolition of our chieftainship I must necessarily go back to the time immemorial . . . when the institution of circumcision was established by providence and state plainly why it was established. The purpose of circumcision was to train the people to be true to themselves, their neighbours and relatives and to help one another in times of trouble. Above all these circumcisions trained men to be loyal to their chiefs, their government and their national movements, to protect their rights and country, and fight for their rights and country when the enemy of their country attacks them. And, on the other hand, the chiefs were taught to rule their people with sympathy. In this institution people were taught to refrain from the commission of theft and adultery as well as all other social offences. Now it was under this institution that Basuto people were able to hold on and protect their rights and country from the encroachments of all their enemies. It was through the spirit of loyalty to their chiefs and brotherhood that they were able to stand by their chiefs through thick and thin . . . and it was through this institution that the chiefs tried all in their power to rule their people in a sympathetic manner.

It was under these conditions that Basuto people lived when the missionaries came with their religion into Basutoland.

When the missionaries started their activities they denounced all the virtues taught Basuto people through circumcision as heathen practices and told the people that the virtues contained in their religious teachings are more sublime than those practised by Basuto. The christian Basuto are demanded to acquire better habits and godly virtues in turn of their denouncement of their social laws. The missionaries of one denomination teach their followers to regard the followers of another denomination as their social enemies. In this way in Basutoland, there are the missionaries of three denominations: namely, Paris Evangelical Missionary Society, Roman Catholic and the Anglican Church (not including the Wesleyan church which has lately started its activities in Basutoland). The followers of each denomination are the social enemies of one another. The promise of godly brotherhood and the sublime social reforms of the best description are not seen but internecine strife and hatred of one group against another.

In regard to politics the christian Basuto are the most disloyal to their chiefs who are entrusted with the right of looking after the welfare and interests of Basuto people. In times of national troubles, when all men are required to render their service in defence of their country, rights and freedom, the christian Basuto are often found in the lists of treacherous and disloyal men. Very often they despise their chiefs. To support this matter, it is better for me to quote some remarks from the *History of South Africa from 1873 to 1884*, Vol. II, page 60. Dr. Theal, in writing of the trouble of disarmament war, says: — 'Before the day fixed, those Basuto who were in the service of the government, most of the converts at the mission stations, Jonathan's clan, and a few others gave up their arms.' Perhaps it is better still to explain why the chiefs and all thoughtful men of Basuto nation abstained from embracing christianity. Notwithstanding the fact that when the first missionaries first started carrying on their activities in Basutoland, the chiefs and the leading men of Basuto nation embraced christianity with eagerness. After the first national troubles which needed the service of all men in defence of their rights, when the missionaries inserted the influence of Christianity upon their followers against matters of such nature, the chiefs and all leading men of the nation who had embraced christianity broke away from the church.

Rev. R. Henry Dyke, in his *Gospel Work in Basutoland*, page 13, says: — 'The missionaries were at this time full of enthusiasm and expectation as conversions had been numerous and the church was zealous in the work of spreading the gospel. Several of the young chiefs and leading men of the tribe were church members and hopes were entertained that soon the Basuto as a nation would accept christ as Lord and King. But alas! political troubles arose and a succession of sanguinary conflicts took place between Moshesh and Sekonyela, chief of the Batlokoa. These conflicts were mostly due to the mistaken policy followed by Major Warden in the Orange River Sovereignty and to his fixing arbitrary boundaries between the natives and the early Boer settlers. The missionaries, in their attempt to bring christian influence to bear upon the conduct of such wars, found themselves at variance with the leaders of the people, and serious misunderstandings followed. The confidence of the tribe was lost to some extent, and a great falling away took place, particularly among what might be called 'the aristocracy of the tribe.' Even after this, the church of Basutoland became more and more democratic and the missionaries developed their work among the people through the people . . . . As a matter of fact, however, the missionaries had to bear in a measure the brunt of broken hopes and lost ideals of the natives regarding the whiteman.'[20]

In this way you will easily realize that religious teaching has some connection of assistance with the colonial administration carried on by the Colonial administrators for their own selfish ends for the exploitation of African nations. This is mainly done by the missionaries to break up the social and political integrity of our national existence and the task of doing this explosion in Basutoland was entrusted to the missionaries by the colonial officers of the government as will be learned from the writings of Dr. Theal.[21]

The Government of Cape Colony, on seeing the inevitable national semi-independence of Basuto under their chiefs under the protection of England to result from the readjustment of the affairs of disarmament war . . . concluded an arrangement with the missionaries of Basutoland, particularly of the Paris Evangelical Mission Society, whereby the future generations of Basuto people would be rendered ready to give up their rights and lose their country through ignorance of true history of the relations and conditions under which Basutoland came under the protection of England. Since that time Basuto people were secretly deprived of their valuable property of letter books of the dealings of Moshesh with the governments of Cape Colony and Orange Free State which were in the hands of the missionaries of the Paris Evangelical Mission Society. This plot of the deprivation of Basuto nation of their national priceless property was effected by the missionaries in sending the letter books of Moshesh at the request of the government of Cape Colony to the Cape Colonial government in 1882. This step was taken as a preliminary step in the attempt of bringing the political annihilation upon the national independence of Basuto under their hereditary chiefs by forcing the darkness of ignorance upon the future generations of Basuto people taught in schools and churches.

Dr. Theal, writing of this matter, says: — 'Early in 1882 the government resolved to have all the authentiç records that could throw light upon the history of the Basuto tribe collected and published, and the duty of carrying out this work was entrusted to me. It was not supposed at the time that the quantity was as great as it was subsequently ascertained to be. The government of the Orange Free State was applied to and with the utmost cordiality opened its archives for our use. A clerk was engaged for some months at Bloemfontein copying documents which had not been supplied to the High Commissioner.

The missionaries in the Lesuto were not less ready to help. The early letter books of Moshesh were in their possession, and these were forwarded to me with many other papers of the utmost value for the object in view. The journals, reports and maps of the first missionaries in the Lesuto were copied and supplied in the most obliging manner.'

It is a political fact that the Cape Colonial Government concluded a scheme with the missionaries of Basutoland to teach Basuto people distorted political ideals to give them a defective education which in practice is worse than illiteracy because of its misleading effects and deceased education has proved itself to be poison to every healthy mind or brain . . . . On account of this scheme, the Basutoland school text books are full of political fallacies aiming at dodging the minds of even able Basuto people into the loss of their political status. In speaking of the position occupied by Basutoland under the protection of England after the disarmament war in 1884 and of the plot to undermine that political status to bring it to ruin, Dr. Theal writes as follows in the *History of South Africa from 1873 to 1884*, Vol. II, pages 79-80: — 'On the 18th of March 1884 an order of the Queen in Council was published confirming the act severing Basutoland from the Cape Colony, and on the same day Lieutenant-Colonel Marshall James Clarke, who had been appointed Resident Commissioner, relieved Captain Blyth of the disagreeable duty he had been performing and direct imperial rule was established in the territory.

'Basuto were of course elated by the change, as it relieved them of all fear of compulsion of any kind being employed against them if they did not choose to obey every regulation that might be made by the representative of the Queen . . . . The imperial administration in Basutoland employed a moral force alone, which would have been of very little value but for the fear of the chiefs and the people that they might be abandoned if they did not at least profess to be loyal. British protection they valued because they knew that if it should be withdrawn they would soon be again in the condition in which they were when Sir Philip Wodehouse came to their relief . . . . To this, to time and to missionary teaching the future of the Basuto was committed.'

Now I wish to point out here that in 1884 Proclamation no. 2B 1884 was put before the Council of Pitso to be considered, but it was rejected by Basuto people on the ground that it weakens and abolishes the birth right of our chiefs to claim chieftainship in direct conflict with the conditions under which Basuto came under protection. But it is under the authority of the same proclamation . . . that His Honour the Resident Commissioner drafted the new laws for the abolition of our chieftainship. This catastrophe has been brought about by pernicious propaganda carried on by the missionaries in their teachings in church and school. This fact is further illustrated by Rev. R. Henry Dyke in the *Gospel Work in Basutoland*, page 6-7, in the following language: — 'Owing to its geographical and political position Basutoland is bound, in the near future, to become one of the most important factors of the 'native question' in South Africa, as its inhabitants form the only large tribe which retains its unity and independence under its hereditary chief. It is therefore of the greatest possible importance that christianity and education should without delay let their power be felt; for out of 460 000 Basuto only one fourth come under direct influence in church and school. What then is to become of the 350 000 who live in heathenism and are increasing in numbers at an abnormally rapid rate?' This quotation is clear enough to show that the missionaries are in great earnestness about the political annihilation of Basutoland under the protection of England. The treachery and hypocrisy of the missionaries as the political enemies of Basutoland is now disclosed in a very clear manner.

Now we have learned from Dr. Theal of how the future of Basuto children was entrusted to the missionary teaching and through their teaching in church and school Basuto people were tantalised with the heavenly like happiness of progress if they may do away with the stumbling block to christianity and civilisation — the chiefs . . . . Under the teaching of this nature, all those Basuto who came under the influence of christianity and education in church and school gradually acquired a deep seated rancour towards their chiefs and their political status hidden from them by the teaching of the missionaries in schools. In 1904, before the South African Native Commission, Rev. Dyke was asked whether there was not yet any outcry for reform of the people associated with the church. These questions were asked because the government officers knew well that in the missionaries was placed the trust of undermining the political status of Basutoland to bring ruin on the National Life of Basuto nation. The following were the questions asked by Sir Godfrey Lagden, the chairman of the Commission, to Rev. Dyke of Paris Evangelical Society.[22] These questions are found in the South African Native Affairs Commission with minutes of evidence, Vol. IV, p.414: —

39612   The powers given to the chiefs in this country by the existing laws or regulations have, I take it, in your opinion, been fairly administered?

I think it is very satisfactory considering and during the last thirty years things have worked very well.

39613   Do you think there is much hardship in the fact that people suffering from injustice are not able to get further redress by appeal?

I think those injustices should be seen to by the existing government, and pressure brought to bear upon the chiefs as a general thing to give consideration to all and not only to a certain number.

39614   You have a great many christians in this country. I believe?

Yes the christians are a considerable number.

39615   They amount to many thousands?

In connection with Paris Society we amount to about 40 000 adults connected with our church, of whom over 20 000 are on the church roll.

39616   Amongst this large class with whom you are so familiar, has there been an outcry or any demand in any shape for a change in the order of things here?

There has been no general demand for it that I know of.

39617   Has the voice of reform in any way made itself felt or the desire for change?

In certain details there are things that our church people would like to be modified.

These questions were asked by a man who knew well that from the christian people will arise the outcry for a general change in the form of present order of things obtained and enjoyed by Basuto nation under the arrangement concluded in 1884 . . . . We shall see how this outcry came to burst out like a dynamite.

Now we have seen that the missionaries through their teachings are entrusted with the means of breaking up the integrity and internal self government of Basuto under their chiefs with their teaching by sowing seeds of discontent and disaffection of the people towards their chiefs. A great many disabilities have been placed before the chiefs to make them hopeless in discharging their duties to the best interests of their people. While these disabilities placed before them the missionaries are taking the advantage of the shortcomings and vices of the chiefs forced on them by the inevitable disabilities placed on them by the Government Officers . . . . With these vices they accelerate the growth of rancour and disaffection between the chiefs and the people and one of the great disabilities was the introduction of the appeal matter. It was well known that much more weight than the chiefs are able to perform would fall on them resulting from this matter and that in the end it would result in great hardship to the people.

It was under these circumstances that in about 1920 there came to Basutoland a man with the purpose of rousing the people to murmur much about the bad management of affairs. This man wrote many articles of criticisms against the management of affairs by the chiefs in one of Basutoland newspapers under the nom de plume 'Mohlokalebitso'. This man collected through his influence all those whose animosity against the present order of things had long been sown through education and christianity as Rev. R. Henry Dyke with others in conjunction with government officers had wished. This man disguises himself as a Mosuto. This man became the adviser and friend to one organisation of the name of Progressive Association of Basutoland. It was during this time that another (probably the same man) of the nom de plume 'Mosotho' wrote an article in the *Friend*, issue of 2nd December 1921, by which he accused the chiefs of gross maltreatment of the people . . . and that the people are being cruelly forced to render free labour for the chiefs in the performance of which some people had been killed with knobkerries and others injured.[23]

Furthermore he levelled a charge of miscarriage of justice at the chiefs courts and the unnecessary delay in hearing the cases. He invited all the white men in Basutoland and in the Union Government to use their influence to bring an end to all these things. These charges were seconded by the late Simon Phamotse and the Progressive Association, composed of christians and educated Basuto, upheld this matter . . . . In 1922, a great Pitso was held in Matsieng as the result of this political outcry for a reform in the order of the political status of Basutoland by the men specified above. It is under these circumstances that His Honour the Resident Commissioner found the pretext of drafting these new draft laws for the abolition of chieftainship.

Now I beg to show that it is not for the benefit of Basuto people that our chieftainship is being abolished but it is for their final political ruin under the pacific methods to bring about the inclusion of Basutoland into the Union Government. This matter is much analogous with the matter of the abolition of chieftainship of the Kaffir chiefs in Cape Province in 1855 by Sir George Grey. The reasons assigned for the abolition of chieftainship of the Xosa chiefs to them were not the same with those explained to the Secretary of the Colonies in London. The abolition of chieftainship brought no good result to the Xosa people but an unspeakable misery and final ruin of their national existence. This matter fits well in our case. In connection with this matter, *A Question of Colour*, page 19 reads as follows: — 'In 1855 Sir George Grey, who succeeded Sir George Cathcart as Governor, effected an important change in the administration of justice among the natives. His reasons for this change he stated to the Home Government, and, briefly put, the system which he found existing was that the native chiefs derived a considerable revenue from what might be termed the fines and fees of the court of justice, — thus exercising sovereignty by appropriating to themselves what should have been a part of the public revenue.

'To remedy this state of things, Sir. G. Grey, as her Majesty's High Commissioner, offered to pay the chiefs and their principal Councillors certain fixed monthly stipends in lieu of the fines and fees they formerly received and in consideration of their voluntarily relinquishing the authority conceded to them by Sir G. Cathcart (in our case by the Home Government in 1884) . . . . They were now permitted to continue to hear all cases brought before them by their people, but they were to be assisted in their deliberations and decisions by European magistrates, who were to be placed with them; and all fines and fees imposed for public offences become a part of the revenue of the Crown as in other countries.' In this case of the abolition of our chieftainship the same reasons are the real motives which actuate the Resident Commissioner to abolish our chieftainship. It is not true that the real motives which work as an incentive upon His Honour The Resident Commissioner to force him to break the condition under which Basutoland was transferred to the Imperial protection in 1884, are the feelings of sympathy and of love to Basuto people because I have ample reasons to show that the most acute grievances harshly affecting the people in Basutoland are rigorously and fiercely and mercilessly applied upon Basuto people by the officers of the Government.

To prove this matter, I beg to state that in 1925 the Lekhotla la Bafo did put before His Honour the Resident Commissioner the tension of heavy tax of £1.5s and showed him that since the Union Government had resolved to reduce the amount of tax to £1 Basuto people will evade the payment of £1.5s by going over to the Union government for some months as workers so that they may get time to pay their tax in the Union Government to return home after that payment of tax. Thus, the revenue of Basutoland will decrease and that when such matter draws his attention he will devise some further atrocious measure to draw money from the people in such a way equal to the economic strangulation of Basuto people by forcing them to pay more money than they are able to earn under the present conditions of closed doors of trade against them. But instead of reducing the hut tax His Honour, through the advice of the missionaries, increased the hut tax by the levy of three shillings upon £1.5s to bring the amount to £1.8s. All those who fail to pay this exorbitant amount are sold for £1.8s to the capitalists who send them to their works under very cruel conditions. Another point of great affliction to the people is the matter of the poisonous dip, which kills the sheep and goats of the nation by the thousands [see Document 28]. We have put the matter before His Honour the Resident Commissioner to use dip free of poison but there is no relief and sympathy shown to the people by His Honour the Resident Commissioner. Moreover, as we had foretold that His Honour the Resident Commissioner on seeing the decrease of the revenue would devise some further merciless means of raising money. His Honour has introduced another cruel measure of the overcharge on all parcels delivered at the postal agencies throughout Basutoland. We have tried to show him this grievance under the most pathetic language but no relief has been made by him. Moreover we have shown him the great hardship applied upon Basuto by exacting ½d per lb. on all wool sold by Basuto but no mercy, no sympathy, no fatherly love, no relief has been shown by His Honour to the poor people of Basutoland.

The government allows the chiefs a certain amount of money as allowances for the tax collected in their wards and if the tax collection in the wards of some chiefs decrease their allowances are reduced. In this way, when some people die leaving their widows and children behind, those widows are deprived of the fields they were ploughing during the life time of their husbands so as to give them to young men who will pay tax to keep up the required standard to give him the right to claim sufficient allowance for his pay. The widows, on being deprived of these fields, may bring their complaints before the notice of the officers of the government but nothing always is done by them to relieve them of this hardship. In this way, these poor widows often . . . resort to making beer for sale in order to earn means of livelihood. But in face of all these facts, His Honour the Resident Commissioner has supported the abolition of the sale of beer. The Lekhotla la Bafo did put this matter before the notice of His Honour and the Paramount chief but no relief has been forthcoming . . . .

Now . . . I wish to draw your attention to the fact that our political existence has been undermined by the teaching of the missionaries in attacking our national and social customs which invigorate the national ties of unity under our chiefs under the guise that those customs are incompatible with the word of god . . . . It is not so but they attack our national and social customs to satisfy their own selfish purpose. It is always the case when the missionaries enter the field of preaching the Gospel to other nations of certain national and social customs to discuss the matter of how they shall deal with the national and social customs of those people who embrace christianity. This matter is eloquently explained in *The Question of Colour*, page 65 in the following language of Rev. A. Kropf: — 'Wherever the Gospel is preached among heathen nations, and souls are saved by the means of grace and brought into the folds of Christendom, a most important question arises, namely, what is to be done with the national and social customs of the converted people? Are they to be allowed, and to what extent, or are they to be abolished, and those who still practice them excluded from membership of the church?'

Now when the missionaries attack our national and social institutions they do not mention that they attack them by their own account not connected with the word of God but they attack them as the national sins which cannot allow those who practice them to see God and his paradise at the hour of death. In this way you will clearly and easily see that God is used as a bait and hell as a bugbear by the missionaries to the people to force them to relinquish their sacred national and social customs to bring about the disorganisation of the people under their hereditary chiefs bound together by their national ties. Under this kind of teaching today, our sick man being our chieftainship is on the point of expiring unless some national effort be made without delay to put our grievances as a nation before the notice of the government of His Majesty King of Great Britain in England. I wish to explain briefly why we must appeal to the Secretary of the Colonies to agitate for the revision of the constitution of the National Council to admit of adequate representation of the common people through their elected representatives under the machinery of Lekhotla la Bafo and also to put before the Secretary of the Colonies our protest against the abolition of our chieftainship by these new draft laws.

Some people advise us not to appeal to the Government of England because they allege that many nations appealed to England without success. They point out that India, China, Egypt and Africa through African National Congress all appealed to the Government of England for redress of their national grievances without success. Hence they deduce that in the same way our case will also prove a failure. Now the viewpoint of the Lekhotla la Bafo is that it would be wrong for us Basuto people who are directly under the protection of England to apply the case of other nations in our matters. We wish to put our appeal of grievances before the Home Government so that if England neglects and disregards our grievances that may be done to us so that we may know the Government of England has neglected our grievances . . . .

I wish to briefly explain the catechism of the Lekhotla la Bafo before you here that Lekhotla la Bafo instructs its members to obey the laws made by the Government officers in Basutoland notwithstanding the fact that some of them are operating harshly upon the people . . . . The Lekhotla la Bafo instructs that its members must be loyal to the King of British Empire in accordance with the conditions under which Basutoland came under the protection of England. Its members must cherish feelings of affection towards their chiefs and do all the services required from them by their chiefs as in the days of the Chief Moshesh and his successors. The members of Lekhotla la Bafo are instructed to respect all those holding positions of authority. Those who are the Government servants must carry out the orders of their masters to their fullest satisfaction and those who are under the shopkeepers must obey and respect their masters and do all that they are ordered to do in a most satisfactory manner . . . so that when the grievances are put before them to ask for redress they may well know that those grievances affect some of the members of the Lekhotla la Bafo . . . . Above all, Lekhotla la Bafo is not up against any kind of organisation of any group of people in Basutoland. On top of this, Lekhotla la Bafo binds most strongly its followers to cherish feelings of love to the ministers of religion. All members are forced to work for the acquisition of high educational attainments and assist the ministers of religion in the matter of promoting sound religious ideas and habits. [See Document 25].

I beg to explain here . . . the harmful propaganda carried on by the ministers of religion to bring about our political downfall and ruin. Lekhotla la Bafo does not mean to carry on its activities against the ministers of religion, but I have explained these historical facts so that the missionaries may be able to reform their ways regarding these facts so that we may be able to carry on our labours in harmony with them. I wish to state here that the missionaries have come into our homes, deceived us in every way under the guise of Christianity. But do you not ever believe that we are not christians. We believe in God the Father, God the son, and God the holy ghost; we endorse the Nicene creed; we believe that Jesus died for us; we believe that God lives for us as for all men; and no condition can the missionaries impose on us by deceiving us about christianity will cause us to doubt Jesus Christ and to doubt God. We shall never hold Christ or God responsible for the commercialization of christianity by the heartless missionaries who adopt it as the easiest means of fooling and robbing other people out of their land and country. If we would indict christianity the bishops of christian religion would stand aghast as history reveals.

. . . I warn you Basuto that in the abolition of our chieftainship is interwoven the opening up of Basutoland to the occupation of Europeans to the complete disregard and elimination of what had been promised to those who would assist in the matter of the abolition of our chieftainship. Those of you who cherish the idea that if they assist those who abolish our chieftainship in their attempt they will get some benefit out of it are quite mistaken; the outcome of the abolition of our chieftainship will be the opening of Basutoland to Europeans to settle and exploit it to their own interests. At that time, when you try to speak about the conditions under which Basutoland through Moshesh came under the protection of England, the officers of the government will tell you that it is on account of your clamour and request that your chieftainship was abolished and with it the conditions under which Basutoland came under protection of England went to the region of oblivion and hence those conditions are no longer in force. Then you will begin to realise that you had been fooled . . . . I quote a view held by many white people in South Africa as explained by Sir Godfrey Lagden in his book of 'Basuto', Vol. II, p.644 in the following language: — 'It is not right, on the plea of misplaced respect for rights of the occupants, that industrious races should abandon rich territories to uncultivated and incapable native populations who will never turn them to account. To deny this right to civilised peoples will

be to suppress all possibility of human progress . . . . For a civilised
nation it is not merely a right but a duty to turn to account those lands
whose value is wilfully ignored by a careless and primitive people.' In
order to show you that the aim and object of all the white people living
in Basutoland and in the Union is to open Basutoland for the occupation of Europeans, I beg to quote the address of welcome to Prince
Arthur of Rev. A. Casalis for Paris Evangelical Missionary Society in
1921 found in *Naledi* of 10 June 1921 which reads as follows: — 'The
education of Basutoland is a very important, and at the same time a
very delicate one. It cannot be neglected either by the missionaries,
nor by any white man living in the country, whose wish it is that the
great social race problems of South Africa be dealt with in a true christian spirit with view to the pacific establishment of a really united
South Africa . . . . We are convinced that the Basutos ought to be
given an education which will render them apt to fulfil their duties as
citizens of the South African Commonwealth.' As I have already
showed, it is through the efforts of the missionaries that Basutoland is
threatened with the final political death blow and ruin. These missionaries were working under the instructions of the white men living
in the surrounding colonies and in order to prove that the whiteman of
the surrounding colonies are working for the political downfall of
Basutoland in order to give way to the settlement of Europeans in
it . . . I beg to quote from *Native Life in South Africa* by Solomon
Plaatje, p. 209-210 the following passage in which Sir George Farrar
before the Transvaal Labour Commission put questions to General
Louis Botha:—

11302   Sir George Farrar: you said that you would recommend the breaking
up of locations like Swaziland, Zululand and Basutoland and the putting of white settlers there?

General Louis Botha: I would suggest that these countries be given up
to the white people to live in . . . .

11337   Farrar: The general tenor of your remarks is that there is sufficient
labour and it only wants a little patience to wait for it that is all?

Botha: I have distinctly stated that there is a greater amount of labour
than has at present been obtained. But there are farmers who have
farms, and have no natives living on these farms. For these people it is
difficult to obtain natives because the natives who are not living on the

farms are in locations. If the locations were broken up the native would be made to live on farms.

11338   Farrar: You suggest that we should break up such land as Basutoland, Swaziland and Zululand?

Botha: Yes I say that such places are a source of evil. It is building up a Kaffir Kingdom in the midst of us which is not only bad for the Kaffirs themselves but is a danger in the future.

11339   Farrar: But take Zululand, for instance; there is a quarter of a million people there. What would you do with them if you break up their territory?

Botha: They would all live on the farms as the white people are doing now.

11340   Farrar: Oh you want to cut up the land into farms, give it to the white people and retain the Kaffirs on the farms?

Botha: Yes.

11343   Farrar: But what will the white people do with the Kaffirs, pay them wages or charge them rent for the ground or what?

Botha: My opinion is that Kaffirs who live in locations should work for the white people and the land should be exploited. The white people would pay them for this work they did and this would civilise them.

11344   Farrar: A nation like the Basutos you would deal with in the same way?

Botha: Yes.

11345   Farrar: They at present occupy the land, we have had it in evidence before us to the effect that every inch of land in Basutoland is occupied and worked by the Kaffirs themselves as their own property?

Botha: That is just my argument . . . because there is opening for the Kaffirs there they go and live there without doing anything.

11347   Farrar: But they do something. They work the whole country, they have lots of grain?

Botha: Yes, for themselves.

11352   Farrar: I have shown you that Basutoland is fully occupied by Kaffirs and they work it. Do you want to apply your scheme to Basutoland?

Botha: I do not know very much about Basutoland, I have never been there personally; but I am acquainted with Zululand and Swaziland, and I want to state this, that in my opinion it is not only wrong policy, but also a dangerous policy to have large tracts of country inhabited by uncivilised races, and to keep them there on the present terms.

11353   Farrar: But these natives lived there from time immemorial. It was theirs before we came here. How can we drive them off the land now, and take it for ourselves?

Botha: I think we are feeling very happy that we drove them from Johannesburg in the olden days. They lived in this country too just the same and the Kaffirs who became civilised under us have improved.

Now, having heard the foregoing quotation, I want to remind you that when Devil came to Eve, the wife of Adam, with his suggestions that if Eve might eat the fruit of the tree of the knowledge of good and evil she might become wise like God himself, it was not because the Devil sympathised and loved Eve and Adam, but it was because he knew well that the result of her eating the fruit of the tree of knowledge of good and evil will be the curse which will bring misery on them and that in such a way he will get time and opportunity to exploit them for his own selfish ends. In the same way, if you allow your chieftainship to be abolished, the outcome of it will be breaking up of Basutoland to allow white settlers to occupy it who will exploit it for their own selfish ends and turn you [into] their slaves and animals of burden and toil, just as you have learned from the above quotation what was being contemplated by the late Prime Minister of the Union Government. He is dead now, but his evil spirit is still ravaging the land. It is on account of his policy that we are today confronted with the question of the abolition of our chieftainship which in fact is the question of the abolition of the present political status of Basutoland . . . .

Now, in conclusion, I appeal to you chiefs one and all to realize that the honour, freedom and welfare of Basutoland are at stake. It is not time for you to take greater interest in the meetings of dances and horse races and neglect to take much interest in the politics of your country. It is your birthright to discuss and think over in your minds the present politics of your country. It is high time for you that you must reform your behaviour towards your people. I want to draw your attention to the fact that your treatment upon the nation is irksome, and unless you do all in your power to reform your treatment to the people, you will render our task more difficult in our efforts to save your rights and powers from ruin and abolition because the nation, tired of your troublesome treatment, will easily be duped by those who wish to deprive you of your rights and powers to allow them to carry into execution their scheme . . . . I earnestly beg you to realize that upon you devolves the trust of keeping Basutoland safe for posterity and this time needs and demands all chiefs and people to sink all their differences of opinion, jealousies and bickerings amongst themselves to face the common enemy with all the seriousness of purpose and effort to save Basutoland . . . .

Now I appeal to you my countrymen and women with all earnestness of my heart to rally to the cause to save our earthly paradise. I want to warn you from the historical hard facts of experience that all white men in South Africa may smile at you and smile around you but deep down in their hearts there is no love for you but that which you maintain for yourselves. This may seem outrageous in a country where we profess christianity and fellowship, but men, in spite of all the religious and moral teachings that man indulges in, when it comes to black man, he is left in the cold to fight his own way through if he is to survive the condition of slave, peon or serf. The only friends that the black man of Basutoland has hitherto are perhaps England and God. Believe me when I state this, because I know what I am talking about. Let no pseudo-angelic, no high sounding philosophy enunciated by the divine persuade you at this time not to act as black men for your own interest and for the good of your posterity. I want to remind you that you are capable of achieving all that may be achieved by members of other races of the world. It is not true the black man of Basutoland along with the rest of his fellow members of Africa is predestined by the providence for the position of hewers of wood and drawers of water for other races of the world. It is through your foolishness that you may take that position, but if you work hard like all the other races of the world, through your achievements you will force other races to respect you just the same way as those races are being respected by other races. It is now time for you to wake up from lethargy of many years under that trickery, chicanery and swindle perpetrated upon you by members of other races for their own selfish purposes to devote your minds into the loss of your priceless property — Basutoland.

My countrymen and women, I appeal to you to realize that this time demands men and women of strong minds, great hearts, true faith and willing hands, men whom the lust of office does not kill, men and women who the spoils of office cannot buy, men who possess opinions and a will, men and women who can stand before a demagogue and damn his treacherous flatteries without winking. Therefore, I appeal to you to support the Lekhotla la Bafo with men and finances to answer the call to duty for lo! Basutoland long asleep, is now regaining consciousness.

> She has heard the call imperative
> Oh Basutoland awaken the morning is at hand,
> No more art thou forsaken,
> Oh Beautious motherland, from far thy sons and
> daughters are hastening back to thee,
> Their cry sings over the borders,
> That Basutoland shall be free, Basutoland redeemed,
> Let it be one and glorious aim of the oppressed,
> By the hopeful sons of Basutoland —
> Come in and possess the land which the Lord
> Thy God has given you under the Protection of
>   England. Why not?

13.

Presidential Address, Matsieng,
21 June 1929, LNA S 3/22/2/3

In order to make you understand the position under which we are deprived of our rights it is better and necessary for me to explain the historical inclinations and tendencies of the man in whose interests our rights are being taken away from us. We are living side by side with the Europeans living in the surrounding colonies and these Europeans came into our countries in Africa with the sole purpose of turning our countries into the commercial fields from which they must enrich themselves in order to benefit . . . their mothers countries in Europe from which they came . . . . We learn this fact from the *British Colonial Policy* by Mr. H.E. Egerton, page 2. But they realise that it is always difficult for them to have the command in their hands, of the wealth of the countries in which they have entered unless the government of those countries is in their power . . . . Therefore, they do all in their power to take powers of government of the countries in which they live either by force or fraud from the indigenes of those countries who are eventually turned into animals of burden and toil for their new and cruel masters.

In order to work for the realisation of these two fold objectives, many wars have been waged under various pretexts all over the world, and many indigenous nations of many countries in the world have been exterminated such as the Red Indians in America, Tasmanians in Australia and the Bushmen in Africa in order to give way for the flourish of capitalism and imperialism . . . . It is often investigated by the Europeans in Africa why the black Africans do not dwindle before the forward march of capitalistic and imperialistic barbarities and exploitation.

Another point I wish to draw your attention is the fact that the missionaries, who have entered our countries under the guise of the messenger of God to preach the gospel to all nations of the world, are the pioneers and herald of the pernicious capitalistic and imperialistic forward march which blasts everything which comes in its way. It is not true that Jesus on the eve of his departure ever said: 'Go ye unto all nations and preach the gospel to them' as it is so stated in the Gospel of Mark, chapter 14, verse 15 . . . . We learn from *Encyclopedia Biblica*, page 1880, section 'G' that in the gospel of St. Mark, chapter 16, from verse 9 to the end of the chapter is an interpolation which means that those verses were inserted by the councils of the bishops in order to find the pretext of sending the spies and pioneers of capitalism and imperialism into foreign countries under the guise of the messengers of God of heaven . . . . In fact the God who sent them into our countries is the evil spirit of capitalism and imperialism which has proved itself to be a curse and scourge to the world. This fact is substantiated by the fact that we learn in the *Naledi* issue of 2 December 1921 of the views expressed by Rev. Dr. Henderson, the Principal of Lovedale Institution, in regard to the incoming of Europeans into South Africa and their taking possession of our countries. On talking of the segregation question, he is reported as follows: — 'If the Bantu people used aright the vast resources placed at their disposal we should not have been here today. The incoming of Europeans to South Africa, and the taking possession of its lands was the judgment upon their failure.' This Rev. Gentleman expresses in clear language that it was and is true that he is the messenger of the God of imperialism and capitalism and therefore all missionaries have proved themselves to be the agents of our enemy — imperialism and capitalism . . . . It is through their labours that many of our countries were brought under the iron heel of imperialistic oppression and capitalistic exploitation and, in Basutoland, they have contributed a large share in the work of depriving Basuto nation of their rights . . . .

Now all the Europeans who have entered our countries in Africa and other countries of the world are making use of the two old latin proverbs 'divide et rege' which means 'divide and rule', and 'Si vis pacem para bellum', which means 'If you wish for peace be ready for war'. All the tactics and manoeuvres of Europeans in this country are directed to bring about and put into effect the division of one nation or tribe against another or the division of the nation against its Chiefs in order to give them the opportunity and time to take the country of that nation under their government so that they may be able to enrich themselves with its products. This is a question which must exercise our minds so that we may get the method and policy to counteract this policy of setting the nation and chiefs against one another.

When we look at the method and policy adopted by our enemies through which Moshesh was deprived of his country now known as the Orange Free State, we find that the subordinates of Chief Moshesh were turned and made his enemies by Major Warden and formed them into a league; and into his league Chief Sekonyela of Batlokoa was added and these chiefs then formed into a league were ordered to cause troubles and wars to Chief Moshesh . . . . It was during these wars and national troubles fomented by Major Warden, who was supposed to be a man entrusted with the power of protecting Basuto nation from the encroachments of the Boers, that he drew up a line of boundary between Moshesh and the Boers and thus gave the Boers the greater portion of Basuto country and helped himself to force Moshesh and his subjects to give up this country to the Boers by means and help of those chiefs who had been turned into the enemies of Moshesh and his people although they were his subordinates. And, in this way, the powers of the government over that country after many long bloody wars shifted into the hands of our enemies the Boers . . . . They have the control of the government over the country and the wealth of its products of the country taken from Moshesh through turning his subordinates into his enemies.

Let me tell you a little story of a man who found a snake one day lying almost dead on account of the effects of cold. This man, through sympathy he felt for this snake, went to it and took it up and put it under his armpit to give it some warmth . . . . In this way a snake recovered its consciousness and life, but immediately after this the snake bit the same man in the armpit and put a drop of poison into the wound and through this poison the man soon died after. This man died through his fault of making a wrong use of sympathy.

In like manner let me remind you [of] the rebellious conduct of Chief Moroke who was turned into the enemy of Moshesh mainly through the help of the Rev. William Shaw of the Wesleyan Church who resided in Thaba-Nchu.[24] When the Boers first crossed the Transvaal River to settle on what is known as the Transvaal, Moselekatsi [Mzilikazi], the chief of the Matabele who had fled from Natal from the inroads of Chaka, fell upon those Boers and killed many of them and captured their wagons, oxen and all their belongings. The remaining Boers returned to Thaba-Nchu at Chief Moroke's residence, and chief Moroke gave them some cows to milk and some oxen to draw their wagons . . . . Through his help under his protection in Thaba-Nchu, these Boers organised themselves and went together with Chief Moroke to fight Moselekatsi and with his assistance the Boers managed to put Moselekatsi to flight from the Transvaal and captured many cattle.

Just as I have explained, Moroke, along with other chiefs, were turned into the enemies of Moshesh by Major Warden . . . . In 1851 he used them as his contingents to put into effect his scheme of humbling Moshesh with war in order to put into effect his scheme of the deprivation of Basuto of their country. Moreover, in the great war of 1865-68 between Basuto and the Boers, chief Moroke assisted the Boers as their ally and through his help Basuto were nearly conquered by their enemies. But after the death of Chief Moroke, the same Boers, who got the Orange Free State through his help and the same Boers who managed to put Chief Moselekatsi to flight through his help, turned and set the sons of Moroke one against the other and inflamed the trouble between them which finally ended in a skirmish betweem them . . . . On account of that skirmish the Boers of the Orange Free State got the pretext to deprive Barolong people of their country which formerly had been Moshesh's. This is the end of the gratitude of the white man, whether English or Dutch, to a black African. If you help a white man to gain something you are promoting him to bring about your own ruin. This is the experience of the

Africans in Africa in regard to the white man's gratitude.

Now it was from the encroachments of these Boers that Moshesh requested the Queen of England to protect him. But at the same time he explained in clear language that he wanted to govern his people by his native laws and customs and that he feared to put his people under something which they could not understand. He did not like the government to send Magistrates because that would be like putting a stone which is too heavy for them to carry. But if the Queen would like to introduce other laws into his country he would be willing. But he would first of all put such laws before his people in council and if accepted by the people he would then inform her that they have become law. These are the conditions under which in 1869 the English Parliament recorded in the Imperial Blue Book, No. C4140 its recognition of his protection under England under the same conditions. In 1884, Sir James Marshall Clarke was ordered by the English Government that whenever he could try to introduce other new laws in Basutoland he must not enforce such laws against the wish and desires of the people and that he must not do anything against the wish of the Basuto nation. These instructions were the guiding principles drawn by the English Government for the guidance of the Resident Commissioner in Basutoland.

In 1903, the council of Pitso was abolished and the present misnamed National Council was established and as you all know the constitution of that council ostracised and gagged the common people and our chiefs are turned into the puppets and dupes of the President of the National Grave known as the National Council . . . . Under these circumstances, His Excellency the High Commissioner, through the advice and recommendation of His Honour, the Resident Commissioner, has issued disloyal and treacherous proclamations of the worst description by which we have been deprived of our rights and our chiefs are turned into the fools and puppets and titulars. We are being taught new deprivations of our rights through incarceration and when we ask the Officers of the Government why they deprive us as a nation of our rights, they usually adopt their fooling tactics of setting one class against another and they tell us that it is our Paramount Chief and chiefs in the National Council who make these proclamations of which we complain . . . .

The purpose of our holding a meeting in Matsieng at the Paramountcy is to consult together and discuss our grievances which result from our being deprived of our rights and freedom by the Proclamations. We ask the Paramount Chief to let us know under what grounds and circumstance our rights and freedom have been taken away from us. We ask him in this way because it is through him that we are being prevented from electing our own representatives to represent us in that political dungeon known as the National Council. Moreover, it is our duty according to the conditions under which Basutoland came under the protection of England to put our matters and grievances before the Paramount Chief for redress and it is for him to see those which it is proper for him to put before the Resident Commissioner to consult him about them . . . .

I announce that Lekhotla la Bafo received an invitation to attend a meeting to be held in Paris from the 20th July to the 31st July 1929 from the League Against Imperialism and for National Independence. Perhaps it is better and necessary for me to say a few remarks about the formation of this organisation. In 1927, the workers of Europe, groaning under the exploitation of the capitalists of Europe, held a great meeting of workers in Brussels into which there were the representatives of the workers from parts of the world. In this meeting an attempt was made by the workers to ameliorate their position but their attempt was made futile by the fact that they realised that it is impossible for the workers of Europe to bring to reason the capitalists of Europe because they have their economic slaves in the colonies who produce wealth for them . . . . In this way they can live quite happily without the workers of Europe if those workers do not submit themselves under their exploitation. For these reasons the workers of Europe realised that their economic emancipation is interwoven with that of the Colonial peoples but they again noticed that without the political emancipation of the colonial people groaning under the iron heel of oppression of foreign imperialism and capitalism, the economic emancipation of the colonial peoples is impossible. Therefore, on account of these facts, the workers of Europe organised this League Against Imperialism . . . . The aim and objective of this organisation is to collaborate with the Colonial Oppressed peoples in their activities to try to secure a place of freedom under the sun. It is why this organisation takes great interest in our struggles for freedom.

Another invitation comes from the Universal Negro Improvement Association under the leadership of Honourable Marcus Garvey to send a representative of the Lekhotla la Bafo to attend a meeting to be held in Jamaica, British West Indies, from the 1st to the 31st August 1929.

The aim and objective of this association is founded on the following new facts: The Africans in Africa and abroad are the most exploited, and oppressed, maltreated, enslaved, down-trodden and despised as well as hated because they have no power behind them to protect themselves from the insults and oppression and encroachment upon their rights and liberties from other nations. The Englishman is respectable not because he is respectable [but] because he has his own Government to protect him, to force respect for him upon other people. So is the French, the German, the Spanish and others who have governments of their own to look after their interests and welfare. Therefore this organisation strives for the uplift of the entire negro race and it aims at setting on foot the schemes and plans, which will enable the negro races to establish a government of their own in Africa, their motherland . . . . It is for this purpose that an international convention of negro people of the world is going to be held in August 1929. I regret that Lekhotla la Bafo through the lack of funds is unable to attend . . . these conferences . . . .

In conclusion I want to draw your attention to the fact that it is not the fault of the English government in England that you Basuto people are being deprived of your rights under the guise of protection . . . . The fault lies with you because you handed the reins of destiny of your country to other people by allowing yourselves to come under the sway of the evil influence exerted upon you to lull you in the lethargy of deception to give your enemies opportunity and time to prevail over you . . . . Now it is up with you to wake up and fight for our rights constitutionally until we appeal in England where we shall learn whether the English Government would confirm these deprivations of our just rights or would revoke them. In the meantime, we have no reason to complain against the English Government, Parliament and nation because we have not yet put constitutionally our grievances before them to redress. I appeal to you, chiefs and people, to support Lekhotla la Bafo with money and strong active men so that it may be able to fight for the rights of people in accordance with the conditions under which Basutoland came under protection.

14.

Presidential Address,
Maseru, 13 October 1929, LNA S 3/22/2/4

. . . I suppose it is necessary to briefly give some few political and historical facts which serve as the motive and incentive of our fight for our hereditary chieftainship under the protection of England. You all know that it was through the more threatening attitude and menace of European robber imperialists of the Orange Free State who had already entered into his country and who were continuously threatening him with the final war of extermination in preparation to taking his country under their control for exploitation, that Moshesh repeatedly asked the British Government to take him again under the protection of England against his enemy who had already encroached upon his major portion of his country. To show that I am not giving a political untruth when I mention that the Boers of the Orange Free State were planning to wage a war of extermination upon Basuto in order to deprive them of their country, I beg to quote some remarks expressed by Sir George Grey in his letter dated 16 August 1856 to the Secretary of Colonies as recorded in Basutoland Records, Volume 2, page 226 as follows: — 'From this correspondence you will find that Moshesh has now, for some time, anticipated that he will shortly be attacked by the people of the Orange Free State, and from the enclosed copy of a letter from the President of that State, in answer to one which I wrote him on the 23 July, copy also enclosed, its Government appeared to have resolved to enter upon hostilities at the commencement of next month, unless certain demands are complied with. What renders the matter more difficult is that the President pointed out in a letter a copy of which I transmitted in my despatch No. 32 of 24th April last, that the real cause of war between Moshesh and the Free State will be the boundary question, whatever other circumstance may be made the pretext for it; and I think it will be very difficult to settle, without a war, a question which I could have wished to have seen adjusted before we left the Orange River Sovereignty.'

Now when Moshesh saw the future political prospects and outlook of his country and nation more and more becoming dark as the days passed away, he repeatedly requested the British Government to take him under protection to protect him with his people and country against his political enemy and opponents until, in 1862, the British Government, through Sir Philip Wodehouse, sent out a commission composed of Messrs John Burnet and Joseph Millerd Orpen to record his wishes and desires in relation to his being taken under the protection of England . . . . Then Moshesh, in 1862, addressing his people before these commissioners, said: 'You must now listen that you may know what I have done for you when I was young and strong; how I have watched over your interests. Now I am old and about to become blind like an old goat. What you have been listening to were only temporary arrangements, but now as I am an old man I am going to make arrangements which will last for ever.'[25] Then addressing the commissioners, he said: 'If the Government sent Magistrates the Basutos will not understand. It will be like a stone which is too heavy for them to carry. What I desire is this, that the Queen should send a man to live with me, who will be her ear and eye, and also her hand to work with me in political matters. He will practice the Basutos and gradually teach them to hear Magistrates, while he is helping me in political matters. He will show them how these things are done in the Colony. He should be a man who will be fully trusted by everybody, and he must know our ignorance and our ways. I fear to put my people under something which they cannot understand, they are like little children who must first be taught the A.B.C. If I can obtain an agent, I will be under the Queen as her subject and my people will be her subjects also, but under me. I am like a man who has a house, the man rules the house and all that is in it, and the Government rules him. My 'house' is Basutoland. So that the Queen rules my people only through me. The man whom I ask from the Queen to live with me will guide and direct me, and communicate between me and the Government. I shall then consider myself to be under the Queen's authority. I shall be like a blind man, but when he directs me I shall be considered wise; when the Agent and I agree as to what is right, I shall carry it out, and he will report it to the Government. I wish to govern my own people by Native Law, by our own laws, but if the Queen wish (sic) after this to introduce other laws into my country, I would be willing, but I should wish such laws to be submitted to the Council of the Basutos, and when they are accepted by my Council I will send to the Queen and inform her that they have become law.'

These above-quoted conditions, having been forwarded to the Secretary of the Colonies with recommendations for the appointment of an Agent to reside with Moshesh, Sir Philip Wodehouse, the

Secretary of the Colonies, in his letter dated 5 June 1862, consented to the appointment of an Agent to reside with Moshesh. But before the appointment materialised, our enemy, the President and Secretary of the Orange Free State, confidentially arranged an agreement with Sir Philip Wodehouse, in his letter dated 19 July 1862, reported to the Secretary of the Colonies of his confidential agreement with the Government of the Orange Free State never to appoint an Agent to reside with Moshesh. This agreement was made in order to provide the Orange Free State Government with necessary weapons and means to put into execution its scheme of war of extermination upon Basuto in order to deprive them of their country. Then, after the great war of 1865 – 68, Sir Philip Wodehouse pretended to come to the help of Basuto, while in fact, he was actuated by the motive of coming to the demand of a share in the spoil wrested from Basuto which was to be partitioned between the Cape Colony and the Orange Free State. The share of spoil wrested from the Orange Free State under the pretence of wresting it for Basuto nation culminated in the annexation of Basutoland to Cape Colony in 1872.

It was after the disarmament war that in 1884 Basutoland came under the direct protection of England enjoying the rights and privileges contained in the conditions laid before the Government for acceptance. It must be to clear you that in 1868, when Sir Philip Wodehouse came to take Basutoland under pretended protection of England, Moshesh pointed his overtures to the commissioners as the conditions under which he had to be taken under protection. But Sir Philip Wodehouse overlooked them and foisted Basutoland into a Crown dependency. This fact alone was accountable for the Disarmament War. Then, in 1884, Basuto people were again granted the privileges and rights embodied in the conditions laid by Moshesh before the commissioners for his acceptance under protection and internal self-government under their hereditary chiefs was encouraged by British Government to Basuto people.

Then again as before our enemy, who did not like to see Basuto prosper under their hereditary chiefs . . . laid political snares and dynamic explosives for the future political annihilation of Basutoland . . . . Through their agents [they] persuaded the English Parliament in 1890 to enact the Foreign Jurisdiction Act which finally put the protectorates under the same category as those territories acquired by England through conquest. This is a step to prepare for the dispossession of Basuto of their country in the interests of our European robber imperialists in South Africa who are blood-thirsty.

In 1903 Lord Milner, as High Commissioner for South Africa and a supreme representative of the King of England to protect Basutoland, laid the foundation stone of an alliance of our enemies in the four colonies of South Africa to unite and build up one strong government whose chief aims and objects were directed against Basuto people to break down the conditions under which they were enjoying the blessings of peace under the protection of England as Moshesh requested . . . . The Resident Commissioner as the man on the spot was turned a spy and agent of our enemies in the four colonies which in 1910 united under one Union Government as the consummation of a commission appointed by Lord Milner in 1903. Under this new order of things created for the political murder and rape of Basutoland, the Resident Commissioner is entrusted with duties of functioning [sic] our enemies with ways and means of how best they can strike a decisive blow for the final death blow . . . and end of political existence of Basutoland. It was through the agency of the Resident Commissioner that in 1909 Lord Selbourne to Basuto chiefs and people spoke in a way more or less adapted to Sesuto custom that in the event of a unification of the four colonies becoming a reality Basutoland would have to be incorporated in such a Union Government because the Union Government would be like a chief's son who is entrusted with the right of looking after Basutoland by the King who is the father to Basutoland. It is why at the present time General Hertzog, the Prime Minister of the Union Government, is trying to get either Prince of Wales or Duke of Gloucester as High Commissioner for South Africa so that during his tenure of office Basutoland may be brought under the Union Government as an appange to him for the dispossession of Basuto of their country. We declare openly that if either of the two sons of our beloved King be brought out here in South Africa as an instrument of our ruin, we shall not accept him as such. But we shall be prepared to accept him as the High Commissioner like all other High Commissioners because Moshesh never entertained the thought of his country becoming an appange to the Crown in any other way than the conditions laid by him before the Government.

Now I have tried to explain the few above historical and political facts in order to make it easy for you to understand that it is impossible for his honour the Resident Commissioner, who by his own actions and official demeanour proves himself to be our arch enemy, to have at heart interests and welfare of Basuto nation so much that he can bring genuine reforms in our Basuto courts of law . . . .

Do you all know that our Resident Commissioner, Sir Herbert C. Sloley, was appointed in 1903 by our High Commissioner, Lord Alfred Milner, to participate as a member in the Commission to gather information from the European inhabitants of the four United Colonies and three protectorates as well as Southern Rhodesia regarding the kind of treatment of cruelty they wished to be applied upon the black Africans; and how far they would like the Africans to be dispossessed of their lands and deprived of their rights; and how far and in what way would the detribalisation of the Africans in the Protectorates be put into effect; and under what best ways and methods would the protectorates be incorporated in the Union Government? The findings of this Commission were that in the Protectorates through the High Commissioner's Proclamations issued from time to time there must be directed a campaign for the complete destruction and the eradication of the social fabric of the Africans in the Protectorates . . . . As the chiefs are entrusted with the right of preserving and looking after the social laws and customs which bind together the people as one harmonious whole upon their chiefs, it was contrived that through a policy of treachery and betrayal the powers enjoyed by the chiefs over their people must be gradually but ruthlessly taken away; and that in the process of putting this policy into effect the chiefs in the protectorates must be deluded to misuse their powers and rights over their people to maltreat and oppress them and that every evil that tended for the division of one class against the other, and for hatred of people against their chiefs must carefully be taken up in order to help bring about the desired end of tribal system in the Protectorates so that it might be easy for the Europeans to take Basutoland to exploit it and enslave its indigents. It is why today we see our social rights, laws and customs attacked from all quarters by Europeans of all different walks of life to destroy them . . . .

Another point noteworthy in connection with breaking down our social fabric to bring about the detribalisation of our political existence as a nation consists in the vilification and pollution of our chiefs by the officers of the Government through enmeshing them in the judicial manoeuvres directed against them to prepare for their expulsion from posts of exercising their duties as judges for their people in cases brought before them. It is why today you see the Resident Commissioner brings into life and resuscitates Proclamation No. 2B of 1884 under the guise of restoring justice to Basuto courts of law.

You all know, I suppose, that under this Proclamation the Resident Commissioner is empowered to appoint chiefs from whichever groups of persons he likes, not only in the lineage of our chiefs but also in the common people. The type of chiefs thus appointed under the powers of this Proclamation would be the worst political sluggards, phlegmatics and what not, whose patriotic consciousness has long been dead owing to the general atrophy applied upon them in school rooms and churches under the guise of giving them education and saving their souls from eternal burning in hell. The chief duties of such appointed chiefs would be to put into effect the ruthless measures contemplated by our enemy — the Resident Commissioner and His Excellency the High Commissioner — who are here to put over and carry into effect the findings of the Lord Milner Commission which had brought about the formation of the Union Government to pursue a uniform Native policy, and which has brought us to face our peril sealed in the South Africa Act in its schedule for the incorporation of Basutoland along with her sister Protectorates in the Union Government.

Let me remind you of the charges levelled by 'Mosuto' . . . that the people are maltreated by the chiefs, are compelled to work for the chiefs' many wives lands without food and without pay, and that the worst of it all is that Basuto are experiencing the heart-rending grievances of gross miscarriage of justice at the chiefs' courts while these people are debarred from appealing to the courts of the local Assistant Commissioners, who are full of justice, without the permission of these malefactors — the chiefs. In support of these views of 'Mosuto', Simon Phamotse said that justice in the Government courts is nullified by the presence of the chiefs' assessors in the Government courts and that if a qualified judge would be appointed to try appeal cases in the Government courts of Basutoland, pure justice would then exist in the Government courts. You know that the Progressive Association upheld these views of 'Mosuto' and Phamotse. It was to carry into effect the views advocated by Simon Phamotse to appoint a qualified judge to try appeal cases in the Government courts that Mr. Patrick Duncan, a member of Union Parliament for Natal, has been appointed to fill the position of a well qualified judge in law by his Excellency the High Commissioner by Proclamation.[26] Now let me ask this question: In what school has Mr. Patrick Duncan been taught the Sesuto social laws and customs now practiced by Basuto and out of which arise disputes and cases to be tried in our chiefs' courts? The answer to this question is a negation . . . . We cannot say anything but declare and announce in . . . unmistakeable terms that we like Mr. Patrick Duncan as our enemy in the Union Government, but we do not like him to dispossess us of our country and enslave us to incorporate our country in the Union Government . . . . We do not like him to have any official connection with us in our country . . . . Therefore, it is our duty as a nation to present a strong agitation before his Excellency, the High Commissioner to take away Mr. Patrick Duncan from amongst us in the Basutoland . . . .

Before I come to the conclusion of my remarks I must give some cursory remarks about our friends — the agents of imperialism and our political enemy — the missionaries and their teaching. You have already learned that our friends, the missionaries refuse to do us the service of holding prayers for us that God may make possible for the Government, chiefs and nation to live in perfect harmony on the ground that religion and politics are incompatible. Now I like to know whether the God of the church is a cruel capitalist and imperialist oppressor, who takes pleasure in the persecution of the poor toiling masses, whose sole consolation is offered in Sundays at the altars of the churches by the ministers of religion which consists in the sacred instructions of slavish obedience on the part of the poor persecuted masses to their cruel and ruthless masters . . . . If the God of the church be merciful and sympathetic both to the powerful and weak, rich and poor alike, and if it is true that he commanded that 'Thou shalt not covet thy neighbours' property or possession' and what not, why does he not instruct the missionaries to direct their labours towards converting the robbers of our rights under Proclamations, and those who work hard day and night to make efforts to deprive us of our possession — Basutoland. Why do the ministers of religion of the church not excommunicate these men who are working in direct contravention of the sacred Commandments? Why in face of the God of the church these settlements are allowed to practice all these enormities upon the poor people of Basutoland and strive for their dispossession of their country? Are the missionaries not aware that the members of their churches are committing grave and serious mortal sins? If they are not the members of their churches why is it that they do not preach the Gospel to them to show and teach them that it is wrong to God for them to covet their neighbours' possessions and that they ought to bring back all of our rights fraudulently taken away from us by them? Why is it that the ministers do not tell the robbers of our rights that if they do not give back to us all that they robbed from us, they will be burned in the eternal fire of hell ? . . .

Let me give you my warning. It is not an easy task to repel a well organised enemy from our country which had the privilege to persuade our protector, England to allow them to apply their treacherous, delusive, destructive and narcotic manoeuvres upon us to bring about our political death while we were being placed under delusions of security. We must work hard day and night to make efforts that your desires and wishes be presented and interpreted by your own representatives to British Parliament, Government and nation that we do not like to see our chieftainship decapitated and destroyed. We like the British Parliament to enact a law providing for the permanent independence of Basutoland of the Union Government. Therefore, let us contribute liberally towards the defence fund against the Government in his actions to bring one of our enemy into our country as a judicial commissioner although he is one of those Moshesh asked the English Government to protect him from their aggression and encroachment.

Another imminent danger frowning over us like a storm-cloud fast gathering strength is in the appeal for rebatement of income-tax for European traders in Basutoland to the Secretary of the Colonies. Some years ago Lekhotla la Bafo protested against the turning of European traders into residents of Basutoland through making them pay income tax but the Government and the Paramount Chief turned a deaf ear to our protests . . . . Today the European traders pretend to have a grievance resulting from the income tax paid by them in Basutoland which is higher than the one payable in the Union Government . . . . Today, after the Union Government has reduced the income tax, the Basutoland Government pretend to refuse to reduce it and for the reason European traders got the raison d'etre to appeal to the Secretary of the Colonies to ask him to reduce the amount of income tax payable. All these views expressed by the European Traders as their grievances are nothing but a camouflage and pretend to give them to persuade the Secretary of the Colonies to indirectly recognize them as the inhabitants of Basutoland, enjoying all the rights enjoyed by all the residents of any country under the British Government as a crown colony. For this reason we must present a strong movement against their being accorded indirect official recognition as residents of Basutoland by the Secretary of the Colonies. I remind you that in April 1868, Moshesh wrote letters to Sir Philip Wodehouse that

Basutoland must be reserved for the exclusive use of Basuto people and that no Europeans should be allowed to have any right at all in Basutoland. Now if European traders in Basutoland would be recognized as the inhabitants and residents of the territory enjoying all the rights as residents of any Crown colony, what is the use of our asking the English Government to protect us from our enemy, the robber, capitalist imperialist of South Africa? If we may not wake up now and present our strong protests before the Colonial Secretary against this movement on the part of our enemy the European traders in Basutoland, we shall be dispossessed of our country and enslaved as the result of their being recognized as the lawful residents of Basutoland . . . . Let us give our protector to know that we are afraid that if he may recognize these robbers to exercise any residential rights in our country we shall meet the same fate as the previous one in the case of the loss of the Orange Free State.

Now my fellow men and women, let us be prepared to meet any form of emergency in defence of our country, whether it be horrors or death and terrorism placed before us . . . . Let us press forward in our peaceful and constitutional fight against the legions of that monstrous destructive enemy, the South African Imperialism which moves along with international world Imperialism to crush the poor toiling masses of the world. Let us vindicate our cause and join hands shoulder to shoulder in our struggle for emancipation from helotry and collaborate with the international emancipation movement in our fight to rescue our country from clutches of her enemy, the South Africa robber imperialists.

When Lekhotla la Bafo appealed to Paramount Chief Griffith for food for one of their meetings, he was naturally incensed. Informing the Resident Commissioner that he would not allow the feast to be held, he complained that he had never heard of someone asking a chief for permission to hold a feast in another man's village and expecting him to feed the gathering.

15.

H.M.D. Tsuene to Paramount Chief Griffith Lerotholi, 7 January 1930, LNA S 3/22/2/4

With respect and humility, we your children ask you to allow us to hold a meeting to thank the Almighty God who caused H.H. the Resident Commissioner and H.E. the High Commissioner to agree to let the nation retain its Chieftainship of birthright and to reject the Resident Commissioner's little book which was going to bring an end to the Chieftainship of birthright. The meeting should be held on top of Thaba Bosiu at the ruins of the village of Chief Moshoeshoe, head of the Chiefs to whom the Lekhotla la Bafo is teaching all the people to cling, who (Chiefs) came out of the loins of Moshesh to keep the agreement which Chief Moshesh made with the British Government.

As on that day, the 12th March 1930, the meeting will accomplish two purposes, namely to thank God for saving our born Chiefs from destruction and to pray for you and all born Chiefs that you be given grace to rule the people in peace which will silence the cries of the people, which cries are the Government's excuse for its wish to do away with the Chieftainship of birthright. Give us permission Chief to hold the meeting on top of Thaba Bosiu. We ask for meat from you for the feast because it is a thanksgiving meeting for the continued existence of Chieftainship. We intend to make a feast although we are poor. We are your children; give us food.

Chief, we would also mention that on the 16th March 1930 we will hold a meeting at Matsieng to make fresh in the ears of the people the rights of the people which we know you look after, which rights without warning we see in the hands of the Government, and after this meeting of reminding the people, representatives will come before you to hear what you have to say about the rights which are in the hands of the Government.

16

Presidential Address,
12 March 1930, Thaba Bosiu, LNA S 3/22/2/4

Since Moshesh, the father, founder, collector and caretaker of this nation passed away through death to the great unknown beyond the grave, it is the first time in the history of this country — Basutoland, as well as in the history of our organization, to hold a meeting on the very spot where our beloved caretaker . . . had put up his residence; for the purpose of raising our national prayers as one man to God through our priests for thanks giving to Him . . . .

You all know that we have just passed through a fearful political storm which had been organised for the purpose of destroying our hereditary chieftainship to give way for the flourish of Imperialism which aims at keeping all the colonial nations under its sway in the conditions of hewers of wood and drawers of water for the few but powerful and well organised class of wealthy Europeans who have entrenched themselves in our countries . . . . This terrible and fearful storm was the regulations issued by His Honour the Resident Commissioner for the abolition of our present hereditary chieftainship . . . . As you all know . . . we as Lekhotla la Bafo contributed our share into the work of waging a struggle in defence of our hereditary chieftainship to rescue it from its enemy . . . . In the meantime, God has crowned our efforts with success. It is for this success, though of course it is an ephemeral one, that we have organised this meeting to thank God for the help He offered to us in our endeavours to wage a peaceful struggle in defence of our hereditary chieftainship. We felt it imperative for us to hold a meeting of this nature here because we are aware of the fact that it is not on account of our powerful struggle in defence of our chieftainship that His Honour the Resident Commissioner and His Excellency the High Commissioner were forced to leave it as it is today . . . . We realise that our weakness is manifest to all . . . . It is only through the powerful hand holding the oil of mercy of God that propitiated the hearts both of His Excellency the High Commissioner and His Honour the Resident Commissioner . . . which has induced them to leave our chieftainship as it is today. For this achievement we must send forth our national thanksgiving to God, the almighty, creator, the most benevolent and merciful one through our priests and all those who have at heart the interests and welfare of this nation, who realize the imminent danger in which we are at the present time. To us this day is a day of joy because it is the day on which we celebrate the important achievement ever attained by us through the mercy of God, that the power of the enemy which had waged its struggle for the purpose of decapitating the head of our political honour, power and glory — our chieftainship, had once more been repelled . . . .

On the other hand, this day we have assembled here for the purpose of offering our prayers to God to ask him to forgive and overlook our national failures or sins, faults and shortcomings which tend to lower and alienate the favour and sympathy of our heavenly father from us. First of all, let me point out some of our national mistakes for which, through prayers to God, we must try and reconcile ourselves with the souls of our departed forefathers who are already before the face of God. Moshesh with his nation was the observer of the circumcision . . . . In Basutoland this institution was looked upon as a sacred one under which all men and women had to be trained. Today, through the missionaries' teaching, this institution in Basutoland is no longer respectable and all those who have come under the influence of the Church and school known as Christianity hold it to pollution and all of those who are under the influence of the missionaries' teaching detest the idea of looking upon the souls of their departed fathers and relatives with their chiefs as having the right to pray to God for their success in their enterprises and undertakings in this world . . . . At the same time they are taught to look upon the souls of the departed men of alien races as filling the position of intercessors before God . . . . This is said to be compatible with Christian religion; but the absurdity of this idea is exposed when you come to consider the time when those who have been taught to renounce the intercession of their relatives already before God and who have adopted men of alien races as their intercessors come to the point of the clash of interests with the children of those men of alien races who are regarded as the intercessors of those who are taught to renounce the intercession of their relatives who are already before God. Do you suppose that those men would neglect to plead the cause represented and fought for by their children on earth and champion through their prayers to God the cause of those who have renounced the intercession of their fathers? Do you suppose, for instance, that the relatives of these robber Imperialist Europeans who are already before God would neglect to pray to God for the success of the schemes and undertakings pursued by their children in Basutoland intended to deprive Basuto nation through fraud of its land and rights [or] to pray for the success of Basuto nation in its struggles to stay the progress of their children from entrenching themselves into Basutoland? No, they would never do it. I earnestly beg you to refrain yourselves from joining the company of those who are reviling the institutions of our departed fathers no matter whether we do not practice them at the present time. Let us look upon those institutions as respectable in honour to our fathers already before God so that they may be ready at all times to join our prayers to God for the success of our national emancipatory movements and undertakings that we pursue in the world for the liberation of our oppressed races. Today we have assembled here for the purpose of offering our prayers as a nation to God to show our national penitence for all the national offences we committed as a nation before the face of God and his saints; our fathers already in heaven . . . .

Now you all see that our political outlook before us is rapidly getting darker and darker as the days pass because the chiefs are now playing into the hands of our enemy through their maltreating the people at the time when the members of the Progressive Association are urging the Government to see what steps he can take to bring about the adoption of those rejected proposals . . . . They point out the fact that the chiefs do not apply the laws of the Lerotholi book of laws in their decisions to cases and disputes laid before them, and they point out that the chiefs apply their own wishes and desires contrary to the Lerotholi laws upon the people . . . . In this way, excessive and exorbitant unlawful fines are imposed upon the people.[27] The treatment of the chiefs upon the people is most vexatious and . . . you all see that our success in repelling the proposed regulations for the abolition of hereditary chieftainship is no better than an ephemeral success . . . . Within a short space of them another storm raging for the abolition of our hereditary chieftainship will burst forth unless [a] very drastic and well organised campaign be waged by this organisation in defence of the afflicted nation of Basutoland with its hereditary chieftainship . . . . We must defend our hereditary chieftainship despite the fact that [it] is more and more becoming troublesome and an unbearable burden to the people and try to reform it in our own interests because it is a part and most important one of the conditions under which Basutoland came under the protection of England . . . . It is the foundation upon which the conditions of our coming under the protection of England are built and if we may let the foundation get destroyed without being repaired by us we shall suffer an irreparable loss of the political status enjoyed by Basutoland as a protectorate under England . . . .

I have explained all these points so that you as ministers may be able to understand precisely every point upon which Lekhotla la Bafo asks you to raise your prayers to God on its behalf. The first point is that you must send forth your prayers taking as well our prayers as Lekhotla la Bafo to God for thanksgiving for the great success He bestowed upon our labours in the past in defence of our lovely and sacred hereditary chieftainship. The second point upon which Lekhotla la Bafo requests the ministers to pray to God for this nation is on the point of national commission of offence by this nation through being deluded and misled by the foreign teaching of European missionaries to revile and renounce the sacred institutions of our fathers, already before the face of almighty God, and look down with contempt and disdain upon them as no longer our intercessors before God . . . . For this delusion we feel ourselves penitent and our hearts are contrite . . . . We wish to reconcile ourselves with the spirits of our dead forefathers, relatives and friends and call upon them to join us in our prayers to God to help us to take up the righteous course of revindication of our just rights treacherously taken away from us by our blood thirsty foes under the mask, garb and disguise of our friends, helpers and agents of our protector . . . . We as Lekhotla la Bafo call upon you, ministers, to pray to God to send down His light of wisdom upon our duped chiefs, principally the Paramount Chief, to refrain themselves from persecuting this nation which is to play into the hands of their enemy . . . .

Now you know that some time ago we as Lekhotla la Bafo did ask the European missionaries of Paris Evangelical Mission Society, Roman Catholic and the Anglican Church to pray God that good understanding may exist among the chiefs, the officers of the Government and this nation; and that God may cause those who deprive us of our rights cease pursuing that policy; and that through pacific methods we may regain our lost rights. But I regret to mention here that they refused to do this service. It was for this reason that then we turned to Basuto ministers of independent churches to come to our help and pray God to make possible for this nation to get a square deal under the chiefs and the officers of the Government [see Document 23] . . . . We did not only ask the Basuto ministers of independent churches but we asked all people of different religious tendencies and habits, Basuto medicine men, diviners, those who still believe and cling to the way of their forefathers in praying God and all those who have at heart the interests and welfare of this nation, as Moshesh had requested . . . . Today we still repeat the same request to you one and all. We ask you to pray God to be near us and help to carry patiently our cross of sufferings which we contemplate to undergo within a short space of time of passive resistance in the attempt to revindicate our stolen rights under Proclamation [see Document 28]. Lekhotla la Bafo appeals to you one and all and says to you: Pray for my soul, pray for my success in the revindication of our stolen rights, for many things are done through the force and help of prayer much more than this world thinks of. Pray for the success of our attempts to unite the African Protectorates under one strong and powerful League of Protectorates to look after the common interests of the Protectorates and represent them before the British government . . . . It was the fervent desire of Moshesh to unite all the South African nations under a union of friendship and mutual help in days of national troubles caused by our common enemy . . . . Therefore, it is our fervent desire to follow in the footsteps of our great martyr, Moshesh, to contribute our share into the works of uniting our African Protectorates under our powerful League of Protectorates . . . .

Owing to the fact that in Basutoland Lekhotla la Bafo is put on trial of persecution and hydra of endless conspiracies to plot for its downfall through the machination of the powers that be, we have resolved to affiliate our organisation with the world organisations of oppressed peoples of the world . . . . We have already informed the Paramount Chief, the Resident Commissioner, His Excellency the High Commissioner, and the Secretary of State for the Colonies that . . . we shall affiliate our Association with the Associations of the oppressed peoples of the world so that they may help us to disseminate the true state of persecution we receive at the hands of our rulers . . . despite the fact that we are constitutional in our activities. For this reason, we have applied for affiliation to the League Against Imperialism and for National Independence whose headquarters are established in Berlin, the capital of Germany, Red International of Labour Unions, Communist Party of South Africa, South African Federation of Non-European Trade Unions, African National Congress and the Universal Negro Improvement Association whose headquarters are now established in Kingston, Jamaica, British West

Indies. Of all these applications we have succeeded in the conclusion of affiliation of Lekhotla la Bafo with the League Against Imperialism and on the New Year day we held a meeting in Mapoteng in which we celebrated for the first time the inauguration of the affiliation of Lekhotla la Bafo with the League Against Imperialism . . . . Henceforth, we shall disseminate the appeals of the League Against Imperialism to the affiliated associations in our meetings and they likewise will disseminate our appeals to the League Against Imperialism . . . . Today every act of persecution and torture we receive at the hands of our cruel rulers will be disseminated throughout the world through the help of this organisation. For this reason I appeal to you Basuto ministers to pray God to bless our endeavours to conclude well founded and permanent affiliation of Lekhotla la Bafo with the organisations of the oppressed peoples of the world in accordance with the aspirations of Moshesh the founder and collector of this nation.

Now my fellow men and women, I send forth my message of appeal to you from the sacred cradle of Basutoland and earnestly beg you to get ready for the great conflict that lies ahead of us. Let us prepare ourselves to follow in the footsteps of our great martyrs who sacrificed their property, their all and finally laid down their lives in defence of this country. Let us get ourselves ready to enter into a fierce but peaceful struggle and campaign of passive resistance and made knee-deep in the blood shed by persecution and sufferings attendant on passive resistance and boycott of foreign cloth that lie ahead of us in defence of our rights, liberty, freedom and country. My call to you, my countrymen and women, is this: You sleepers, away, the day and hour of danger has fallen upon you, come together and use naught your power to cut asunder the shackles of bondage riveted upon you by your political enemies. You have in your command power enough through peaceful organisation to force and dictate your will to become the rule of the day. You will bring your enemy upon his knees and adore you within a short space of time and obey your commands to him if you only prepare yourselves to undergo any amount of hardships and persecution and welter in prison cells and keep at bay the legions of hell from doing further harm in your country . . . . Therefore, my fellow men and women, let us resign ourselves to the will of martyrdom . . . and be ready to take up our cross of sufferings in revindication of our cause and rights and freedom. For this reason let us keep ourselves near to the will of God . . . who will purge every feeling and tendency of cowardice from our hearts and give us enough courage and patience to undergo our sufferings with clean conscience. For this reason I appeal to you, ministers of Basuto nation, to raise and offer your prayers to God for us and for this nation as a whole so that God may bestow his blessings upon us and crown our efforts with success . . . .

The centrepiece of Lekhotla la Bafo meetings was the Presidential Address, but the meetings also featured prayers, songs, discussion of association business and political action, and comments on current issues from the participants. The participation of women, albeit in small numbers, was a notable departure from male-dominated traditional pitsos. The following statements are taken from police accounts of meetings.

17.

Seeiso Lesiano: Although my father is the son of Molapo, I make a speech because I can see that our country is suppressed. Some people will not dare to give out their opinion for fear of being imprisoned. The National Council has been built with a view to deprive us of our right. This country belongs to the Basuto as a nation, not to Moshesh alone . . . . Moshesh in his time always consulted the nation in any matter concerning it, and yet our present Moshesh does not consult us simply because of money paid to him by the white people. I have often brought complaints before the A.C. [Assistant Commissioner] Leribe and he has always given me the same reply that he cannot interfere in matters concerning the natives, but when bloodshed occurs he (A.C.) intervenes. The National Council is not for the nation but for the interests of the chiefs. Members of the National Council go there only for the sake of money paid to them, and they do nothing good for the nation. If we were all of the same feelings as Josiel Lefela our deliverance would be sure. In conclusion I appeal to all the Basuto to unite and seek their own way of deliverance because our chiefs have thrown us away.[28]

We are under the flag of Lekhotla although I was born in the house of Moshesh. We must sweat before we can get any good. White people knew that the cry of the P.C. [Paramount Chief] would be very big and listened to by the King and therefore found a means of shutting his mouth. There is a house at Maseru which is called National Council. It is there where Basuto are clipped. Moshesh before he died cursed the white man's liquor, but it (brandy) comes into Basutoland through permits. Although you, Basuto, are not allowed to make sesuto 'joala'. I wish to know why we are paying tax and why you say that Lesotho belongs to Moshesh and not to Basuto. The P.C. gives orders now without consulting the nation because his mouth is smeared with jam. I blame Griffith and not the whiteman that we are being placed in Gaol like this on account of Sesuto beer. There is no nation that is (experiencing) slavery like the Basuto nation.[29]

Mikael Monathi: I recall to mind a public pitso which used to be held by the Basuto, which 'pitso' was wiped off by the establishment of the National Council. At this 'pitso' the nation was consulted, but today the members of the National Council never inform us as a nation of what they are going to discuss, and on their return they never tell us what was discussed. The nation has been killed since the National Council was established, tax was increased to 25/- and shortly afterwards to 28/-. With regard to the dipping tanks, our sheep are killed and yet we get no compensation as dip-supervisors often say that they have not died through dipping.[30]

Mikael Molelekoa: There is a saying in Sesuto 'son-in-law, come quickly, because the stock of your parents-in-law are being captured'. In 1869 Moshesh asked the British Government to protect him and his people under certain conditions, because he did not like to come under the Union Government. General Hertzog now wishes to take away the three protectorates from the direct protection of the British Empire. I call all those who wish to fight for our rights to come forward and be given badges so that they may be arrested wearing the badges of the Lekhotla la Bafo.[31]

I regret to see none of you, men of Leribe, trying to help themselves. Why is this so? Are you still keeping something back even after being injured in your property? Women, ask these men to give you their trousers so that you may join Lekhotla la Bafo. The Government is against cruelty to animals but they make cruelty to people.

Dip-Supervisors kill our sheep through dipping. He (Government) forbids us from owning bastards and Persian sheep. How is it that your Government see our cruelty as your own?[32]

When I was still in the Government service in Bechuanaland a certain woman had three daughters. One day she sent one to go and pluck mealies from lands. She went and plucked the mealies. On her way home she went to a tree which was nearby to rest under its shade as the sun was very hot. When she got under the tree she put her basket down and a snake called 'Mokoepa' (a venomous snake found in Bechuanaland) leaped down from the tree and struck her on the head and she dropped down dead. The mother sent another one to go and see the cause of her delay; when she passed by the tree she saw her sister lying under the shade of the tree, and she thought she was asleep. She went to her and when she was about to stoop over her to wake her up, it leaped down and struck her on the head and she fell down and died. The third was sent and she was also killed in the same manner as her other two sisters. Their mother became anxious about her children and a thought struck her that her children might have been killed by 'Mokoepa' so she cooked porridge and poured it hot in a clay pot and carried it on her head when she went to see her daughters. When she arrived at the scene the snake leaped down and plunged its head in the hot porridge and its head became peeled off and it died. This woman was compensated with £500 for having killed this enemy. This story reminds me of General Hertzog, who is the snake called 'Mokoepa' and should be killed. I refer to you women and request you to do like that woman, who killed that enemy. I wish you would do like her.[33]

Daniel Makhakhe: A native to a European is like a drilling iron which after being used is left outside and exposed to rains.[34]

Rev. C. Monathi: Moses did not stay for the comforts of Egypt but carried on the work of freeing his nation from bondage.[35]

Rabase Sekike: We have missionaries who preach Heaven and Hell. Satan reigns in Hell which is a place of torment. Now our father Moshesh told us that to him the Boers and their Government represent Satan and His Power. You have noticed that the European painters always paint Satan black, and God white. This shows how hateful we are to these people. It shows how the Government represented by Mr. Sims and others are wolves in the fold dressed in sheep skins. We object to the H.C. [High Commissioner] staying in Pretoria, because we and the P.C. [Paramount Chief] were not consulted. If the P.C. was consulted and agreed, he is also to be blamed because he did not consult us the Basuto. Seeing that by the treaty between the British Government and Moshesh the H.C. was meant to be a buffer between us and the Boers, we fail to understand why this Chief does not come and stay with us. During the Great War we went to fight for the King, while the Boers rebelled. But today these traitors are more favoured by the Government than we who were loyal. The Boers say that if, when they come to Heaven, they find the native there they will bid goodbye to God and His Heaven. When a white man advocates anything you always crowd around him and believe him, as witness the French missionaries who talked us into trusting them, and then stole the Diplomatic documents and sent them to the Cape, thereby helping their brothers to defraud us of our rights and land. You still go to them and reject us, who are working for your well-being.[36]

Roma 'Neko: You are requested to contribute towards the expenses entailed by this 'Lekhotla' in the transactions in connection with your welfare. It is your duty to extend monetary aid in order to safeguard your own interests. Another matter to which I must draw your notice is the fact that the present boundaries of this Territory are the result of Gen. Hertzog's predecessor's actions. Now again, Gen. Hertzog is the prime mover in the matter of the H.C.'s appointment. His only interest in the Territories is that of a destroyer. Moshesh said: — 'The Queen will rule my People through me and Her Representative will only be the mouth-piece by which we shall communicate.' But Gen. Hertzog, from whom we fled when we made this agreement, occupies the primary position in deciding how we shall be governed. The missionaries have done a great deal to divide us by preaching denominationalism amongst the people. Let us all be 'Basuto' and fight for our rights, not with sticks but with our tongues. Let us ask that the Representative of our King should live amongst us and not amongst our enemies.[37]

Thaba Matasane: My complaint is against the National Council. They never consult us when they go to their meetings. They are paid out of the people's tax, but they never speak for the Nation. When they come to the Council Room they make the unanimous announcement to the Government: — 'Chiefs, the Basuto have authorised us to agree with all that you propose'. Let us unite to fight this evil.[38]

Mashapha Jokonyane: When an epidemic disease spreads about, every endeavour is made to find suitable remedies. England has betrayed its trust, for while she continues to live on our bounty, she makes no return. The Government has ordered the store-keepers not to buy our produce, but still insists on our paying taxes. The Government also steals part of our resources in the form of the duty of 1/2d per lb. on wool and mohair. (Here followed the telling of the fable of the 'Lion and the Hare'.) The Government will come to the same fate as the 'Lion', viz. by being outwitted by the weak and timid 'Hair' [sic] — the exploited Basuto. If we refuse to pay taxes and the Government imprisons us, how will it be able to feed so many of us.[39]

Lebina Hlakane: Let us leave the God of Paul and Peter and pray to our own Gods — ancestors. At the R.C. [Roman Catholic] Church certain people were excommunicated for attending a Zulu heathen ceremony, and when they asked for forgiveness they were told that they could not be pardoned because they had the Lekhotla la Bafo as backers in their supposed evil-doing.[40]

Maphutseng Lefela: The two races composing the population of the Union of S.A., united in order to make it more easy to incorporate the Native Territories. England was consequently juggled into making certain promises which paved the way to the realisation of this object. Are you then prepared to sit under this affront? We should appeal to France, Germany and the United States to demand an explanation from England, why she has broken her solemn promise to this nation. In India, at the present time, the Government is experiencing the most difficult reverses. The Indians will no longer tolerate the tyranny of the officials, but the Government is unwilling to rectify its mistakes or to give the reins of Indian Administration to the Indians. The Indians, therefore, say: 'In that case we will starve you by refusing to pay taxes and by boycotting your trade.' The result is the present depression of trade; because the Indian Commercials have no market for their merchandise. The Government will eventually step out of India. As we are speaking, a Commission is sitting to devise other means of governing India. Are you afraid of fighting for your liberty and that of your chiefs, even though that leads to imprisonment. The Government depends on its existence on our bounty in the way of taxes, and if we refused to pay, it (the Government) would not be in a position to feed so many of us during our imprisonment. If we collected sufficient funds we might bring over some of our brothers in the U.S.A. to come to our aid as doctors, teachers, etc., thereby crippling the white man's activities in his work of enslaving us.[41]

Sentle Moshoeshoe: We are tired of the oppression under which we have suffered for many years. We are like lost sheep without a shepherd.[42]

Khotso Silas: The whole nation is troubled. We have many grievances: — 1. Dipping tanks are a source of trouble. We receive some good from them but we are bound to pay for them. Whatever good we may get from the Government the payment for it indirectly always exceeds by far the value of what we have actually received. There is too much going to gaol over these dipping tanks. It is time a stop should be made to it.

2. Tax is another trouble. The amount of tax we pay is too high for our poorer classes. Why should the rich and poor be taxed alike. The 3/- education levy has made no improvement at all in our schools.

3. The third thing is the laws that are made for us. We are never consulted upon any laws that have to be made. The laws are merely rammed down our throats.

4. The new laws form another menace to the advancement of this nation. We are strangled like dogs. All good Governments consult their people in the making of their laws. These proposed new laws are repugnant to Native policy. Why should we be killed like cats by being put in a bag and then killed. The Government is very cruel to us.

At the treaty of Mokema — which was made between Queen Victoria and the Paramount Chief Moshoeshoe — it was agreed to protect Moshoeshoe and his people and not to annihilate them. We want the chieftainship of Basutoland to remain as it is.[43]

Lesooa Makeanyane: Money is a terrible sin. Our chiefs have forsaken us for the sake of money. The Government has failed and so have the missionaries. Let us ask God to help us.[44]

Samuel Mohoanyane: The making of the laws of this country is in the hands of a few white people and the majority of the inhabitants — the Basutos — have no voice in the legislature. We are told that our sons must pay tax at the age of 21 years but we are not told when they have to leave off paying tax. It is a question of the survival of the fittest. We have old men of 60 to 70 years old who are still paying tax. I think we ought to be exempted from payment of tax at the age of 50. We are told when to start paying tax; I think it is only fair that we should be told when to finish off.[45]

Halefetsane Moshoeshoe: I regret to see that the chiefs have not attended this pitso. We were one day called by our chiefs to attend a pitso in which we were asked to help England against her enemies, and this was the day when the chiefs sold their liberty. I say our chiefs will never see Moshoeshoe nor will they ever see God. If we have to die to maintain our liberty I am prepared to die with the members of the Lekhotla la Bafo.[46]

Sam Monyatsi: Although we have said volumes of words against our chiefs we wish it to be plainly understood that our grievance is not at all directed against the chiefs but against the Government. The government has deprived us of our chiefs. They were taken away from us in 1903. Our chiefs are prompted by the Government sometimes, to go wrong. Our grievance is against the political dungeon at Maseru. It is our burial place instead of being our birth place. All you people . . . stand on your feet and help the Lekhotla la Bafo.[47]

Mophetheane Seleka: Basutoland is not a conquered territory; why should the inhabitants thereof be treated as if they were slaves. If we pray to God he will help us.[48]

Nyepe Mokoaleli: We are slaves but someone has come to deliver us from bondage. Tax is being increased year in and year out. Our sheep no longer belong to us. We are daily being sent to prison for losing our own sheep. We are between two hot fires — the traders on one side and the Government on the other. We are being sheared to the bone. When are we going to be free to trade in our own country?[49]

Alice Metapanyane: All the public money of this country goes to buy motor-cars, and public duties have been neglected. Where is an orphanage for Basutoland?[50]

Emma Aaron: True wisdom is obtained in the fear of God. Let us first pray to God and then we shall be wise. We have been told that tax was increased in order to meet education expenditure, but instead of increase in education we find increase in motor-cars.[51]

Libenyane Jobo: We are doing propaganda work in the hope that perchance God may listen to our cries. All the crime in the territory is due to the taking away of our chiefs from us. No sooner we have considered one law than another is brought up for consideration. The government is working in concert with the missionaries. The Government shears us and the missionaries our wives. The chiefs have until now not yet held any pitsos for the consideration of the new laws by the people. The 100 members of the Council earn their livelihood by the sweat of our brows. We should all be treated alike. There should be no discrimination. Moshoeshoe said 'protect me with the lice of my blanket'. Let us all be members of Council in turn, so that we all may share in the eating of the revenue of the country. The chieftainship of Basutoland has to be abolished, because we hear that chiefs will now be appointed. Why do away with Moshoeshoe's family? If they have done wrong let us pay 'sethabathaba' to ransom them.[52]

Joseph 'Neko: All the trade of the country is now in the hands of our natural enemies — the Dutch people. A Dutch transport rider gets 18/- per bale from Makhaleng shop whereas a Native transport rider only gets 6/-. The whole scheme is designed to fatten the Dutch people and kill us. Every male person of this territory pays almost £2/10- a year in Government taxes and Church taxes.[53]

Rev. C. Monathi: The efforts of the Boers to regain their national independence was crowned with success, because they did not tire of organising and pleading their cause, until they are today in control of the reins of government over their English conquerors. You should organise to the same end.[54]

Zabulon Rakuoane: The Government is as cruel as Chaka.[55]

Moshosho Sehlare: Rex has killed our chiefs. Before the advent of *Rex* our chiefs were very dignified persons, who were the spokesmen of the people, but today they have become insignificant because their place is taken by *Rex.*[56]

Josiel Lefela: We oppose the law made for the prevention of growing and using dagga. This law was made simply because it was observed that the Basuto would become rich by the sale of dagga as the Government is against any sort of trade which might bring good to us, as in the sale of kaffir-beer. Dagga has been used since the days of Moshesh and it is known to have no ill effects to the life of a human being.[57]

. . . [I]t may be well for you to know that the God of these missionaries is worshipped in banks, in pounds, shillings and pence found as the result of the exploitation of our lands being taken in possession of the Europeans for whom the missionaries are their pioneers. Now the most disquieting fact is that the missionaries in teaching our people declare to have been sent by God through the Holy Ghost while in their hearts they know the God who sent them to our African Nations.[58]

Although whites typically characterized members of Lekhotla la Bafo as 'mad-brained Natives' and 'half-educated revolutionaries', who represented the thinking of only a handful of Basotho, it is evident that the organization's leaders were articulating the feelings of a large number of people.[59] The following document lists grievances that Chief Boshoane collected from his people to present to the National Council.

18.

Grievances of the people of Qopana Letsuela's ward, 24 September 1928, LNA S 3/22/2/2.

Our grievances are as follows:

No. 1. The first grievance is with regard to the nine month's contract for which a person is taken before a Police Officer in Basutoland to swear that before the expiration of nine months he will not return to Basutoland.
No. 2. He swears that when he arrives at the mine he will have to pay the following amounts: — 1st Tax money. 2nd Railway fare. 3rd Money for Food. 4th The doctor's fee. When a person completes paying off these amounts and falls sick he is taken to the hospital and will

not be released and the period of his contract will be at a standstill until he either recovers or dies. No compensation is made either to his children or his relatives.

No. 3. Now we should like to know what is a contract, whether it is the money or the period of months because it is only right that when a person has finished paying off his advances he may go and seek better employment.

No. 4. Here is another important grievance. All the work on the mine — good or bad — is performed by Natives and the white people merely point a mark with their fingers. The grievance is that when there is a fall of rock in the mine and there are many Natives killed and two or three Europeans the compensation given to the Europeans exceeds by far that of the Natives. Now we should like to know what the cause of the difference is or whether the Natives have done wrong by performing hard labour or whether the Europeans receive preference because they merely point with their fingers. . . .

No. 8. The nation's grievance with regard to the 8/- in the tax. The nation asks the Government to remove the increase of 8/- because we have been deceived. We were told a College would be built for us where our children would be taken to; but we find that more hardships were being placed upon us. In the old days a child reached Standard VI whilst he was yet in the mission school at home and was only paying school fees, but today when a child passes Standard III it is said that he should be taken to a higher school like Koeneng Station. This child will continue to be fed by his father, and this is a great hardship.

No. 9. Grievance regarding the Scab Act. The Nation requests the Government to abolish the dipping tanks in Basutoland because dipping spoils the wool by cleaning it and therefore making it lighter than before and the result is there is no price. As for scab the flock owners will treat their own flocks in the same way as the Dutch people whose flocks are not treated by the Union Government. Further more these dips have put some of our people into difficulties by being always punished on unreasonable grounds. . . .

No. 11. Here is the Nation's grievance. We have a grievance because the Veterinary Officer stays only in Maseru. Our stock die whereas we have the Veterinary Officer. According to custom we Basutos usually eat the flesh of our dead animals; but on account of the absence of the Veterinary Officer if a beast dies it has to be buried for it is suspected of having died from anthrax. This done without the beast having been examined by the Veterinary Officer. Cattle killed by anthrax are eaten. It is a mistake to bury them because they are buried before they are examined.

No. 12. Another grievance is about transport in Basutoland. Again we request the Government to repeal the law which states that oxen inspanned to a wagon should have a leader for all the time they are on transport from one shop to another. Here is another grievance: The motor-car drivers are not always careful enough to hoot the car while the wagon is yet at a distance to give the front wagon time to stand aside. Another thing is if a wagon meets a motor car on a narrow road we ask the Government that the motor car should always rear [move backwards] as it is easy for it to do so and the wagon cannot.

No. 13. Another grievance is with regard to the purchase of merchandise. We ask the government to look into the matter of the heavy prices charged by shops. We were told that the difficulty [high prices] was caused by the European War and were promised that after the war the pre-war prices would be restored when an Austrian rug did not cost more than one pound.

It is now some years ago since we pointed out this difficulty to the Government but there is no change. Members of the National Council brought us an answer to the effect that the Government was unable to place a price upon the merchandise belonging to traders.

Whereas the high prices charged by traders have still placed Basutoland in a position in which it may be thought that the European war was still on, and the result is now extreme poverty in Basutoland caused by the traders, we request the Government to allow us to look for hawkers from among our black people who are beyond the seas.

We ask that all medicines for general diseases amongst horses should be stored in all the Government Camps because the traders charge us 2/6 while the Government charges only one shilling. We request the Government that widows should be maintained as heretofore. They should not be deprived of their lands. These widows should remain under the control of the chief and bring up their children under that control. We do not refer to those who stay in towns because they have already removed. We ask the Government to made a law to protect the women whose husbands have turned them into widows although they are still alive. The men throw away their wives and children and throw upon the woman the responsibilities of bringing up the children. The women have to find clothing for themselves, to clothe the children, to take the children to the doctors for treatment when they are sick and to plough for them. These men eventually break bonds with the whores with whom they have been living in the Union and they come home to drive away their wives and then marry some other woman with the cattle belonging to the children of the discarded wives. We request that women be protected from such men. The protection should be to the following effect — a man who has discarded his wife and children should never be allowed to have any more right to his wife. The children must belong to the woman and the husband's relatives who were helping the woman.

We again ask the Government to make a law for the protection of barren women against the heirs, so that whatever is bought by the barren woman or given to her by her husband during the husband's life time, the heir should not put his hand to such property. According to the existing law regarding the heirs and widows the heirs help only their own mothers and treat the barren women with cruelty for they have no sons to sympathise with them. We therefore ask for a legal protection against this cruelty on the part of the heirs.

The nation's grievances about the trader's shops which have filled Basutoland is another thing. These are the shops that make it impossible for good prices to be given for Basuto grain. One trader has as many as fifteen trading stations in one district, and so he cannot give different prices against himself. Some have as many as five shops, and some four while others have three shops. We ask the Government that every trader in Basutoland should be allowed only one shop. There should be different shop-owners so that better good prices may be obtained.

19.

Maphutseng Lefela, 'Justice for Basutoland, an appeal to world democracies, workers and peasants', *Inkululeko*, January-May 1941.

How Basutoland Came Under the British

Basutoland is a country which claims the protection of the British Government under certain conditions. These conditions were proposed and put forward before the Imperial Government by Moshesh on behalf of his people and Country.

On the other hand the British Government gave its word of pledge to accept the Basuto people under its protection if they were prepared to pay a tax for all administrative expenses. The Imperial Government was not prepared to pay any money from the Imperial Treasury towards the administration of Basutoland.

The Basuto accepted this condition because it relieved them from the fear that the use of money from the Imperial Treasury might at some future time, be construed as a purchase of their rights and national property.

Moshesh had told the British Government that he wished to govern his people by his own native laws and customs. If the Government wished to introduce other laws he would be willing but such laws should first be handed to him. He would then put them before his people in their council. If the laws were accepted he would inform the Government that they were now part of Basuto law.

Moshesh also laid down that his country was to be protected for the Basuto only, and that Europeans would not be allowed to hold land or own any rights of citizenship in it. He explained that the selling or renting of land was a practice unknown to the Basuto. If he sold or ceded any part of his country he would be regarded as having robbed his people. Again, he said that the custom of his people would not let a chief do anything affecting the people without first calling them together and giving them an opportunity to express their opinion.

The historian, Dr. G.M. Theal, wrote: 'When Moshesh spoke of his wish to come with his people under the broad folds of the flag of England he certainly did not mean that he desired an English officer to fill his place, or that English laws and customs should supersede the laws and customs of the Basuto. What he wished for was protection against opponents, with full liberty to govern his people as he liked' (*History of South Africa*, Vol. V, p. 56). This quotation gives the exact wishes and desires of the Basuto nation. On this point the British Government gave pledges without number to the Basuto, that as long as they remained loyal, their wishes would be respected.

Basutoland under British protection at first enjoyed the rights of self-determination and semi-independence. But owing to the work and dangerous narcotic influence of the Christian missionaries, combined with the bullying and deceptive manoeuvres and tactics of the representatives of the Imperial Government, the rights and powers of the people and their chiefs have been steadily usurped.

The Policy of Divide and Rule Pursued

After it had been agreed that the Basuto should manage their affairs under the chiefs in accordance with their customs, under the protection of the British Government, a Proclamation was issued in 1881. This laid down among other things that only chiefs appointed by the Resident Commissioner would have the right to try criminal and civil cases, and that they would have to act according to rules and regulations to be issued from time to time.

The Proclamation was put before the National Pitso of the chiefs and people. They rejected it. But instead of being thrown out, it was put in the book of Basutoland Proclamations to be used against future generations who would not know the true state of affairs in regard to the Proclamation.

The British Government saw that as long as the people had the right to meet with their chiefs in national convocations to shape their political affairs, it would be very difficult to insert the thin edge of the wedge to break down the semi-independence of the Basuto.

The Cape Colonial Government proposed that the Basuto should be persuaded to abandon their Pitso, which would be replaced by a Council of chiefs and headmen organised and managed on the lines of civilised people's councils. A verbal promise was made that this Council would adhere to the rules of custom which supported the Pitso, for this alone was satisfactory in its functions and work to the people and chiefs.

At first the Basuto refused to act upon this suggestion. But owing to the repeated persistence of this idea for 20 years, they at last agreed during the lifetime of Lerotholi. Therefore the present misnamed National Council was established in 1903. Since it was constituted the people as a nation have been muzzled and gagged. The Resident Commissioner is the President of the Council. He has the power to disqualify and dismiss any member for no offence whatsoever and without having to give a reason. In this way all those who have at heart the interests of the nation have been removed. Moreover the Resident Commissioner is empowered to appoint the members of the Council, who number 100.

The chiefs have been divided from their people by this Council. The people cannot now raise their voice and advise their chief what they wish him to do. The chiefs meet together, without their people. That is not in the way of a Basuto custom, and it is bad. The people have no say in their own matters, and the chiefs have been weakened because they do things without the support of their people.

Missionaries Attack Basuto Customs

After 1881 after the trouble over the guns the missionaries intensified their mission work. They worked hard to compel their followers and school children to throw aside the institutions of ancient days. Those who came under the influence of the missionaries were compelled to do away with polygamy and circumcision. Polygamy is the source of rapid increase of the people. Circumcision inculcates the military spirit with duties of civil life. That is why the missionaries said they were evil.

True historical records were sent to the regions of oblivion. Instead false records were introduced into schools. This was done in order to impart to children a diseased and defective knowledge which is more harmful than illiteracy. The Christians were taught to do away with worldly riches and affairs, and that it was better for them to lose their country and gain the happy life beyond the grave. In fact all those who came under missionary influence became and are nothing but political phlegmatics and pedantic dilettanti whose souls are so dead that they themselves never said: 'This is my own, my native land, for which I must sacrifice all of my belongings and even my life.'

All the best educated men and women come under this category. This is the reason why, through the fear of revival of race consciousness, the priests of the Roman Catholic Mission urge the Paramount Chief and Resident Commissioner to join hands and crush the Lekhotla la Bafo under the pretext that they are rooting out Communism in Basutoland. For the members of the Lekhotla la Bafo, though not Communists, are working to bring back to the Basuto their pride and love of independence.

After the abolition of the Pitso, a Board of Education was set up through which certain powers of the Chiefs were entrusted to the missionaries. Under this Board education has been kept down at a scale suitable for hewers of wood and drawers of water, understanding as little as possible of the language of their taskmasters. In many schools the children are taught from sub-standard A to standard III. In more than three-quarters of such schools, mostly in Roman Catholic schools, the children receive their instruction from half literate teachers. These have little knowledge of Sesuto reading and at the same time are not able to utter a single correct English sentence. As long as they are able to teach the catechism in Sesuto, it is enough.

Government aid is given only to schools under the direction of European ministers. The schools under ministers of Native Separatist Churches are not entitled to receive grants from public revenues. Yet these revenues come from taxes paid by the people who belong to the Separatist Churches. The ministers of the Separatist Churches are not allowed to become marriage officers, who are made by Proclamation. This right is the monopoly of ministers of Churches under the Europeans. Native ministers are therefore not allowed to marry the members of their own Churches. It is also through the missionaries that many oppressive Proclamations have been issued, such as those making unmarried men pay poll tax, in 1911, and making polygamists pay twice and three times as much as other men.

Rights Taken from the Basuto People

Basuto chiefs have been deprived of their rights and powers over trading matters which they formerly exercised in the interests of the people. These powers are entrusted to European traders who are able to make their voice heard by the Government through a Board of Licences. It is through this Board that Basutoland has been made a fortune-hunting reserve for Europeans. The Basuto are refused trading rights in their own land.

Other powers have been taken from the chiefs and entrusted to Europeans organised under the Agricultural Department. It is under the name of this Department that the Authorities issued a Proclamation for the decimation of the flocks of sheep and goats as a result of which many families are living on the level of starvation. Owners of sheep and goats are subjected to monthly tax at the rate of 3d. for 45 animals under the pretext of dosing them to destroy intestinal pests.

Many Europeans have been introduced in Basutoland to live as residents under the Veterinary Department, which is a sub-section of the Agricultural Department. The Europeans under this Department make their living as parasites upon the tax exacted from the people. These are dip inspectors and their servants. Through this Department the movement of livestock into the Union is restricted, but the movement of stock from the Union into Basutoland is not placed under very stringent restrictions because the animals are imported principally by European capitalists. •

The Paramount Chief

At all times, when the people through the instrumentality of the Lekhotla la Bafo asked the Government Officers why they promulgated Proclamations which in fact infringed the pledges given to the Basuto respecting their wishes, the officers replied that the Proclamations were issued with the consent and in consultation with the Paramount Chief, who was declared to possess sole rights over Basutoland.

The Paramount Chief was allowed to exercise arbitrary and autocratic powers over the Basuto people and country. This was and is incompatible with our national customs. According to our law the chief is the servant of the people, to carry out their decisions arrived at in national meetings. Again, these despotic powers are inconsistent with the democratic laws which the British Government claims to uphold.

The local Government officers ascribe the abnormal and autocratic powers of the Paramount Chief to a legacy from the native customs and laws of the people. This is false. The Paramount Chief is held up above the decisions of the National Council. He is regarded as having power to alter or annul the decisions of the National Council. That is against Basuto law.

In 1929 the Resident Commissioner tried to abolish the hereditary chieftainship and replace it with chiefs appointed by the Resident Commissioner in terms of Proclamation 2b of 1884. The National Council rejected this suggestion. The hereditary chieftainship remained, as it was before under national custom. But without the consent of the National Council the Paramount Chief has allowed the Resident Commissioner to abolish the hereditary chieftainship. It is replaced by chiefs appointed by the Resident Commissioner, and with powers of jurisdiction defined and restricted by regulations.

In a manner incompatible with our national custom, the Paramount Chief has deposed Chief Seeiso Maama and Chief Joel Motsoena and reduced the former to the position of a common man. Chief Joel Motsoena has been made a sub-chief under Chief Letsie Motsoena who, according to Basuto law, is under Joel Motsoena in rank. Chiefs Molopo Maama, who has been installed in the place of his elder brother Seeiso, and Letsie Motsoena, have been appointed to their ranks under Government Proclamation, while the chiefs who were downgraded have been refused the right to institute legal action in the courts.

A Joint Association of Protectorates
to Look After Their Common Interests

As far back as 1926 the Basutoland People's Association known as
Lekhotla la Bafo tried to organise an association to look after the
common interests of the Protectorates. This was after Chief Sobhuza
II of Swaziland had prosecuted his case against the Swaziland Corporation for dispossessing the Swazi people of part of their land. The
decision of the Privy Council in that case brought to light the fact that
under the Foreign Jurisdiction Act the British Government had the
same rights in a protected country as in a country acquired by conquest. The Crown could make Orders in Council even when they
subverted and annulled the conditions under which the people had
accepted British protection.

The Lekhotla la Bafo addressed letters to Chief Sobhuza II, thank-
ing him for his bold action in taking the case to the Privy Council, and
the Chief Tshekedi Khama of Bechuanaland. To these chiefs we
suggested that owing to the disclosures in the case against the
Swaziland Corporation, an Association of Protectorates should be
formed. The first important step of the Association would be to put
before the British Parliament our request that the Crown should not
have the right to issue perfidious and treacherous Orders in Council
which subvert the status of our Protectorates, and deprive our people
of their rights over their lands to open them to European colonists.

Chief Sobuza replied accepting our suggestion. A communication
was sent by us to the Resident Commissioners of the three protectorates. The Resident Commissioners of Swaziland and Bechuanaland
refused us the right to enter into their Protectorates. In 1931 we
appealed to His Excellency the High Commissioner. We requested
him to make a provision allowing us to organise an Association of this
kind, and to consider the advisability of erecting his headquarters in
one of the Protectorates and taking his advisers from among the people
living there. The High Commissioner dismissed this appeal.

Finally we appealed to the Secretary for the Dominions. We asked
for the right to organise this Association so that through its
instrumentality we might be able to put our protest against the incorporation of the Protectorates in the Union, and place before the
Imperial Parliament a request for the repeal of the Foreign Jurisdiction
Act. We asked for the same facilities to organise the Association as
those he had allowed for the creation of a Permanent Joint Advisory

Conference in which the three Resident Commissioners meet three representatives of the Union Government to study the ways and formulate the methods by which our Protectorates may be transferred to the Union.

20.

Rabase Sekike to Chieftainess 'Matsaba Seeiso, 30 May 1943, MA 1/33 1937-1946

It is with due humility and respect that we beg to address this letter to you as our advice and prayer on behalf of this nation to you in connection with the Government order executed through you that this nation is placed under compulsion to plant trees in the dongas and other places without getting any remuneration for the sweat of their brows.

In order that you may understand the difficult conditions erected by this order compelling people to give free labour to tree planting scheme for as long as the work remains to be done, we have the honour to point out that the men and women are all compelled to work from six o'clock in the morning to five o'clock in the evening, working hard for all twelve long hours without being given an interval for food or rest to gain breath. The people during these hard times of famine are not given time to go and earn for their living or to go and buy some necessaries for their living. Those who may do this are being in danger of being fined . . . . The women are not given time to prepare some food for their consumption during the time when they are at work because as soon as dawn comes all the people are by order compelled to go to work, men and women alike . . . . In the evening the women are not given time to go and prepare food for the next day of work before it is dark in the evening. Above this there is no wages for this work.

These conditions of slavery are applied upon the people under the pretext that according to Basuto customs the chief has the right to call his people to do for him some work by way of giving free labour to the chief. But in connection with our customs the people are provided with some food to eat during the time they are at work of this nature. To verify our statement, we have the honour to quote the following

passage from Rev. E. Casalis book titled *Basutos*, pages 162-163:—
'The Basutos assemble every year, to dig up and sow the fields
appropriated for the personal maintenance of their chief and his first
wife . . . . The chief generally makes a point of being present, and he
takes care that some fat oxen are prepared for the consumption of his
robust workmen'. . . .[60] Moreover . . . we quote the following
passage from the Transvaal Labour Commission of 1903 in which the
late Resident Commissioner for Basutoland, Sir Herbert C. Sloley,
gave evidence before that Commission in which speaking about
Basuto work said:— 'Among themselves the native wishing his field to
be ploughed, or weeded, or reaped, would invite his neighbours to
help him, providing for them a little feast in the shape of a few pots of
beer or some other food. I mention this by way of showing that cash
payment for labour is a new thing among them, and as a reason for
the exercise of patience in dealing with the question (vide Transvaal
Labour Commission, p.202)'. Now it is not a slanderous statement to
state that your order compelling people to work for no wages without
any food being provided for them has created conditions of slavery far
worse than the conditions under which prisoners in gaol live. The
prisoners are much better than your people compelled to work without
food, without being given an interval for rest, because the prison
authorities are bound by law to provide prisoners with rations of
porridge and beans or cabbage and potatoes for their breakfast and
supper every day. But your people are by order put to work without
wages, without food and without rest. This work takes them for as
long as they have to fill up the dongas with planting trees. These
people are not given time to go and do some work of their own even in
summer when the people are engaged in cleaning their fields of obnox-
ious weeds or in spring time when people are ploughing their
fields . . . .

Now we have the honour to have to point out the fact that today
you as a woman have ascended the position of paramount chief does
not alter the position of women under your rule. According to our
customs the powers of your administration fall upon and affect men
only. The women are under their husbands. For this reason it is not
right for you to create such a change of far reaching and disastrous
results without first consulting Basuto nation of the measures that are
inevitable to be applied on the women under your rule. For this reason
we advise you to make use of your administrative powers on men
alone as usual and have the women remain the mothers of the next

generation as before. Again we ask you to love mercy and give us to know the benefit that will eventually accrue from this scheme of tree planting.

In conclusion we ask you to consider with favour our position that you may ask the Government to be prepared to pay wages to all the people engaged in tree planting scheme, that the women must not be included in this work, that the trees must be protected by you through the chiefs like all other trees planted by Basuto nation in this country.

21.

Maphutseng Lefela, 'Basutoland, Basutos and Europeans', *Umsebenzi*, 31 October 1929.

. . . The policy adopted by the local agents of British South African Imperialism in Basutoland in regard to European traders, who came into Basutoland under the provisions of the law of trade enacted by Moshesh in 1859 . . . which provided that no European traders in Basutoland shall have the right to sell the sites and houses erected for trading when they feel tired of their work, was to sell the sites and trading houses to other European traders in a secret manner. But since the chiefs have been bought over this transaction is nowadays carried out publicly . . . . The chiefs are now completely enmeshed into the network of political and legal intrigues, and are not anything but titulors [sic] and puppets and agents of oppression of their people in the interests of their enslaving masters. The local officers of the Government perfidiously turned the European traders residents of Basutoland through making them pay income tax notwithstanding the protest of the Lekhotla la Bafo against their being turned into residents of Basutoland.

Today these land grabbers, being aware of their insecure hold of the rights of Basutoland as residents owing to the intensified struggle of the Lekhotla la Bafo against their being recognised as residents of this territory, pretend to disagree with the local agents of imperialism — the Resident Commissioner and the High Commissioner — on the question of rebatement of the income tax to bring it into the same level with the Union Government income tax. For this discrepancy they determined to appeal to the Secretary of the Colonies to lodge their request for the rebatement of income tax. The indirect danger of this appeal is that the Secretary of the Colonies, in reducing the income tax payable by them in Basutoland, will have indirectly recognised them as residents of the territory. Therefore, they will goad the local officers of the Government to do everything in their favour to enslave the people in their interests. Lekhotla la Bafo has lodged its protest before the Secretary of the Colonies.

Today Basuto people are deprived of every trading right in favour of these European traders while heavy direct and indirect taxes are imposed on them and hence poverty overtakes the people in an alarming manner, while at the same time those who own sheep and goats are having them decimated by poisonous dip under the pretext of healing the scab. The ultimate resort for Lekhotla la Bafo will be to organise the people to form cooperative agricultural unions through which to enable Lekhotla la Bafo to come to terms with some other sympathising agricultural associations of the world regarding the importation of agricultural implements into the territory so that the people of Basutoland may have nothing to buy from these European traders shops for the period of three years or so . . . . At the same time the people through Lekhotla la Bafo are working hard to raise funds for the establishment of trading houses and big industries to enable the people to wage their struggle against these land robbers so that they may easily evacuate Basutoland because their terms of activities will have ceased to exist. This is the only ultimate resort to defend our rights against their being given to these land robbers despite our peaceful protests.

22.

Rabase Sekike to 'Matsaba Seeiso Griffith, 2 February 1941, MA 1/33 1937-1946

On account of your father having signed schemes for the sale of Basutoland so that it might be taken out of the hands of Basuto people for Europeans, you and we together see the furrows which waste the fields of the people . . . . Even those which have already grown crops are being laid waste under a narcotic saying that it is the prevention of dongas or shuts . . . . This work is being carried out with the money from England from the 'Colonial Development Fund'; moreover, with this money, dams are being constructed all over Basutoland in order to prepare for cotton growing and others of similar nature . . . . Fences are put up enclosing the land and fields of the nation without the consent of the Basuto people and also to grow on the mounds creeping grass and lucerne, etc, etc for which Basuto people are being heavily fined if their animals fed on them. Basuto people are prohibited owning animals which they like — except only those allowed them by the Government. All kinds of barbarities perpetrated upon Basuto people are applied upon them under the guise that is the Paramount Chief who allowed such atrocities to be applied upon them by the Government. All things which according to conditions of protection Moshesh requested that they must be reserved for Basuto people in secret your father in law signed documents yielding them to Europeans. It is why the Government fools those Basuto people who support the chieftainship of your father in law, N. Griffith, and of Seeiso as well as yours with praises that they are supported by the Government because they are right. Whereas the fact is that through the chieftainship of the family of N. Griffith the taking of Basutoland out of the hands of Basuto people, the suppression of hereditary chieftainship of the family of Letsie II because through it according to the conditions of protection Basutoland and all things belonging to it have to be restored to Basuto people. It is why the Government declares that it was arranged that chieftainess Mahali Letsie II must never ascend to the position because she is a woman, but today, despite the fact that you are a woman, owing to the long felt need of the Imperial Government to take and deprive Basuto people of Basutoland, you are installed and vested with the powers of the Paramount Chieftainship because through you the policy of privation will easily be effected. It is why you are installed independently of your lawful and legitimate guardian according to our laws and customs, namely Chief Bereng, and you remain under His Honour the Resident Commissioner so that you may work in colaboration [sic] with anything but flunkies and licks spittles who are his favourites so that through you the final privation of Basutoland may be carried out.

In 1872 the Hermon congregation of the Paris Evangelical Mission Society laid the foundation for a thriving independent church movement in Lesotho by breaking away from the mission church. Independent churches gained much popularity in the twentieth century largely through the inspirational leadership of prophetic figures like Walter Matitta, who developed a close relationship with the movement of Josiel Lefela. He and other independent church leaders shared common views on the role of European missionaries who stood accused of subverting the social and economic fabric of Basotho society in alliance with colonial officials. These ministers did not see a distinction between religious and political life. As Rev. Raymond Mohono put it, '. . . it is our duty not to accept the precepts of European religion unless its tenets are in agreement with the political welfare of the Basuto . . . . Other National Churches have evolved from the natural revulsion of the common people against oppression by the ruling classes — religious and political. We are always protesting against the tyranny of foreign missionaries.'[61]

23.

Statement of the African Federal Church Council Conference, Teyateyaneng, 29-31 May 1931, LNA S 3/22/2/6.

We Basuto ministers of various denominations have originally been under European missionaries who have churches in Basutoland and SA but owing to the hypocrisy of European missionaries, more particularly revealed and manifested in the treatment of discrimination and differentiation meted out to their followers in their churches, we gradually became discontented and eventually separated from their churches. But however, we realised the value of taking up the work of God upon our own shoulders to work among our own people in the land of our birth Basutoland and Africa as a whole. Like all people in any part of the world who are under the protection of their Governments, we hoped and expected to receive the protection from our Paramount Chief and chiefs as well as the Government protection so that our work in this country may not be hemmed in by disabilities invented for the purpose of nullifying our work in this country.

Moreover as we know that the desire of the late Chief Moshesh was that European missionaries might teach Basuto people how to manage the work of God amongst themselves so that after having been able to manage this work of God independently of European missionaries they may be able to carry on the work amongst Basuto people independently of European control. And again we know that the promise of these European missionaries to Chief Moshesh and Basuto nation originally was that they had come to teach Basuto people the word of God, they would then retire and leave the work in the hands of Basuto people to it themselves. For this reason we had hoped that our breaking away from European churches would be taken as the right step towards the fulfilment of the promise given by European missionaries to Moshesh with his people and that the chiefs would be more encouraged and pleased with our work to see the sons of Basutoland carrying on the work of God amongst the sons and daughters of Basutoland and of Africa as a whole.

But alas! we became the target of revilement and scorn and all sorts of wickedness and objection were and are attributed to us. The bed and source of all these malignant and aspersive allegations attributed to us are the European missionaries in this country, and on account of the fact that many chiefs are now their followers, for they are Christians in their churches, our chiefs have become the victims to this spirit of hatred and revilement. The Government has not escaped from the malignant spirit of hatred fathered by the European missionaries. Now we are being denied all the rights that are indispensable to all missionaries and ministers and when we try to appeal to the paramount chief and chiefs we get no redress and when we appeal to the local government officers we meet the same fate. We are told that those rights which are denied to us are the monopoly of European missionaries in this country.

For this reason as we have no one to come to our help we turn and appeal to Lekhotla la Bafo to help us with whatever help it may be in its power to give us and therefore we whose names are signed hereunder authorise Lekhotla la Bafo to take up our grievances and try all the best it can to seek for redress on our behalf in all our grievances. The chief points of our grievances are that we are refused the right to buy Communion wine by the Government on account of the request submitted before it by European missionaries in Basutoland. We are compelled to buy it through European missionaries. We are refused the school grant for our schools notwithstanding the fact that our followers pay 3/- levy for education.

We are compelled to put our schools under European missionary schools that they may be taken as schools of those missionaries and that religious and moral teaching should be conducted according to the discipline framed by those European missionaries . . . .

The chiefs are pursuing a rigorous campaign of depriving us of our sites for church under flimsy pretexts. This is being done by the chiefs in order to please European missionaries of three denominations in this country whose aim is that our churches must be uprooted to leave the field of work for the flourish of their own churches. The chiefs are encouraged to do this by the Government.

We are refused the right of marriage officers and we have applied for this right for several times to the Government but our applications have all been dismissed by the Government because this is the monopoly of the European missionaries of three denominations in Basutoland.

We are refused the right of selling European medicines by the Government but this right is preserved as a monopoly for European missionaries by the Government.

When a matter of immorality happens amongst the members of our churches, the churches in which such matters happened are said to indulge in matters of promiscuous sexual intercourse and such of our churches are said to be the same thing with the Zion Apostles Faith Mission Church of Rev. Edward T. Lion whose church has already been banished from Basutoland. This allegation is being ascribed to such of our churches in spite of the fact that such of their members who are found guilty of the infraction of the churches rules and discipline have been excommunicated and, this shows that the aim of this malicious allegation ascribed to such of our churches is that such churches must be banished from Basutoland. But a wonderful fact is that these questions of immorality are not only confined to happen in our churches but we have seen such instances happening in some of the European churches in this country but such matters were left in the hands of such churches to settle and were never subjected to such humiliating indignities and disparagement of aspersion.

. . . The Lekhotla la Bafo will undertake to handle those questions which affect our respective churches from the secular point of view which assume the political character to disable our religious work and the Lekhotla la Bafo will not be taken to have the right upon the shaping of purely religious matters of our respective churches. On the other hand the Lekhotla la Bafo will have the authority upon such matters which after having been passed by the accredited members of the African Federal Churches Council at its general conference will be ratified by our respective church assemblies through the signatures of the directors of our respective churches authorising the Lekhotla la Bafo to wage its struggles on our behalf in connection with such matters in question.

Signed by   R.M. Mohono, President
               R.S. Moltoli, Vice President
               L. Leboane, Secretary

24.

H.M.D. Tsoene to Lord Passfield, Secretary of State for the Colonies, 18 June 1930, LNA S 3/22/2/5.

We have much respect to have to address this letter to you on the subject of Education in Basutoland. At the very beginning of the coming in contact of Moshesh and his nation with Europeans with their achievements through civilisation. Moshesh was inspired with the keen desire of getting them means of procuring Education for his nation which would lift up Basuto nation to the same standard and level of progress and civilisation with European nations. But unfortunately for him his hands were quite full of political matters that he got no time to put his hands into the work of making a substantial beginning for the introduction of sound Education in Basutoland. But, however, the missionaries had promised him that they would educate Basuto people to the highest Educational attainments but all this has been nothing but a camouflage.

   Chief Lerotholi, in pursuance of getting a real sound Education for his nation, consulted his people about the project he had contemplated to set on foot that he had got one man, namely Mr. Wright Dude, an American Negro, who had promised him that in the matter of Education he would recruit the best teachers in America for the universities — one for Technical Education and the other for other branches of sciences — he wanted to establish. For this reason he asked his people to support him in this undertaking and he therefore started the erection of buildings for technical school at the place called Rakhoiti's. He intended to put the other university at Qeme. At this juncture the Resident Commissioner of Basutoland intervened and persuaded Chief Lerotholi to trust the whole scheme in the hands of the Government. The Resident Commissioner in persuasion told Chief Lerotholi that if he only would collect funds for the establishment of such universities in question and entrust them to the local Government, the local Government officers are greatly interested in the matter of giving Basuto people a real and substantial education and they would get the best teachers for the universities in question. For this reason Chief Lerotholi agreed to entrust the whole scheme to the local Resident Commissioner in his capacity as the representative of the Government. Therefore he removed the site from Rakhoiti's where the foundations had been laid to Maseru. Then Chief Lerotholi asked his people to contribute money and cattle towards the funds collected for this project of these two universities and the people willingly responded to contribute cattle and money which realised £3500. Then the Resident Commissioner made it impossible for Mr. Wright Dude who was then in Cape Town to return to Basutoland. Owing to this arrangement Chief Lerotholi consulted His Honour the Resident Commissioner that no more European traders should be allowed new sites for the erection of Buildings for trading purposes because Basuto young men trained in these two universities would need much field for turning to practical account all the knowledge they gained at these schools. But Chief Lerotholi died before this scheme was properly handled and organised and for this reason it was easy for the Resident Commissioner to ruin the whole scheme and make that school what it is today, which is a government workshop . . . .

Since then the . . . system of education has been pulled down to put the other which the missionaries . . . thought best suited Basuto people to make them good and reliable servants for Europeans and to make them ready to yield their country to become the commonwealth of all other races . . . . The missionaries are working hard more than ever before to teach the Basuto Christians how to sing hymns and pray kneeling down all the time. The religious meetings are of such frequency that through kneeling down the knees of all Christians have grown up deep horns in preparation to offering the last prayer before the son of God who is said to be on the threshold of doors of heaven for the second coming to bring an end to the earth . . . . Therefore, good preparations are being hard impressed in the churches to urge Basuto Christians to do away with earthly riches and wisdom because before the face of God it is all folly according to the missionaries' teaching in Basutoland.

We pay excessive and exorbitant hut tax squeezed out of us in an oppressive and cruel manner, but with the money squeezed out of a barbarian and savage nation, the local officers of the Government appropriate a large amount of money by which the children of local European officers of the Government are taught in schools whose mothers and fathers are well civilised and have a history of two thousand years of civilisation behind them. But the children of the barbarian and savage Basuto nation, as we are so contemptuously degraded by some local Europeans, are left helplessly ignorant without the very rudiments of a real education other than making them good and reliable servants and devout Christians.

Now on 28th May 1930, through our delegates, we asked Mr. T.B. Kennan, the Assistant Commissioner, why the local officers of the Government are importing Europeans into Basutoland in an inconsistent manner to the conditions under which Basutoland through Moshesh came under the British protection. He said that those Europeans against whom we complain . . . came into Basutoland to hold positions which require civilised men, well qualified for the posts they hold in benefit to Basuto nation. There is no other way to take because Basuto people through the lack of education to qualify them for such posts are hopelessly ignorant. For this reason, as we realise that the local officers of the Government have ruined the enterprise and project of Chief Lerotholi for better education with the ultimate aim of exploiting our state of backwardness in educational attainments; while they have appropriated our money to teach their children; while ours are forced into a state of ignorance and backwardness, and have thus failed to use aright the trust of imparting civilisation to other backward races of the world, we beg and pray you to open the door for our children to go abroad to England and other countries of civilised world for education in all its branches so that our Basuto people in ten years time hence may have men who are well qualified for various posts obtainable in the civilised world.

25.

A letter of instructions to the delegates of Lekhotla la Bafo, 22 December 1930, LNA S 3/22/2/6.

1. You, delegates are instructed to hold your meetings in peace compatible with the white and green flag which is the flag of peace and hope. If you find some people trying to cause some trouble or impediment to your holding a meeting, you must face the situation peacefully and calmly and if you find that some people are bent on causing trouble you may insist on holding your meeting . . . . After you have asked the chief or headman together with the representative of the Government to quell the trouble but in vain, you may close the meeting but write down the causes of the trouble.

(a) You go out for the purpose of holding meetings which have been called by the Lekhotla la Bafo at the headquarters and the chiefs and the Assistant Commissioners of the districts have been duly informed. But, if by consultation you may be asked to hold meetings at the places of some chiefs, sub-chiefs or headmen where there are members and where there are none, you may do so . . . .

2. In all the matters in the agenda and which may not be in the agenda which you may find necessary to make speeches upon in order to make necessary explanation for the people you must at all times keep in mind the instructions of the Lekhotla la Bafo that the people must be guided to say their complaints with respect. You must not preach seditious doctrines that the people should overthrow the chieftainship of the sons of Moshesh, but you must advise the people to remain under the chieftainship of the sons of Moshesh. You must teach the people to remain under the permanent protection of Great Britain upon Basutoland over Basuto people and that the Government should put into effect the protection over Basuto nation through the Paramount Chief and chiefs in accordance with conditions laid by Moshesh before the Government for protection under England.

(a) You must teach the people that Lekhotla la Bafo is the medium through which the people with respect must say their complaints regarding the points where the chiefs have done away with the measures by which the people were satisfied in their application and also in regard to the powers which the Chiefs have sold away to Europeans which have been entrusted to them by the nation without consulting the people.

(b) You must teach the people that in matters concerning which the Government no longer complies with the conditions upon which Moshesh came under British protection and in cases where the Government has deprived the chiefs of their powers which are invested upon Europeans under various departments and in regard to such powers wrested from the chiefs by the Government, it is no longer possible for the chiefs to champion the interests of their people because the chiefs have been turned into policemen . . . . It is hightime that the people should be prepared to say the whole truth of their grievances and organise themselves to wage a peaceful struggle against the Government by getting the means of taking legal proceedings against the Government in the Courts of law to end before the Privy Council when they are well prepared to handle such a situation. The people must be prepared to fight against certain laws after sufficient funds have been collected such as the dipping regulations and the Proclamation for hut tax . . . . Such laws will have to be fought against after sufficient funds have been collected and the date and time to commence the struggle will have to be made known beforehand . . . . This will have to be done not that there should be any trouble but that there may arise cause of taking legal proceedings in the courts of law to end before the Privy Council in England. No delegate must encourage the people to break the laws administered either by the chiefs or by the Government. It does not matter how harsh such laws may be. The people must obey them all so that it may be easy to understand that those which will have to be contravened are meant to be made the means of taking legal proceedings under constitutional ways in a respectful manner.

(c) You must teach the people to remain under the permanent protection of British Government . . . . In cases where an appeal is to be made to the nations of the world to ask them to go and pray British Government for Basuto people, this must be done in a loyal manner to British Government.

(d) No man must encourage the christians of various denominations to hate one another nor hate the non christians. The delegates must teach the people to help one another, but in cases where the missionaries teach religious matters and education, must be attacked in a peaceful and respectful way.

Lekhotla la Bafo reserved its most searing invective for colonial officials who raised its ire. In this document, R.B. Smith, an Assistant Commissioner, comes under attack, but the colonial official who was most consistently vilified by them was J.H. Sims, a long-time Basutoland civil servant, whom they described as 'an Angel of Destruction' and the 'worst malefactor the world has ever seen and a most wicked despot whose cruelties know no bounds and are without parallel'.[62]

26.

Maphutseng Lefela, 'One oppressor less for Basutoland', *Umsebenzi*, 30 November 1929.

Basutoland has got rid of one of our worst blood thirsty foes whose record is one that has no equal or parallel in regard to the manner in which Basuto people were treacherously deprived of their rights. Basutoland came under the protection of England on the ground that no Europeans should be allowed to come into Basutoland to live as residents owing to the fear that if Europeans would be allowed to live in Basutoland the same old perfidious and treacherous tactics would be employed by those Europeans to deprive Basuto people of their country in the same way as the Orange Free State was taken for Europeans under the guise of protection. Now Mr. R.B. Smith was one of those officers in Basutoland who are expected to close the door of Basutoland against the entry of Europeans into it. But instead through his treacherous labours, and during his administration many Europeans of different situations of life have been imported into Basutoland to become residents. Of these there are European doctors — Dutch and English doctors in Maseru and other places who do not like to touch Basutos who want medical examinations but only order them to put away their clothes and look at them from a good way off and then ask them a few questions. No proper and careful treatment is received at the hands of these men.

The wicked officer of the Government in the person of Mr. R.B. Smith together with His Honour the Resident Commissioner and His Excellency the High Commissioner has deprived our chiefs of their powers over their people in regard to public health. On account of this fact many people who through sickness are unable to work hard for themselves, have not been taken out of the roll of taxpayers because their chiefs are no longer regarded as worthy to recommend the sick people to be cancelled from the list of the taxpayers, but when they go to these cruel doctors who cannot touch them they are told that they are in good health and therefore they cannot be taken out of the list of the taxpayers. In this way many sick and incapacitated people are groaning under the heavy yoke of tax.

It was under the administration of Mr. R.B. Smith that through Proclamation Nos. 31 and 32 of 1928 the residences of the local Assistant Commissioners in Basutoland were brought under the pale of Municipal regulations of the Union Government and many people in their places are being subjected to cruel laws obtaining in the Union Government. Basuto people living in these reserves are not allowed to own more than eight head of cattle.

Moreover, Basuto people are deprived of their rights of free trade. The trade of Basutoland is made a monopoly of a mere handful of European traders and during the administration of Mr. R.B. Smith many Basuto people have been arrested and persecuted although they were working in compliance with Proclamation No. 28 of 1928 which allows Basutos to trade without licence in hides, skins, horses and bones as well as products of Basutoland. Through the Wool Export Duty Proclamation Basuto people are being robbed of ½d per lb. on all wool and mohair sold by Basuto people and the traders are collectors of this money. With the help of this money many Dutch tatterdemalions have been imported into the territory to carry out the nefarious work of the extermination of the flocks of sheep and goats of the Basuto nation through poisonous dip under the guise of healing the scab. Under the method in which this dipping operation is being carried out all those who own sheep are turned the slaves of these Dutch tatterdemalions under the title of dip inspectors.

During his administration another act of robbery was introduced which is the extra charge of 3d per lb. on all parcels delivered to Basuto people at the inland postal agencies through out Basutoland. This extra charge is made in spite of the fact that these parcels had been sent out to their various destinations at the expense of the sender. This act of robbery has hit hard many poor Basuto people.

It was the same notorious man who proscribed the members of Lekhotla la Bafo as outlaws and closed correspondence through His Excellency the High Commissioner. There is no proper communication between Lekhotla la Bafo and His Excellency the High Commissioner at the present time. And again, it is the same man who in 1928 issued a circular notice to all the principal chiefs in order to prevent Lekhotla la Bafo holding meetings throughout Basutoland; and that people strictly ordered not to contribute any money to our Association. That is why Lekhotla la Bafo is the poorest organisation in the world in spite of the fact that the people like and sympathise with it. These are but a few instances of the wicked and nefarious official acts and character of this heartless agent of Imperialism. At the present time the whole nation is seething with discontent, and is groaning under a heavy yoke of oppression created by Mr. R.B. Smith. We hope the successor to this man in office will not follow in his footsteps. We shall not tolerate his kind again.

27.

Maphutseng Lefela, 'British imperialism in Basutoland plot to suppress "League of the Poor" ', *Umsebenzi*, 15 August 1930.

About half a year ago the Secretary for the Colonies in London, England, in reply to complaints submitted to him by Lekhotla la Bafo . . . stated that letters should be addressed not to him but to the Resident Commissioner, the local representative of British imperialism in Basutoland.

The Resident Commissioner evidently took this as a hint to get busy suppressing the poor people in Basutoland. He began by ordering the chiefs (through the assistant commissioners) to prevent meetings of the Lekhotla la Bafo in their respective wards. If the league carried on its meetings in spite of the prohibition of the chiefs, the latter were encouraged by the Government to intervene indirectly and secure the dispersal of the meeting, by inciting the people against Lekhotla la Bafo.

When the Commissioner found that this plot had failed as a result of exposures made by Lekhotla la Bafo, and that the people refused to be led astray, he tried a new plan. He sent letters to the chiefs of Basutoland, ordering them on one pretext or another to send him their official signatures (produced by rubber stamps) on blank pieces of paper. We learned that the object of this was to fill in these blank papers with various petitions to the assistant commissioners, asking them to request the Government to deal with Josiel Lefela (organiser of the League) whose movements were alleged to be creating feelings of hostility between Europeans and Basutos as well as between the people and the chiefs. These fake petitions also asked that the Lekhotla la Bafo should be suppressed.

The chiefs were required to send in three blank papers containing their signatures, in order that copies of the 'petitions' might be sent to the High Commissioner in South Africa and the Colonial Secretary in London.

The plot to deport Comrade Josiel Lefela without trial and to suppress Lekhotla la Bafo is thus laid bare. Fortunately we have discovered the plot before it has materialised. The people of Basutoland will rally on the League of the Poor and ensure that this nefarious plot is nipped in the bud.

28.

Maphutseng Lefela, 'Passive resistance in Basutoland, our last resort to fight against oppression', *Umsebenzi*, 31 January 1930.

. . . The worst of all proclamations in vogue in Basutoland are the regulations for dipping our flocks of sheep and the method of collecting hut tax in Basutoland; also the trading regulations which have made trade in Basutoland a monopoly for European traders. And besides these measures, they are also subjected to the cruel laws of the local Assistant Commissioner; by this I mean that the Assistant Commissioners are free to set aside the laws in vogue if the local Europeans do not wish to see them applied but prefer to see the reverse of such laws i.e., what is unlawful, applied upon the people. These unlawful applications are rigorously applied upon the people in just the same way as the laws in vogue.

For this reason Lekhotla la Bafo . . . informed the Secretary of the Colonies that owing to the practice of applying unlawful measures upon the people by the local Government officers we should within a short space of time preach the doctrine of passive resistance of all unlawful measures applied upon the people while at the same time we preach obedience to all written laws no matter how harsh they may be, until we get the means of putting our grievances before the English Government for redress 'in a constitutional manner' — despite the fact that we have no accepted Constitution of our own. Moshoeshoe said before the Government the condition that he wished to fill the same position as a man who has a house. The man owns the house and all that is in it and the Government rules the man. In this way he made it a condition that Government would govern his people only through him as he said Basutoland was his house and the people were the furniture of the house. Now as this condition has been subverted without our knowledge, we being politically gagged, we on the 21st, 22nd and 23rd June 1929 [see Document 13], held a meeting at the Paramountcy in Matsieng at which we laid down all our rights and powers of the chiefs over the people, now taken away from their legitimate owners and invested in the European Imperialists; and asked the Paramount Chief the circumstances under which those powers and rights which had been entrusted to his care had been taken out of his care to be invested in cruel European Imperialists. The Paramount Chief asked us to give him much time to think over the nature of the reply he would give us. For this reason we have resolved to hold a meeting in Matsieng on the 16th March 1930 for the purpose of waiting on his reply on those points. As the matter is of national importance, we extend our invitation to all sympathising organisations to send fraternal delegates at their own expense to attend this conference, and the other to be held in Thaba Bosiu on the 12th March 1930 [see Document 16]. We wish to have some outside friends when the Paramount Chief gives us his last word for we know for certain that his reply to us will be nothing but an evasion.

Then, after this reply from the Paramount Chief which as anticipated will not improve matters, we propose to enter into a campaign of passive resistance against this yielding of our rights on the part of the Paramount Chief to the European Imperialists, to fill his position over us as a nation to administer cruel laws to oppress us in the interests of the South African Imperialists. According to the conditions under which we came under England, the Paramount Chief is our ruler who must rule us in accordance with our desires and wishes as a nation. He has now sold this right entrusted to him without our knowledge. We shall now set out powers entrusted to the Paramount

Chief which are already in the hands of European Imperialists by virtue of Proclamations. All these Proclamations are in contradiction to those Proclamations imposed on the people as unlawful measures, and it is against these unlawful measures that we shall organise the people to offer peaceful resistance so that we may be arrested. We shall call upon the Paramount Chief with the Resident Commissioner to come and tell us the circumstances that forced him to sell the powers entrusted to him on conditions which England pledged herself to observe. As we wish to carry this case to the Privy Council of England we shall first of all collect funds towards this purpose and for the purpose of subsidising the families of those imprisoned for passive resistance. Our programme of passive resistance will begin with unlawful measures forced upon the people in regard to the dipping regulations.

29.

H.M.D. Tsoene to Mr. Tardien, Prime Minister of France, 1 April 1930, LNA S 3/22/2/4.

It is with due respect and humbleness that we beg to lodge our prayer before you to request you as Prime Minister and your Government to assist us and put our prayer before the Government of Great Britain to have mercy upon us and consider our request before it which we have put before Lord Passfield, the Secretary of the Colonies with a request to put it before the British Government and Parliament to ask them to wait and give us time in the event of the Union Government putting a request before the British Government and Parliament for the incorporation of Basutoland into the Union Government, to put our case to explain before the British Government and Parliament the reasons why we are afraid of our country being incorporated in the Union Government and why we do not like to be taken out of direct protection of the British Government.

. . . We ask you in this way because the Union Government is preparing to put a request before the British Government to make provision for this incorporation in pursuance of the promise of the British Parliament to the Union Government which gave them the right to provide for this incorporation of our protectorates in the Union Government through the South Africa Act . . . . The same British Parliament promised us to protect us in accordance with our desires which are that we must remain under the permanent protection of England. We wish to learn whether it is compatible with the civilised international laws of civilised christian nations to violate pledges accorded by powerful nations for the protection of small and weak nations to hand them to the mercy of the crushing hands of those very Governments against whom protection was sought and secured under conditions and pledges.

We appeal to you because we are unable to lodge our cries before the British Government in a constitutional manner because the local Resident Commissioner has strictly ordered our Paramount Chief and Chiefs to see that the people do not contribute any money to our Association so that we may always remain without the necessary funds, and in this way we find no other way of making our views heard and known to the British Government so as to enable the Union Government to make arrangements with England which empower it to deprive us of our rights while we are thus disabled to make our views known to our protector.

Section 151 of the Act of Union of 1909 provided for the possibility that one day the British would transfer the High Commission Territories to South Africa. One reason why the transfer was never made was that Africans in the Territories were adamantly opposed to being handed over. Numerous deputations of chiefs from Swaziland, Lesotho and Botswana made their way to London to make this point.[63] Lekhotla la Bafo was just one voice among many on this particular issue, although its call for a coordinating body, a League of Protectorates, was a novel one.

30.

E.L.D. Masupha to Sobhuza II,
Swaziland, 10 July 1926, LNA S 3/22/2/2.

It is with great honour and respect that we beg to address you this letter wherewith we convey our views to you on the question of your case against the encroachment and eviction of your people from a portion of your territory made by Mr. Allister Mitchell Miller which you prosecuted until you appealed to the Privy Council of England.[64]

It is with great respect and honour that we beg to express our feelings of deepest sympathy with you in this matter and above all we put our thanks before you for your great courage in displaying that laudable quality which we regret to notice that it is now rare in our African chiefs of keeping a watchful care over the rights of their nations and with this quality with which you have distinguished yourself as the lover and caretaker of the interests of the African people in Swaziland. Your appeal to Privy Council brought into light a very important question affecting the Protectorates in common and it is on account of that very important matter that we beg to address you this letter.

It is with great honour and respect that we beg to put before you knowledge that [we] have learned from the *Mochochonono* of 21 April 1926 which has culled the same from the *Friend* of 16 April 1926 that Lord Haldane is reported as follows: 'His Lordship emphasised that orders in Council issued under the Foreign Jurisdiction Act made jurisdiction acquired by the Crown in a protected country, indistinguishable from what might be acquired by conquest, and this view was supported by reference to the case of Sekhoma in 1920, and Southern Rhodesia in 1919. The Crown could not, excepting by statute, deprive itself of the freedom to make Orders in Council, even when these are inconsistent with previous Orders.'

It is with respect that we beg to point out that from this statement quoted above the protectorates are under the same category of policy with those territories which had been acquired by England through physical force regardless of the fact that the Protectorates have come under the protection of England under certain conditions agreed upon in conventions. But this fact has been unknown to the Protectorates until today when this fact is explained in the pronouncement of the judgment in your appeal case.

It is with great respect that we beg to put before you our advice on this situation is that you as the Paramount Chief of Swaziland may consider the advisability of putting before the Paramount chiefs of Basutoland and Bechuanaland the scheme of establishing a Conference in which the Protectorates would consider together the matters which affect them in common so that these Protectorates may be able to voice their views before the Imperial Government on such questions of common interest . . . .

It is with respect that we beg to state that the establishment of such a conference would be useful for both the Protectorates and the Imperial Government because if the principle of such a conference would be acceptable to these Protectorates who ought to be stationed in London who ought to study all the questions affecting the Protectorates . . . . This way has been very helpful to the Indians who have stationed their representative in England to study all those questions which affect India.

It is with respect that we point out that this kind of Association would be useful in making it possible for the Protectorates to make representations before the Imperial Government on such questions which are important to be laid before the Imperial Government so that England may know the views under which the Protectorates wish to be governed by her.

. . . It is with respect that we again beg to point out that after the establishment of an Association of this kind it is desirable for the advisability of putting before the English Parliament the complaint of the Protectorates as a whole against the point explained by Lord Haldane that under 'Foreign Jurisdiction Act made jurisdiction acquired by the Crown in a protected country, indistinguishable from what might be acquired by conquest' so that the English Parliament may be able to learn our views and wish as regards our relation with England . . . . It is very probable that the unanimous protest of the Protectorates against this Act may bring about a change in the statute which may either amend or repeal this Act. If there be any difficulty in this point the most important matter would be to educate the English people the source of our complaints as Protectorates rests on the fact that our countries asked England under certain conditions to accept them as Protectorates so that they may be different from such countries acquired by physical force by England.

31.

H.M.D. Tsoene to Chief Tshekedi Khama,[65] 12 April 1930, LNA S 3/22/2/4.

. . . we have . . . come to you to ask you to join hands with us in the matter of collecting the necessary funds to enable us to send our representatives to England to voice and represent the interests, wishes and desires of our respective protectorates and to establish a permanent office of the representative of our respective protectorates in England to represent the interests, wishes, requests and grievances of our respective countries before the English Government, Parliament and nation.

You must remember that when Sir Charles Warren warned your father, Chief Khama, to throw in his country under the protection of England as a step against the German encroachments upon your country, Bechuanaland, your father, Chief Khama, agreed to put his country under the British protection under the assurance given on behalf of the British Government by Sir Charles Warren that England would protect Bechuanaland for Bechuana people to enjoy the blessings of peace under their hereditary chiefs.[66] It was never made a condition by Sir Charles Warren to Chief Khama that England would afterwards dispose of Bechuanaland and hand it to other European Government in South Africa, whose cruelty is unparalleled even worse than that of the Germans on account of whom Sir Charles Warren asked Chief Khama to throw his country into the British protection.

Again in 1895, Mr. Chamberlain wrote letters to Chiefs Khama, Bathoeng and Sebele after their visit to England to assure them that Bechuanaland would always remain the property of Bechuana people and that no white man can live in Bechuanaland protectorates unless he lives under the conditions laid before him by the chiefs of Bechuanaland . . . . The contents of these letters are recorded in one of the Blue Books in England.[67] But it would be our folly to let our countries slip out of our control while England has given us sound pledges for protection and it is up with us to stand up and organise our people to make financial contributions to enable us to voice our protest against the incorporation of our respective countries into the Union Government . . . .

We have the honour and respect to have to explain to you that, following upon the strain of language expressed by His Excellency, the

Earl of Athlone, the High Commissioner, which he pressed hard upon you to yield a portion of your country to European Syndicates to dig it, we cannot possibly avoid the crushing manoeuvres and measures directed against us — prompted by the feelings of jealousy by other races of the world — unless we can keep pace with modern civilised progress to prove to the world that we are able to stand our own under the present conditions. We can only come to this position through hard work on our part being done by us to protect our rights and countries. For this reason we earnestly beg you to take our request and appeal to your serious consideration and attention to make a united front movement together with us against the imminent danger of the incorporation of our respective protectorates into the Union Government.

32.

Maphutseng Lefela, 'Lekhotla la Bafo has planned that there should be established a Council for the purpose of looking after the rights of the Protectorates', *Umsebenzi*, 31 July 1929.

In the year 1926 the Lekhotla la Bafo learned the judgment of the case between Chief Sobhuza II of Swaziland and Mr. Allister Mitchell Miller of Swaziland Corporation, which was before the great court of England, namely the Privy Council. In this case Chief Sobhuza II of Swaziland disputed against Europeans of Swaziland, whose head is Mr. Allister Mitchell Miller, who entered Swaziland by permission of Chief Umbandini which granted to them gold mining, provided that they quite understood and knew that they had no right whatsoever to regard themselves as having any right to the country (land) of Swaziland besides the right (concession) of mining where they were given. Now in 1924 the Europeans were turning away Swazis who lived there paying rents. Chief Sobhuza took the step of disputing against the Europeans for this behaviour of theirs. Mr. A.M. Miller answered for himself that he was given the right to the land by law of the High Commissioner's Proclamation of 1917 which was made by the High Commissioner by power conferred by the Order-in-Council of

November, 1907 which has given the High Commissioner the power to deprive the Swazis of the land and to call it 'crown lands'. The judgement of the Court was given for Mr. A.M. Miller in South Africa, and Chief Sobhuza II appealed to the Privy Council of England where he explained that in accordance with the way in which Swaziland came under the protection of the Government of England the Government had no right to make Orders-in-Council giving the High Commissioner power to deprive Swaziland of their land, because the Government of England did not take Swaziland by conquering it in a fight (war) or in any way excepting protection through which Swaziland came under England. For this reason it is wrong to deprive the Swazis of their land under the law which is contrary to terms of the agreement of the protection under England.

Lord Haldane, in delivering judgement in the case, examined the laws of the constitution of England in connection with the protectorates under England, and stated that under the power of the Foreign Jurisdiction Act the Government of England has the power to make Orders-in-Council even if they were contrary to previous Orders-in-Council; the Foreign Jurisdiction Act gives the Government the power to make laws which do not differentiate between countries conquered by arms by England and countries which came under England for protection. And the Crown cannot deprive itself of the power to make such laws unless it is deprived of the power by a law (an act) of Parliament. For this reason, judgement in the case is for Mr. A.M. Miller.

Owing to the above judgement, the Lekhotla la Bafo on the 10th July 1926 wrote to Chief Sobhuza II of Swaziland and to Chief Tshekedi Khama of Bechuanaland that as it had learned the danger of the Foreign Jurisdiction Act at the time of the trial of the case between Chief Sobhuza II and Mr. A.M. Miller the protectorates should form a 'Lekhotla' (Council or Body) for the purpose of looking after the protectorates under England. And by authority of this Lekhotla, the Parliament of England should be requested to repeal the Foreign Jurisdiction Act. Chief Sobhuza in his letter of the 26th July 1926 agreed with this motion. Thereafter the Lekhotla la Bafo met with difficulties which disabled its progress in this matter.

Today at the meeting of the Lekhotla la Bafo which assembled at Mapoteng from the 24th May to the 26th May 1929 the Lekhotla la Bafo placed this matter before the nation, and the nation agreed that is proper that the Lekhotla which looks after the rights of the protectorates should exist and that by power of this Lekhotla, the Parliament of England should be asked to repeal the Foreign Jurisdiction Act. And the meeting has agreed that this should be made widely known in native newspapers of South Africa and in newspapers of the workers of the world to the societies which are fighting for freedom and rights of down-trodden people who live in slavery. The Lekhotla la Bafo puts this matter forward for consideration by black people who live in the protectorates, so that they may help in advice and money which will make this matter get on, for the Lekhotla la Bafo is bound to print booklets which clearly explain this plan and which should be sent to Swaziland and Bechuanaland and all societies which are fighting for the rights of the down-trodden. Further, the Lekhotla la Bafo should send out messengers who should confer with Chief Sobhuza II of Swaziland and Chief Tshekedi Khama to make arrangements for a meeting which should be held, at which representatives from Bechuanaland, Swaziland and Basutoland will consult together about the way in which a Lekhotla of this sort can be established.

The Lekhotla la Bafo has consulted the High Commissioner, the Resident Commissioner of Basutoland, that of Bechuanaland, that of Swaziland, the Paramount Chief of Basutoland and all the chiefs of Basutoland, that it is speaking to Chief Sobhuza and Chief Tshekedi Khama that they the chiefs should be careful and found a Lekhotla of this sort, and if they do nothing in this matter the Lekhotla la Bafo will continue (get on) in the work of establishing the Lekhotla which looks after the rights of the protectorates.

The Lekhotla la Bafo informs all people that if its messengers will be stopped from entering Swaziland and Bechuanaland to meet with the chiefs of those countries to arrange for the meeting consulting about this Lekhotla, the Lekhotla la Bafo will call the chiefs to meet with the representatives, in the Union. If still forbidden, the Lekhotla la Bafo will consider which way to take to further the project, because it is impossible for us to leave our rights and have them transferred to Europeans while no explanation of our fault is given to us under the protection of England. We wish to persevere in this matter until we place our request before the Government and nation and Parliament of England, as the Lekhotla of the Protectorates, is that the law Foreign Jurisdiction Act may be repealed and obliterated from the books of the laws of England for the Government of England is not looking after the rights and welfare of South African Europeans only but in like manner looking after the rights of the black people of the protectorates. The reason why we continue to be deprived of our rights is that we allow our affairs to be represented to our Mother, England, by our enemies, and they represent them badly and in a way which places us in danger of being deprived of our rights; it should quite understand from us its children of the protectorates that we do not wish that it may deprive us of our rights.

Although Garveyism did not take root in Lesotho to the same degree it did in South Africa, it still found an avid disciple in Josiel Lefela. Along with Theal's *Basutoland Records*, Garvey's works were quoted extensively by him in speeches.

33.

E.L.D. Masupha Moshesh to President Calvin Coolidge, United States, 2 July 1927, LNA, S 3/22/2/2.

We, the peoples of Basutoland in South Africa assembled in our congress known as 'Lekhotla la Bafo' (Commons' Association) have the great honour and respect to have to put this prayer of ours before your consideration for the release of Honourable Marcus Garvey from Atlanta Prison without deportation.

We the African Negroes regard Honourable Marcus Garvey in the same light as Jacob did to his son Joseph who was sold as a slave and served as such in Egypt after Jacob found out that he was still alive and the same Joseph had the claim of share in his father's patrimony. In the same manner we regard Honourable Marcus Garvey doing well with his movement to rouse the negroes of the world to a race consciousness and nationalism to build a Government of their own in Africa their motherland.

As Joseph saved his father Jacob and his brothers from the clutches of the great famine we look to the negroes of America for help to save us from the great famine of the lack of Western culture which is ravaging Africa and which has made the African negroes an easy prey to other nations of the world well equipped with modern culture.

We regard the imprisonment of Marcus Garvey as tantamount to the imprisonment of the African negroes in the prison of ignorance and slavery under the most barbarous conditions to delay the day of freedom of mind and body to come to us in Africa.

We pray your Excellency to exercise your executive clemency on Marcus Garvey and release him from the prison cell because he committed no crime in rousing the negro peoples of the world to race consciousness. By releasing Marcus Garvey from prison your name will be enshrined in the hearts of the negro peoples of the world with love and your name will be amongst the names of those heroes who defended justice to prevail in the world.

Moreover we pray you to release Mr. Garvey from prison on account of the appalling condition of his ill health and even if he had committed a crime we would be obliged to request you to have mercy on him and release him on account of his ill health which seems to be aggravated by the condition of his confinement in prison.

We have informed our Government and our chiefs of this prayer we put before you for the release of Honourable Marcus Garvey.

Over the decades Lekhotla la Bafo kept up an active correspondence with a wide range of organisations and governments around the world. The message that they sought to convey varied little as they appealed for help in pressuring the British government to pay heed to their grievances. In this extract, H.M.D. Tsoene elaborates the conditions which led to the founding of the association.

34.

H.M.D. Tsoene to Aboriginal Protection Society, 16 July 1932, Anti-Slavery Papers, Rhodes House, Oxford University.

Chief Moshesh as the collector and founder of this nation had established a parliament known by the name of 'Pitso' and it was through its medium that he was able to consult his people all about the administrative and political measures which had to be enforced . . . . He had no power to enforce his desires which are in conflict with the popular desire of his nation upon his people . . . . On the contrary he was bound to follow the wishes and desires of his people in his administrative measures in vogue. He was made the caretaker of the rights and interests of the people and the country was not regarded as his own property but he was entrusted with the right of looking after and preserving it for his people as a nation . . . . Thus the people were the makers of their own destiny. Chief Moshesh had taken upon himself obligations which he was bound to observe and he had no power of abrogating the divers customs practised by people of different tribes . . . . Through the 'pitso' as his parliament he was able to check the causes of the misrule which might affect his people through application by the chiefs under him because in this parliament every person was allowed to express his opinion upon the administrative and other matters which needed public attention . . . .

Now, since 1903 this parliament was abolished and there was constituted the present National Council whose members are composed of the chiefs and the headmen who are their favourites . . . . All the people as a nation are debarred from making representation in this council for they have no representatives in that council . . . . For this reason this nation is muzzled and gagged in all administrative and political matters but the nation is deprived of the right chief Moshesh had established for it. On account of this fact, since 1919 from time to time we petitioned the Paramount Chief to constitute the Common's Council wherewith this nation may be able to make its grievances reach the attention of its rulers in a lawful way. But he dismissed all of such petitions and told us as the petitioners that if we might not desist he will have to destroy the present status of Basutoland as a protectorate and yield it to European system of Government so that this nation may be exploited to groan under repression and oppression. But he himself alone would live happily for he would purchase a farm to live upon. Today the Paramount Chief has resolved to eliminate the political associations from this territory by his secret orders to the chiefs to deprive the members of the associations of their fields and they would have nowhere to appeal for justice for he has wooed His Honour the Resident Commissioner to support him in all these absolute and autocratic measures and decisions. Thus the Paramount Chief has infringed all the conditions which Moshesh had taken upon himself as obligations to observe and respect in order that good relations may always exist between himself and his nation . . . . His position has fallen upon him by way of legacy inherited from chieftainship of Moshesh, but he destroys all measures which Chief Moshesh had created for the maintenance of good relations between

himself and the people and has become a tyrant of the worst
description. . . .

35.

Maphutseng Lefela, 'South African imperialism, a menace to Basutoland', *South African Worker*, 30 September 1929.

It was Sir George Grey in 1856 who first introduced the idea of a
united Government of the imperial South African colonies to present
a common front to crush the defenceless Basutos under Moshesh as
the preliminary step in the building up of a real white South Africa. In
1903 Lord Milner, as High Commissioner for South Africa, took a
step further to materialise the idea of united South African colonies
under one government and appointed Sir Herbert C. Sloley, then Resident Commissioner of Basutoland, as a member of the South African
Native Affairs Commission to gather information from the white
inhabitants of the four colonies and three Protectorates as well as
Southern Rhodesia as to what form of civilised barbarities and
enormities they wished the native Africans to be subjected to, and to
what extent they should be dispossessed of their lands, exploited and
enslaved; under what form of treachery and betrayal should the
Protectorates be brought under the iron heel of exploitation and
oppression under the united South African Government. Sir Herbert
C. Sloley treacherously, as the man on the spot, supplied the Commission with the best methods and plans of treachery to be adopted as to
the policy under which Basutoland, under the guise of protection,
would be exploited, and its native inhabitants enslaved. Then this plot
having been concluded, England was persuaded to allow the European
Imperialists in South Africa to use their treachery and hypocrisy to the
best of their ability to take the three Protectorates under their united
Government. Practically the High Commissioners and Resident Commissioner are the arch enemies of Basutoland, a protectorate entirely
to be reserved for the exclusive occupation of and use by Basuto
people only.
  The following few historical facts being the policy pursued by the

representatives of the King of England in Basutoland, it is why His Excellency the High Commissioner robs by Proclamation Basuto people of their rights and privileges, and exterminates, through the agency of poisonous dip, the flocks of the nation. Now the Resident Commissioner of Basutoland, on seeing Lekhotla la Bafo organise the people to fight for their rights under the protection of England, adopts unconstitutional and unlawful oppression to stifle and crush Lekhotla la Bafo while it works for the realisation of white South Africa . . . . Our members are being subjected to the unlawful and vicious laws of some of the local Assistant Commissioners whose cruelty has no parallel nor equal. Some of our members are being prosecuted notwithstanding the fact that they were working in compliance with the written law. The friend and sympathiser of our organisation, Mr. J.T. Gumede, in the Union is being unlawfully debarred from entering into Basutoland, while the swindlers and robbers of our rights, liberty and freedom are being imported in various ways into our country.

All these facts are the index to more calamities and atrocities yet to follow in the process to crush and stifle Lekhotla la Bafo, and therefore it is the urgent need and necessity of Lekhotla la Bafo to appeal for affiliation to all sincere organisations of the oppressed peoples of the world, and no time should be lost in putting it into effect. The incentive of our taking this step is the ever growing volume of reports of our members, who went into the Union Government as workers, who are being brutally treated; some of them are flogged while others are shot down with impunity by their cruel and blood thirsty bosses. These bosses take this attitude because they know that our chiefs are nothing but titulars, dupes, puppets and parasites on the local Assistant Commissioners who are our worst enemy . . . . Hence, they cannot do anything to protect their people against maltreatment, flogging and such like on the part of their bosses. By this affiliation we shall be able to entrust our members who are in the Union Government to such organisations as the Communist Party, which looks after the interests of the workers so that with its help we may be able to disseminate the truth throughout the world and cooperate in our defence measures.

Several African visitors to Basutoland in the 1930s reinforced Lekhotla la Bafo's analysis of the situation in newspaper articles. One was Keable 'Mote, who was born in 1898 in the Leribe district of Basutoland. Educated at Grace Dieu Institution in Pietersburg, South Africa, he joined the ICU in Bloemfontein in 1924 and subsequently served as its provincial secretary in the Orange Free State. He was known as the 'Lion of the Free State' for his fearless attacks on the government. Another observer was a leading Communist Party and African National Congress activist, J.B. Marks (1903 – 1972), who attended a meeting of Lekhotla la Bafo at Thaba Bosiu on 27 March 1937. His views were published on his return to Johannesburg.

36.

Keable 'Mote, 'The awakening of Basutoland', *Ikwezi le Afrika*, 18 April 1931.

I have recently paid a visit to this country, the country of my birth, and in view of Mr. Ballenger's [sic] articles I made a point of making certain observations in regard to the administration of justice, also the political, economic and educational affairs of the British policy operating in that territory.[68]

. . . There are remarkable changes in the attitude of responsible European officials which is far different to the days of 'Mussolini' Bosworth Smith, who hated all the educated Basuto young men, only favouring those who supported his officialdom. The present Resident Commissioner, Mr. J.C.T. Sturrock, would make himself a true friend of the Basutos if only he would not allow Chiefs to oppress and enslave peasants.

Educationally Basutoland is backward. Even some of the Missionaries still retain that old philosophy that if a Native speaks English he has attained the standard of an educated man. The result is that men and women are only given a smattering of English in order to be able to interpret. That is why the Chiefs will not educate their children, for they are not prepared to be servants as they are the chosen 'Sons of the Crocodile' (Bara ba Mokoteli). Educationally the Basutos are starved as a race and there are no avenues of employment for the educated.

Politically the Basuto has no voice in the administration of their country. Missionaries arrived in the country in 1833, nearly a century ago, and yet we have no graduates from any University except in a few isolated instances. One may ask why? Simply because the educational qualification of the Basuto is to make clerks of all Natives. Since the days of the late Simon Phamotse the Natives have clamoured for their political rights, but the Chiefs have refused with an insult similar to that made by the President Kruger to the British subjects before 1899. Today the 'Lekhotla la Bafo' and the 'Basutoland Progressive Association' are struggling, although the latter body is defunct and does not exist because Paulus Mohai, who is the founder, has been deserted by all officials who have gone fishing for Government jobs. The 'Lekhotla la Bafo', headed by Mr. J. Lefeela [sic], is the only radical organisation although this is run on extreme democratic lines, but still it is carrying on the battle for liberty. The Basutos are not satisfied with the present representation in the National Council where the Chiefs and their pals never utter a word unless they want money for their kith and kin. The chiefs have contravened the pledge of the founder and leader of the Basuto race — Moshesh. They will never agree to alter their attitude and allow educated and intelligent people to deliberate with them. As a matter of fact, as far as I can remember, none of the present members of the National Council are able to read the political horizon and understand anything about economic laws. The policy of the Chiefs is that of the survival of the fittest, the bottom dog to remain the hewer of wood for the Chief and drawers of water for the aristocrats.

Economically the Basuto is in a hopeless position this year as their wool and mohair have had the bottom knocked out of the price and every Native journal in Basutoland has hair raising letters from aggrieved Natives. What is needed in Basutoland today is encouragement by Government to organise peasants on a co-operative basis, the authorities to provide the initial capital and run the show, allowing the Basuto more say in the administration of major affairs.

The Resident Commissioner should approach the High Commissioner to make a proclamation with regard to necessary reforms based on democracy, allowing the Basuto to form political parties with a Prime Minister, rather than to continue to allow Chiefs with a few educated Natives, to form a so-called House of Lords. The Chiefs of Basutoland have become men at the expense of the poor Basuto. Chiefs are tax collectors and are looked upon as 'detectives' by the rank and file. The chiefs tour round in big motor cars and have no association with the peasants. In consequence they have lost the confidence of the people, but they cannot see it. With the deportation of some of the radicals from the Union the day of revolt will be hastened unless Government makes a change in their policy of ruling the race. The chiefs have the authority to collect and make Sethaba-thaba (tithes), notwithstanding that they get regular pay from the Government and well fit their pockets.

In the Chiefs kraals there is much miscarriage of justice since the Chiefs never sit in the 'Khotla' but are mostly in their 'Malapa'. In short, they are domestic scions. The Paramount Chief Griffiths has made slaves of the Basuto race, making them plough and hoe patches of lands (masimo) without food or payment. In some of the districts of Leribe and Rafolatsane, cases where sons of Chiefs have ill-treated the peasants have been reported. The Chiefs collect money by means of fines, and all this is their private property. I have known a Chief who has quite recently raised the sum of £90 per week, and was fared by the Government to visit the Coast for three months. Let the Chiefs keep and publish a proper record of the fines collected weekly when it will be possible to compare his salary, compensations as members of the Basutoland National Council, allowances for being good detectives of the Government, and their annual gratuity. I am voicing the complaints of thousands of my countrymen who groan under the burden of oppression. The Basutos are asking for an Imperial Commission it being alleged that the poor are deprived of their livestock by Chiefs in an unreasonable manner, and when complaints are referred to the Paramount Chief he takes no heed of them and the result is generally fighting and bloodshed. The Basutos require the door of European jurisprudence opened.

In many cases the Chiefs are the culprits and their indunas plead and defended them in the most heinous cases. Indunas are being bribed up to this day since the Chiefs will not employ educated clerks as these demand pay for services rendered, whereas the illiterate only need to be fed on meat. The result is corruption and bribery are on the increase and the ends of justice defeated. Amongst Basutos there is deep-seated complaint that the policy of the British Government is to oppress the weak. European traders and some of the Government officials are accused of befriending the Chiefs in order to exploit the peasants. The Basuto is not allowed to trade in the Reserves and yet this is a Basuto country. An agitation is afoot at Maseru to start a campaign on a national scale, and I have been invited, with Mr. Jac

B. Crutse, of the Bantu Social Agency, to assist. Since my return to the Union I have placed the facts before several social workers, and they are agreeable to devote their time in the interests of the country of our birthright.

The Basutos have come to the conclusion that changes are inevitable. They are seeking the assistance of their Union friends with a view to bringing concerted action to place the facts before the British public. This is substantiated by the fact that at the last European conference held in Bloemfontein several influential delegates came from Native territories, and as the Union Natives are also sharing the same difficulties as their compatriots. The Resident Commissioner is to be asked to press for a proclamation forcing Chiefs to accept a reasonable change in the democratic election of members to the National Council, this body to have executive powers and a say in the administration of the finances of the territory. The future lies in the powers to be conferred on the National Council with young educated men having a say in the affairs of the country. The Cooperative movement must be on the lines of self-determination. The Basutos want a monument of the late King Moshesh to be erected at Thaba Bosigo, and that a uniform change of chieftainship be immediately brought about in the election of members of the National Council. The Chiefs should be deprived of their autocratic powers, as serious trouble is brewing.

Will the High Commissioner go into these details?

37.

John B. Marks, 'Misery of the People in Basutoland', *Umsebenzi*, 10 April 1937.

In theory Basutoland is still a British protectorate. But in reality it has been reduced to a colonial Reserve by British domination through indirect rule. The whole of the superstructure of Basutoland is lock stock and barrel in the hands of the imperialist lackeys. Griffiths, the contemporary paramount chief is executing his duties as an imperialist agent to the best of his abilities.

Basutoland industrially is still unexplored and agriculturally undeveloped and thus cannot provide a field of labour for its own population. So it serves as a hinterland for labour power for the industries of the Anglo-Boer imperialiths in South Africa. The few thousand Natives who are employed in Basutoland receive very deplorable wages. The highest amount paid to them is 1/- per day. Despite these meagre wages all male adults are obliged to pay 28/- per year for tax. And from time to time they have to pay tribal levies. Peasants failing to pay their taxes are having their cattle and other livestock confiscated. Some of the chiefs are nearly always in a position to buy the best of the confiscated animals. Thus they accelerate, in many cases, the confiscation of animals for which they have a liking. This attitude is very much detested by the peasants.

British Finance Capital

The Basutoland government has accepted and is still accepting big loans offered them by Britain, and this has given Britain an opportunity to extend her sphere of influence inside the country. Above all the loans have been taken without the knowledge of the mass of the people. The mass of the population is only drawn into the forefront when the question of keeping down the interest on this money had come to the surface; in order to keep this down the collection of taxes and the confiscations have been intensified. This ruthless attitude pursued by a government comprising imperialist lackeys is strongly resented by the people and this has resulted in widespread mass discontent among the common population. This discontent expresses itself at this stage in a serious anti-Griffiths movement, headed by the Lekhotla la Bafo (Commoner's Association). It is clear that unless this critical situation is remedied serious conflicts are unavoidable.

Living Conditions

As a result of heavy taxation and the confiscation of property the majority of the peasants are verging on the brink of starvation. At present they live on one meal a day consisting of mealies and pumpkins. The wholesale confiscation of their cattle has disabled them to plough their plots. Thus not unlike the Natives in the Reserves they find themselves at the mercy of the recruiting agents, and so we see hundreds of thousands are forced to come and sell their labour power to the mining magnates at 1/8 per day. And behind them they leave thousands of women and children, victims of starvation and other miseries. Meat today is a luxury among poor peasants.

The Way out of Misery

The way out of this deplorable situation can be found in the unity of the Basuto peoples, which must express itself in a determined struggle against British imperialism and its lackeys, a section of the corrupted chiefs. The struggle against the paramount chief must be closely linked up with the struggle against British imperialism. It should be remembered that Griffiths is but an individual in the hands of British imperialism. So in order to defeat him successfully the system of which he is a tool must be simultaneously defeated.

Resist the tax collectors and you fight actively against Griffiths and his bosses. 'United we stand, disunited we fall.' Down with British imperialism and its lackeys in Basutoland.

38.

Rabase Sekike to Mr. Gromyko, Soviet delegate to the United Nations, 28 April 1948, MA 1/33 1946–1951.

It is with feelings of profound respect and honour that we beg to address you this letter wherewith we convey our humble and respectful petition to you with a request that you may have mercy with us and put before the Trusteeship Council our petition that the Trusteeship Council may take steps and ask the British Government to cease from applying measures, laws and policy of defraudment of our rights and land, to give it to Europeans to colonise it in pursuance of the Foreign Jurisdiction Act surreptitiously passed in the British Imperial Parliament in 1890 which empowered the British Government to apply to the Protectorates such laws as will ultimately put the Protectorates in the same category as those territories acquired by England through physical force of arms, which by virtue of conquest, such territories are treated as crown domains.

We appeal to you because we tried to lodge our appeal and petition before the Trustee Council through the Right Honourable Mr. Trygve Lie, General Secretary of the United Nations Organisation [see Document 41], dated 2-6-46, with a request to put the same before the Trusteeship Council. On the other hand we are being encouraged to learn in the newspapers that Mr. Semakula Mulumba of Uganda lodged

his appeal through you before the Trusteeship Council for consideration his appeal. For this reason as it is practically the Government
which you represent, which stands to champion the cause and interest
of the oppressed races of the world before the United Nations
Organisation, we find ourselves obliged to appeal to you with our
request that you may have mercy with us and take up our appeal and
petition and put it before the Trusteeship Council . . . .

Prior to the Second World War, the British had considered, but
refrained from placing a ban on Lekhotla la Bafo. But when Josiel
Lefela began speaking out against the conscription of Basotho to serve
as soldiers, the colonial administration quickly moved to jail Lefela
and several of his followers on charges of sedition and banned
meetings of Lekhotla la Bafo until the end of the war.

39.

'Basuto people want arms and freedom. Lekhotla la Bafo support Soviets', *Inkululeko*, October 1941.

In his brilliant Presidential address to the Basutoland People's
Association (Lekhotla la Bafo) at Mapoteng on the 31st of August,
the President, Mr. Rabase M. Sekike, analysed the international and
home situation and outlined the tasks of the people of Basutoland.

In stirring words Mr. Sekike declared the solidarity of the Basuto
people with the people of the Soviet Union, 'today when almost the
whole fighting capacity of the German armies is fighting against the
Soviet Union of Russia'. In Russia, Mr. Sekike pointed out, 'all things
are owned by the workers and all production of every description is
being utilised in the interests of the workers. In this way in Russia
every person owns the means of supporting his life, every person has
some work to do for which he gets his own personal remuneration,
and thus there are not to be found any persons remaining without
work to do, and thus the problem of people starving owing to want of
work to do is unknown in Russia'.

The Basuto leader then described the Communist International, 'which is organised on an international scale, without any discrimination based on colour, race or creed', as an 'international parliament of workers and peasants of all countries', where 'the people of different language, different countries, different colours and political standing, are accepted and treated as equals and comrades'.

Broken Pledges

After describing the international events leading to the present war, in which he stressed the folly of the policy of appeasement based on the hatred of the capitalist States for the Soviet Union, the President gave a short survey of the political relations of the Basuto people with the British government.

He pointed out the shabby way in which the Basuto nation had been dealt with by the Imperial Authorities, and gave a sorry picture of broken promises and the undermining of the independence of a free people.

Conscription in Basutoland

On behalf of the Basuto people, comrade Sekike complained bitterly of the system of compulsory military service being disguised as volunteering. Either, he said, conscription should be announced, in which case he would like to know if there was 'a law giving the Government the right to compel the people to enrol for the army', or else they should enrol on a volunteer basis. This 'concealed conscription', said Mr. Sekike, 'is a calumny upon the Basuto people'.

Military Training

The Lekhotla la Bafo demands 'that a full course of military training must be undertaken and completed before the Basuto army may leave Maseru'.

'We demand that Basutos must be taught and trained as wireless transmitters, pilots, observers, and other things such as parachutists. We demand that the training of the Basuto army must not be based on the same lines of instruction as the Union Natives'.

In South Africa, the Lekhotla la Bafo points out, the Africans are not given military training or arms. Comrade Sekike said 'you can imagine how men who do not know how to handle and load a gun and fire it can be expected to fight against men in the field such as the other scientific armies maintain. It is like sending babies in the mother's arms to fight against full-grown men'.

'We wholeheartedly agree', said the President, 'that under the system of recruiting volunteers it is our bounden duty to enlist for army service, but we demand that our African soldiers must be placed on the same footing of equality as the European soldiers, so that they may be entitled to receive the same training as the European soldiers'.

Basutoland Must be Represented at Peace Conference

In conclusion, Mr. Sekike pointed out that the blood of the Basuto people was being shed on the battlefields and that this blood of the people ought to buy back their freedom and independence which had been taken away from them in the same way as Hitler, through his military power, deprived Poland of her independence; likewise France, Belgium, Holland and other countries.

'At the same time when Hitler compelled England to co-operate with the Russian Government in her defence against the German invasion, Great Britain made it known that she is fighting for restoring liberties to the countries brought under the crushing iron heel of the military power of Germany. In the same way', declared the Basutoland People's Association, 'we demand our freedom which has been taken away by force and fraud by England from us, and we shall ask that provision be made to allow us to send our representatives to the Peace Conference'.

40.

'Basutos in conference: appeal to UNO', *Inkululeko*, May 1945.

The conference of Lekhotla la Bafo, national organisation of the Basuto people, has decided to send delegates to UNO to appeal against the violation of the terms of protection of Basutoland by the British Government. The conference was held at Mapoteng, Basutoland, on April 4-7, and attended by delegates from branches of the Lekhotla la Bafo throughout the territory.

Among the delegates were chiefs and representatives of chiefs who were unable to attend, ministers of African churches, teachers, herbalists, workers and peasants. There were a number of fraternal delegates, including Mr. E.T. Mofutsanyana Editor of 'Inkululeko'. The Basutoland Government was also represented.

Mr. Rabase Sekike, vice-president of the organisation presided over the conference. After a very brief and inspiring speech, welcoming delegates to the conference the chairman called upon Councillor Josiel Lefela, Executive Committee member of the Lekhotla la Bafo, and its official representative in the Basutoland National Council, to read the presidential address and lead the discussion.

Councillor Lefela, who kept his audience keenly interested throughout, spoke for three and a half hours. He reviewed the work of the organisation during the war period and the difficult situation under which it functioned.

Cllr. J. Lefela Speaks

He quoted the sedition case against the secretary of Lekhotla la Bafo, Mr. Maphutseng Lefela and others, the internment of some of the leaders of his organisation, including himself, and the banning of the organisation merely because it demanded the arming and training of Basuto soldiers. This, he said, was immediately followed by the banning in Basutoland of 'Inkululeko', the organ of the Communist Party of South Africa, and the only newspaper which published and still publishes the views of Lekhotla la Bafo at a time when all other papers suppressed them.

Mr. Lefela spoke at length on the history of Basutoland from the time of the invasion of South Africa by the settlers. He described the events that led to wars with the Basuto nation, and the efforts of the late Chief Moshesh who appealed to Queen Victoria for protection and not oppression. Since the agreement between Chief Moshesh and the British Government, it had repeatedly been broken by the latter, until the Basutos had no longer any rights left. The chiefs were deprived of their rights, of the land, and people, and turned into foremen for the British Government.

Cllr. Lefela called upon the Basuto people to close their ranks and to unite. They should, he said, appeal to the United Nations Organisation for the restoration of their rights. There was thunderous applause when the speaker called upon the Basutos to unite with other South African Non-European organisations, in particular, the Indians 'who have proved themselves to mean what they say'.

Tribute to Communists

The speaker paid tribute to the Communist Party of South Africa and other organisations here which struggled for the lifting of the ban on Lekhotla la Bafo and the release of its leaders. Despite the Government's order forbidding the organisation to raise funds, the conference unanimously decided to go on with this activity.

One of the chiefs who has recently been deprived of his position by the Government, will be the leader of the Basuto delegation to UNO.

To your 'Inkululeko' reporter, it was clear that Lekhotla la Bafo has won the support of the masses of common people, as its name applies. The delegates represented many thousands of people from all parts of the country.

More than that, today this organisation is supported also by an increasing number of chiefs, who contributed greatly to the conference.

One of the chiefs who spoke at the conference appealed that every Mosotho should join Lekhotla la Bafo, as the only organisation in whose hands lay the salvation of Basutoland.

41.

Rabase Sekike to Trygve Lie, Secretary General, United Nations, 2 June 1946, PRO, DO 35/1177.

It is with feelings of profound respect that we address you this letter whereby we lodge our appeal to you whereby we invoke your aid, that through your intercession you may approach British Government on our behalf that she may cease carrying on war of treaty abrogations of her pledges as a protector over Basutoland and thus that Emergency Regulations may be brought to an end, and that our Association known under the name of Lekhotla la Bafo may be released from restrictions imposed upon it under which the organisation was prohibited holding any meetings during the war . . . . After the cessation of hostilities when peace has been restored, and when all nations are freed from Emergency Regulations, British Government is still rigorously applying war time measures upon Basuto people, and our organisation is prohibited from holding any meetings in this country . . . .

After the conclusion of the war on 20th May 1945 we petitioned the local Resident Commissioner to release our Association from the prohibition of holding meetings as all other Associations in Great Britain which had been placed under certain prohibitions owing to Emergency Regulations have been released. But to our profound amazement our Association was informed in a letter no 3/43 dated 10 Nov 1945 as follows: 'With reference to your petition which you asked me to forward to the Resident Commissioner last June I am directed to inform you that Basutoland legislation corresponding to Regulations 18A and 18B has not yet been repealed by the High Commissioner. His Honour is not prepared to recommend to the High Commissioner that Josiel Lefela be released from his undertaking to refrain from taking any further part in subversive activities.'

Josiel Lefela is our member who was interned during the war and was released under suspended detention on 24th December 1944 under the condition that he must not participate in any political meeting.

Now we have the honour to ask you that, as all the nations of the world have entered into a new era of peace, freedom of press, and freedom of speech and freedom of assembly, you may put before the Security Council of UNO our request that it may take steps and negotiate with the British Government that our Association may be enabled to hold meetings to pass resolutions wherewith to ask the Security Council of UNO to ask the British Government to reconcile her policy with treaty obligations and pledges which she has violated and infringed.

We declare that British Government places our nation under war time laws in order to enable her to carry out her policy of political strangulation and defraudment of our land, the abolition and suppression of the powers of hereditary chieftainship which is the basis of our internal self government while the world does not know that England is carrying into force measures unbecoming of her world wide lip [sic] reputation. Under these circumstances we ask you that you may put our request before the Security Council of UNO that it may intercede and entreat British Government to lift up war time measures and laws to enable our people enjoy the blessings of peace which every nation has bought with so precious blood and sacrifice.

42.

Maphutseng Lefela, 'Taxes up in Basutoland', *Inkululeko*, 18 February 1946.

At a recent stormy session of the Basutoland National Council it was decided by a majority to increase the hut and poll taxes from 28/- to 30/- for every Mosuto living in Basutoland, even if he is destitute. Those regarded as 'better off' are to pay 40/-.

Besides the Councillors, delegates from Johannesburg, representing the Sons and Daughters of Basutoland and the Protectorates Workers' League were allowed to appoint Mr. Nchee as spokesman for the interests of Basuto workers on the Gold Mines and elsewhere in the Union.

The Council rejected completely the Administration's proposals regarding destocking and 'land improvements'.

Then followed the discussion of the proposed tax increases.

District Councillors Opposition

The nine representatives of the District Councils opened the debate on this matter. All of them, with the exception of the Mokhotlong District Councillor opposed the 30/- tax proposal.

It should be understood that these Councillors were not expressing their own personal views, but were acting upon the mandates given them by their respective District Councils, which had passed resolutions opposing the proposed tax increases. It must be stated that the District Councillors resisted pressure from the Government District Commissioners, and faithfully represented the views of their electors in this matter.

Some District Councillors, including those from Quacha's Nek, Mafeteng and Tayateyaneng [sic] went further. They raised points which greatly irritated the President of the Council.

European Officials

The matters which raised the President to anger were those raised by District Councillors relating to the salaries and appointments of European officials.

The Mafeteng District Council had placed a resolution on the order paper calling for the removal of a number of European officials, including all post office clerks, and District Commissioner's clerks, and (barring one of each at the capital, Maseru) all District agricultural officers and police officers.

Quacha's Nek demanded that detailed figures be made available regarding the salaries paid to European and African officials, Councillor Ntuote supported their proposal. Addressing the Council said:

> 'Before the increase of taxes can be discussed in the National Council, I submit that the Government should produce a Staff List, showing the salaries of both European and African staff working for the Government.'

Pointing out that before agreeing to increased tax burdens on the people, the Council had the duty to consider reduction of expenditure, he concluded:

> 'Here in Basutoland the salaries of Europeans are being greatly increased at the expense of the Basuto. This is an important matter, and we should not permit it. It signifies the bondage of our people.'

Rising, in terrific anger, the President of the Council (the British Resident Commissioner) refused to allow the Council to discuss the salaries of Europeans.

Not the Council's Business

> 'The salaries of Europeans is a matter for the High Commissioner and the Secretary of State for Dominions,' he told the Council. 'It is not one for the Council to discuss. The duty of the Councillors is to discuss the increase of taxation, not to call for the salaries of Government employees'.

Now, when all other Councillors spoke on tax proposals, they accepted the increase. They did not follow the wishes of the people on the grounds that as leading figures of the nation they should see that taxes were increased because 'the country was being developed towards self-Government' and services would be extended and improved.

When the motion for higher taxes was put to the vote, it was carried.

In this connection, it should be remembered that the representatives of the people are only nine, and of the remaining 90 most are Government flunkeys and supporters.

43.

'Forced labour in Basutoland', by Watchman, *Inkululeko*, 3 December 1945.

British Government in 1938 through the instrumentality of Proclamation No.61 of 1938, abolished hereditary chieftainship of Basutoland. The procedure under which the Government accomplished this was strictly surreptitious and clandestine, and when it had become an accomplished fact the new type of chieftainship by warrants was forced upon the chiefs in the National Council, after Seeiso Griffith was in his loneliness forced to sign for the abolition of hereditary chieftainship and for the introduction of the new type of chieftainship, which is proclaimed by the High Commissioner in the Official Gazette. Those appointed as chiefs are given warrants wherein their powers are defined.

New Chieftainship

With the abolition of hereditary chieftainship went down into the region of oblivion all that was inherent with it, because the new type of chieftainship is a part and parcel of the European machinery of Government. After its abolition the women were forced to take upon themselves the duties which under the late Native chieftainship were only performed by men. Today the women, and children are compelled to plant trees in the dongas and other places from six o'clock in the evening working hard for twelve long hours without getting any ration for food. The supervisor in this work is a Government hireling working under the Agricultural Department as a Demonstrator.

No Remuneration

In 1945, the British Government constrained, in the Special Session of the Basutoland National Council, members of that Council to accept the proposal by the Government for the establishment of National Treasury. It was formerly promised by Government that offices of this treasury would be built by the Government with the help of public revenues throughout the territory. But today it is not so. The Government through the Paramount chieftainess has issued order in circular letters to the District chiefs to order them to compel their people under them to dig up stones, carry them, and build the offices of the treasury. In this heavy and onerous work there is no remuneration, no ration for food, no tools to work with and no clothing; but their overlords are paid for supervising and driving these unfortunate muzzled slaves into their hard labour.

On this point in the last Special Session of Basutoland National Council, His Honour the Resident Commissioner in the Summary of Proceedings, paragraph 19, in his capacity as the President of the Council, is reported as follows: 'The President in his closing speech endorsed the words of the chief Councillor and made two comments which he felt council should note. Firstly Councillors appeared to be under the impression that the establishment of the National Treasury would absolve the Basuto of their civic duties and that every person performing any public service would be entitled to payment. This impression was dangerous and if it gained hold would lead to disaster. In every country the citizens had civic duties to perform in the common interest and without payment, and the Basuto must retain the idea of National service.'

This slavery forced upon the Basuto nation at the time when all nations great and small, are at liberty to choose any form of government they like, is the prize by which His Majesty's Imperialism rewards Basuto nation for all its labour and sacrifice in the last global conflict. What a shameful betrayal of the people as a nation by the Government in applying worst forms of slavery which during the war were loudly denounced.

Whether the British called Basutoland a 'colony' or a 'protectorate' was of the utmost importance to Lekhotla la Bafo for if Basutoland were termed a 'colony', it believed the country could be opened up to white settlement. The British explanation that Basutoland retained its protectorate status even though it might be called a colony in some publications did little to quiet Lekhotla la Bafo's fear that they were being sold down the river.

44.

Rabase Sekike to E. Bevin, Secretary of State for Foreign Affairs, Great Britain, 9 May 1948, MA 1/33 1946-1951.

Our delegates pointed out . . . that at present our country is no longer called a protectorate but a crown colony . . . . The meaning of 'colony' is defined in a book titled 'British Way and Purpose' 'prepared by the Directorate of Army Education' which appears in the consolidated Edition, Chapter IV, page 485, by Vincent Harlow as follows: – 'The proper meaning of the word "Colony" is a place to which settlers from the mother country go with their wives and children and make a permanent home. Newcomers swell the ranks; they intermarry; farms, villages and towns spring up, a new community is born speaking the same language as the parent state and organised on similar lines.' It was after he was given this definition of the word 'colony' which is now applicable to our country instead of being kept for the use of the black people only under British protection as was so requested by Moshesh and guaranteed in a pledge by the British Government in several treaties.

Now we have the respect to have to explain to you that we do not take this refusal as emanating from the Paramount Chief's independent conviction, but we take this refusal as emanating from His Excellency the High Commissioner through His Honour the Resident Commissioner through the instrumentality of the Paramount Chief, because under the Indirect Rule created ever since the promulgation and enforcement of Proclamation No.61 of 1938 and No.62 of 1938, the Paramount Chiefs, chiefs, sub chiefs and headmen are subjected under continuous routine of instructions and disciplines as to how they may rule their people in accordance with the wishes of their European official instructors. In the Explanatory Memorandum to Basutoland Native Administration Proclamation No.61 of 1938 and the Basutoland Native Courts Proclamation No.62 of 1938, page 3, section 5, it is stated as follows: – 'It will be seen then that essentials of the form of government known as Indirect Administration are that the British Government must rule through the Native Institutions which must be regarded as an integral part of the machinery of Government, that there must be general advice and control on the part of European officers and that it is the duty of the Administration to educate the Native Authorities in their duties as rulers.' According to this above quoted section His Excellency the High Commissioner and the Resident Commissioner used the Paramount Chief as their instrument through which they made their refusal effective because the Paramount Chief does everything in accordance with their advice and control as an officer of the Government.

Again we say that this refusal emanates from His Excellency the High Commissioner because in the Appendix to the same explanatory memorandum, section 2, it is stated that under sections 8 and 15 the Paramount Chief is empowered to make rules and issue orders which in previous times has to be made and issued by His Excellency the High Commissioner with either Proclamations or Government Notices. For this reason it is not aspersary to state that this refusal by the Paramount Chief to prevent our Association from asking for national levy from the people of Basutoland is an order from His Excellency, the High Commissioner through the Resident Commissioner. Moreover, in the *Nigerian Principles of Native Administration and their Application* by Donald Cameron, then Governor of Nigeria, it is stated as follows: – 'I propose therefore that for the future the Resident should exercise in Nigeria the same functions as he exercises elsewhere in the British dependencies, that is function openly as the adviser of the Native administration a directing interest in its day to day affairs. He should sit with the chief and his council when it meets and advise them and direct them in the daily acts of the Administration. The Council should meet at regular intervals as may be arranged with the Resident and the chief should obtain the approval of the Resident before issuing any orders that are not in accord with the approved policy, that is, policy approved by the Resident. All orders will continue to be issued in the name of the chief in order that his authority in no way be impaired in the eyes of his people, no direct orders to the people will be issued by the Resident or the administrative staff, and the Resident will be directed to take the greatest care that the religious scruples and racial suceptibles [*sic*] of the chief and his people are respected.' It is material for you to remember that these two proclamations which introduced the system of Indirect Administration had been copied from Nigeria and the principles of this administration in Nigeria are more applicable to Basutoland Administration.

The year after D.F. Malan became Prime Minister of South Africa in 1948, he raised — as had every South African prime minister before him — the issue of having the High Commission territories incorporated into the Union. By doing so, he resurrected the fear of many Africans that the British would finally accede to his request.

45.

Maphutseng Lefela to Dr. Malan, 26 February 1950, MA 1/33 1946-1951.

It is with due respect and honour that we beg to address you this letter whereby we inform you that we have learned from the South African newspapers that you are determined to ask the Union Parliament to ask the British Government to hand over to the Union Government the three protectorates of Basutoland, Bechuanaland Protectorate and Swaziland. In this respect you have such a right to claim the incorporation of our protectorates into the Union Government because the British Government offered as a pawn these territories to the leaders of the four South African Colonies to hand them to their United Government if they might agree to her proposal to them to form a federal or United Government. This proposal had been accepted and materialised in 1909 when the four South African colonies formed one United Government to include in the constitution of the Union Act clauses relating to giving the Union Government the right to ask the British Government to hand over to the Union Government these three protectorates.

Now we have the honour to have to inform you that long before the Union Government was born, at the time when your forefathers crossed the Orange River and came into our countries, after it became apparent that their designs were directed to usurping and raping our territories under the connivance of Great Britain, Basuto people, through their Chief Moshesh, asked the same British Government to protect them from the imperialist usurpation of our territories by the Boer emigrants . . . . British government agreed to take them under her protection against the imperialist designs of the South African colonists. For this reason we have a right to have to ask the British Government to rescind her promise given you to hand over country Basutoland to your Government. If she refuses to do this we have the right to pray her in the International courts and organisations now available for her perfidy that she might unsay her promise and tell you to desist demanding her to hand over our country to your Union Government. Under these circumstances we have the honour to have to ask you to wait pushing matters for the incorporation of our country into the Union Government to enable British Government to decide what final steps she has to take in this case. . . .

We find it imperative for us to pray British Government in the International Organisations and courts of the world now available because under the Union Government the African tribes have not the right to appeal even to the British courts and organisations in Great Britain against the ruthless laws of discrimination of the Union Government of South Africa. But even if a violent coup d'etat of incorporation may be applied both by the Union Government and the British Government we shall be obliged at all costs to appeal against that measure to the World Organisations and courts to seek for international help from other big powers of the world because under the British Government the King or his representatives cannot be sued in their own courts of law.

On account of the fact that it has long been devised that as our country, Basutoland, is an enclave in the centre of the Union Government provinces, far removed from the sea harbours, if Basuto people refuse to submit to incorporation plans, the Union Government must adopt retaliative measures of with-holding and cutting the commercial supplies of garments and food so as to compel Basuto people as a nation to sell their country for the supply of commercial commodities to enter into their country . . . . Now, in order to guard ourselves against this danger, we find it incumbent and convenient to correspond with other powers on this subject as a precaution so that we may solicit their help in case we are confronted with this difficulty.

On this question of unfaithful and perfidious role played by British Government in her dealings with us in offering our country as a pawn to cover up her own crimes and misdeeds of her political blunders and misrule on the Boer people in the past, in 1947, among other things, we addressed an address of welcome to His Majesty the King wherewith we asked him to rescind and unsay the promises made by his British Government and sanctioned through him to the South African colonies that in the event of their agreement to her proposal to form a federal or united government, she would hand over our protectorates to them. For this reason we have the respect and honour to have to ask you to wait for a little while to enable the British Government to consider our requests and petitions to rescind and recall her promises to you to leave our countries to remain as protectorates as our forefathers requested her.

We have sent this letter to the British Foreign Minister for his information and consideration and to the United Nations Organisation and various other powers of the world with a request to pray the British Government for us not to immolate the status of our countries on the altar of atonement for her own political crimes and blunders to the Boers in the past; and that she may leave our countries as protectorates; and that if she tired to continue her protection over our countries she may give us to know and let us seek protection from other powers of the world to protect us from the inroads and aggressive measures employed by other hostile and inimical nations against us.

46.

Maphutseng Lefela to Trygve Lie, Secretary General, United Nations, 26 February 1950, MA 1/33 1946-1951.

We have the honour and respect to send you a copy of our letter addressed to the Right Honourable Dr. Malan, the Prime Minister of the Union of South Africa, on the matter of our protest against the movement and attempt by him to incorporate our country into the Union Government.

We ask you to put this matter of our protest before the Trusteeship Council and ask it to ask British Government to rescind her promise to the Union Government to hand our country to the Union Government because the reason why Basuto people through Moshesh asked British Government to protect them . . . was because the Boers emigrant colonists proved to be dangerous through their encroachments upon the land and rights of Basuto people . . . . Therefore, British Government agreed to undertake the duties of a protector over our country, Basutoland. The conditions of protection gave British Government no power to exercise political rights such as she has usurped through fraud and deception coupled with cynical surreptitious stealth . . . .

Now as the United Nations Organisation had been established for the simple reason of preventing any powers from usurping and raping small or weak nations of the world by depriving them of their political powers and rights in their own countries in the interests of the usurpers, we hope that the United Nations will leave no stone unturned in the matter of making British Government and the Union Government cease in their enterprise of making these Protectorates of ours come under the sway of the Union Government against the will of their inhabitants . . . .

Today when the Union Government is making representations to British Government for the incorporation of Basutoland into the Union Government, Europeans living in Basutoland will be made clamour for the incorporation of Basutoland in the Union so that British Government may have cause to deprive Basuto people of their land and political rights for Europeans in Basutoland and the Union Government. This is similar to the manoeuvres and tactics employed by Hitler when he took Czechoslovakia because the Germans were a superior race. Under these circumstances we pray that the United Nations Organisation may help Basuto people by championing their cause that the British Government may rescind and unsay her word of promise to the Union Government to hand our protectorates to her dominion to form her part and parcel.

As the introduction of Europeans in this territory has been brought in violation of the provisions of the treaty of Touwfontein dated 30 June 1845 which prohibited the introduction of Europeans in Basutoland and as the imposition of taxes upon the Europeans again is inconsistent with conditions of agreement as stipulated by Moshesh in 1862 and again is in contravention of the law of trade as was published in 1857 by Moshesh, we demand that the United Nations Organisation may ask the British Government to send all these Europeans out of Basutoland together with all the money they paid as taxes to the Government so that we may remain safe from all the troubles inherent in their paying taxes in our country, so that the Union Government will have no cause of interference with our country's affairs.

It is appropriate to remark here at this juncture that the disannexation arrangements which severed Basutoland from the Government of the Cape of Good Hope in 1884 had stipulated that the Government of the Cape of Good Hope had to subscribe annually a sum of £20 000 to Basutoland administration in lieu of the custom duties of the traders from the Government of Cape Colony for their merchandise sold in Basutoland. This fact gave the Government of the Cape of Good Hope the pretext to meddle and interfere in the affairs of Basutoland. In order to give Basuto people complete freedom from the Government of Cape of Good Hope in financial matters, the British Government through Sir Alfred Milner proposed in 1898 to Chief Lerotholi, then Paramount Chief of Basutoland, that he should agree to increase hut tax from 10s 3d to £1 payable by every adult male, so that the Government of the Cape of Good Hope might terminate her contribution of £20 000 to Basutoland Administration. Thereafter Basutoland remained safe from any interference by the Government of the Cape of Good Hope in connection with financial matters of this territory. But the same British Government contemplating to create our protectorates into Colonies in 1936 began to invest huge sums of money into Basutoland, Bechuanaland Protectorate and Swaziland from the British treasury under the powers of Colonial Development and Welfare Act. Despite the fact that we tried to protest against this measure, British Government cynically ignores and overlooks our protests. Under these circumstances we pray you that you may put this matter before the Trusteeship Council and ask it on our behalf that it should ask British Government to withdraw all the moneys paid into our country as income and poll taxes paid by the Union European Nationals living in Basutoland as traders and various other posts so that the Union Government may have no claim of interference in the affairs of our territory through her European Nationals living in our country. In like manner all the money paid by her from the British Imperial treasury to Basutoland Administration may be refunded so that the British taxpayer may have no claim to exercise political rights in our country.

P.S. To clarify before the Trusteeship Council that the funds paid by the British Imperial Government into our countries is most dangerous to us the black inhabitants of these territories, which are paid under the Colonial Development and Welfare Funds Act, under the pretext that these moneys are imported as such in these protectorates only for combating soil erosion for the sole aim of developing these territories as a loan for gratis not to be paid back by the indigenous of these protectorates is a sheer lie. Let us quote an elegant speech made by General Hertzog before the Union Parliament in 1936 in connection with these huge sums of moneys imported in these protectorates at the time of the Union Government taking over these territories as is published in the *Daily Despatch*, East London, Friday, 12 June 1936, page 9 as follows:

'If the British Government is to continue spending money on developments there, we shall have to take over the territories together with the commitments undertaken there, so if we spend this money now it is only what we shall do ultimately,' he said. 'I was told in England that after two years, a beginning could be made with taking over of the first territory. After another year, the second territory would follow and so on, until within a comparatively short time all the territories will have been handed over to the Union. This was all on the understanding that the British Government's undertaking not to press anything against the will of Native will not be violated and, as an indication of our intention and willingness to further the interests of the Natives in those territories, we contributed this £35 000 for combating soil erosion.'

In paragraph 12:

'What my friends opposite do not understand is that if we are to take over these territories — I do not think that any one of us questions the wisdom of this — we cannot expect the British Government to go on spending money on developments there,' said General Hertzog.

After the Second World War, British colonial administrators and Lekhotla la Bafo stepped up their attacks on each other. When, on 30 August 1947, a fire broke out in a student dormitory at Pius XII College at Roma killing three students, the British used the long-standing enmity between Lekhotla la Bafo and the Roman Catholic Church as a pretext for accusing Lefela and a number of his associates with setting the fire. It was no coincidence that their jailing came as they were doggedly probing the manner in which the British were arresting leading chiefs implicated in the *liretlo* (ritual murder) cases.

47.

'A New "Reichstag Fire" Plot Behind the Basutoland Arrests', *Inkululeko*, August 1948.

News reaching *Inkululeko* from Basutoland provides conclusive evidence of a deeply-laid plot on the part of the British authorities designed to stamp out the Basuto people's movement for national freedom, especially the Lekhotla la Bafo — progressive peasant organisation — and to establish a fake 'Communist menace' as an excuse for repressive measures.

Central feature of the conspiracy is a plan, strongly reminiscent of the Nazi 'Reichstag Fire' trial, to accuse members and supporters of Lekhotla la Bafo of burning down the 'Roma' Roman Catholic school last year.

Already a number of leading members of Lekhotla la Bafo — including Mr. Josiel Lefela, perhaps the most deeply respected leader in Basutoland — have been arrested. Men have been starved in prison and even tortured to try and get them to sign false 'confessions' implicating Lekhotla la Bafo in the burning. In one case, it is believed, they were successful in exacting such a 'confession'.

Inspired from London

It is believed that this manouevre has been directly inspired from London, where the British Government has instructed its colonial administrators throughout the world to manufacture 'Communist plots'. The purpose of these instructions is, firstly, to fit in with Bevin's pro-American and Anti-Soviet foreign policy; and secondly, to justify the brutal repression of the people of the Empire in their struggle for freedom and a better life.

In Malaya the British administration is engaging in full-scale military measures to beat down the patriotic Malayan movement against intolerable poverty and for national freedom. In Burma a similar situation is developing. In each case, the British try and label all the people's leaders as Communists.

The same thing is taking place in Africa. Wherever the people organise for a better life, in Nigeria, the Gold Coast, in Rhodesia, the authorities use force against them and then pretend they have found a new 'Communist plot'.

Lekhotla la Bafo

Lekhotla la Bafo (The Association of Poor People) is now being referred to by the authorities as the 'Communist Party of Basutoland', and wild slanders such as 'Moscow agents', etc., are being flung at its leaders.

Actually, Lekhotla la Bafo is a long-established patriotic organisation whose membership includes wide masses of the people of different shades of political life. There is no such body as the 'Communist Party of Basutoland', and while some individual members of the Lekhotla la Bafo may be Communists, the organisation itself aims solely at the freedom and independence of the Basuto people.

During the war a number of leaders of this organisation were interned. Their offence was that they demanded the proper arming and training of Basuto soldiers so that they might be more effective fighters against Nazism.

Wider Aims

The sinister plot of the Basutoland authorities has wider aims as well. A number of chiefs have also been arrested, including men who had no connection with Lekhotla la Bafo.

It is understood that charges of 'ritual murder' are to be brought against some of them, and that the administration is determined to victimise all chiefs who are not prepared to adopt a servile attitude to the administration.

Attempts are also being made to implicate progressive Indians in the territory, in the alleged arson. Men who supported the Passive Resistance movement in the Union are threatened, although it is well-known that Union Indians contributed towards the appeal for aid for Roma College after the fire.

48.

Malei Peshoane to Trygve Lie, United Nations, 25 July 1948, Department of State Papers, Basutoland, 1940-1949, National Archives, Washington, D.C.

It is with due respect and honour that we beg to address you this letter whereby we lodge our appeal before you with which we convey to you our prayer for help at this time of our dire need of international intervention between us and the British Government which has given instructions to her subordinates in this territory to contrive a most harmful artificial and aspersive conspiracy against our Association in order to get the pretext to destroy the lives of many of our innocent members to be sentenced to death in the next criminal session of the British High Court in Basutoland . . . .

. . . [T]he Roman Catholic Church which wields a considerable influence plays the role of an irreconcilable enemy to our Association which is being characterised as a menace as it is being called a part and parcel of the Communist Party maintained through the pecuniary help from Moscow. In order to hatch a plot against our Association, the Roman Catholic priests had their college building and dormitories set on fire in August or September 1947. In this building three Basuto students were incinerated while trying to rescue their books and other belongings. This fire is ascribed to have been set by members of Lekhotla la Bafo and upon this allegation a plot has been set up by the Roman Catholic priests and the Government officers in order to entangle and enmesh the members of our Association into an artificial and technical criminal machination, so as to get the pretext of destroying their lives in order to give British Government a free hand to expel Basuto people from the face of the soil to plant European settlers without anyone standing in opposition to such a scheme.

In pursuance of this plot on the 15th April 1948 a man named Mokeka Monyamane was arrested. On 22nd May 1948, another man named Harold Velaphe was arrested. This man is a member of our Association. After his arrest he was transferred from Leribe gaol to Teyateyaneng gaol on 25th May 1948 and spent the night without having been given any food. He was kept in solitary confinement in a cell which has a concrete floor and the roofs have holes to let in draft, and therefore the cell proved to be excessively cold. In this cell he was given no blankets, and at day time he was not allowed to come out in the sun. On the 26th May 1948, Lieut. Col. Castle, a police officer, having with him Sergeant Moefanyane Maitse and Sergeant Detective Sebolai Tsepande read out to him a written statement which after the reading he was ordered to affix his name on it so that through him as crown witness the other men whose names appear in the document may be charged and prosecuted. This man felt himself unable to affix his name to the document. On the 27th he was given no food and at lunchtime he was given two pieces of beef to eat. After some time he felt a strong stomach ache which he felt like having his bowels getting cut off near the pelvic cavity. At last in his agony he drank his own urine at the time when a foamy matter congregated at the mouth. After this he vomited and purged a bloody matter. While he was in this condition there came to him again the police officer and his two assistants and the District Commissioner Matsepe. Again the same statement was read to him and after perusal he was ordered to sign his name on it but he refused. Then the District Commissioner, Mr. Pott, told him plainly that his refusal to sign it would lead his life to disastrous end which would result in his loss of life but if he agreed to sign it he would save his life. He was further told that even if he might lose his life yet his name would be used as signatory to the statement so that through it the other men whose names appear in the statement may be prosecuted. After this he found himself no longer able to resist and therefore he signed the statement.

The statement which he thus signed under compulsion when it was read out to him, comprised the following points:

'Josiel Lefela, President of Lekhotla la Bafo, sent out two parties at different intervals to go and set fire to Roman Catholic building in Roma at Maam's. He ordered that care must be taken to see that when the building is set on fire that must be done while the pupils are not inside the building. He said that the building must be set fire because the Roman Catholic priests have taken control of the Paramount Chief and the country. The first batch was taken by Mr. Razak T. Surtie with his lorry which had taken four gallons of petrol. This batch was under the command of Kelebone Rametse, but the names of his party are not yet known.

'Mr. Razak T. Surtie came back to fetch the second batch whose names are as follows:

1. Mokeke Monyamane
2. Harold Velaphe
3. Josiel Lefela
4. Rabase Sekike
5. Roma Neko
6. Pakalitha Mokhethea
7. Montsel Konka
8. Nephtaly Mosuane
9. Lebina Hlakane
10. Razak T. Surtie
11. Mahomed T. Surtie

'It was agreed that Josiel Lefela must not himself go to Roma and the setting of fire on the building was to be carried into effect on the 30th August 1947. This batch was sent to Roma by Mr. Razak T. Surtie with his lorry as a driver. Again he had taken four gallons of petrol, but when they were near to Roma Kelebone Ramotse met on the way this batch in a lorry and told the batch that his batch had already completed the work. Therefore the lorry came back with Kelebone Ramotse. In this second party Roma Neko and Lobina Hlakane were the men who were ordered to set the building on fire.'

After he had signed this statement he was given some food and two blankets and a pillow. After some time Sergeant Detective Sebolai Tsepano told the culprit, Velaphe, that the statement he had signed was prepared and drafted by him taking it from one woman Melongvana Ananiase Felatsi in Mapoteng who told all the matter whose contents are produced in writing which is the statement he had signed.

On the 27th June he learned from one policeman that he would again be taken to solitary confinement in a cell where he would be given poisoned food to bring about his death so that in his absence through his name the other men might be prosecuted because he was suspected that in court he would reveal that he was compelled to sign the statement of the crown witnesses. Under these circumstances during the night, the culprit deserted the gaol and came to Mapoteng where he revealed all things relating to his torture, cruel treatment, threats and the ministering to him of two pieces of poisoned beef. After he had finished to put this report before us, he was rearrested by policeman named Moiloa Nthola No. 425 on the 2nd July 1948.

On the 15th July 1948 the following members of our Association were arrested: These are:

1. Josiel Lefela
2. Roma Neko
3. Rabase Sekike
4. Razak T. Surtie (not a member)
5. Metsel Konka
6. Pakalitha Mokhethea

These are all charged with murder of three students who were incinerated in the building, and the setting the building on fire.

As this artificial crime is a plot contrived by British Government to enable her to put to death our members charged under this artificial criminal machination so that she may be in a position to fulfil her pledge to the Boer leaders who demanded her to give our country to them in return for their acquiescence in the unification of their provinces to form the Union Government, we appeal to you that you may have mercy upon us and approach the British Foreign Minister to consult the Dominions Secretary to agree to our proposal that before this case may be put through the preparatory examination stage that a Judicial Commission to be composed of the nations of the Permanent members of the Security Council and other members of the Council may be sent out to investigate the conditions of treatment meted out to culprits detained and kept in solitary confinement to find out whether their treatment and conditions imposed upon them which induced them to take the position of crown witnesses were not in conflict with prison regulations, whether illegal coercive measures and manoeuvres were not employed against these culprits to compel them to take position of crown witnesses in matters about which they have not the least knowledge.

Again we request that a court other than the present British High Court in Basutoland may be constituted under the Statute of the International Court of Justice so that it may be permissible for the Judge and his assessors to be appointed from nationals of other foreign states to try this case so that justice may be found to all parties concerned. We ask in this way because this is not a factual criminal machination arising between two states related to one another by alliance in the attempt by British Government to usurp the political semi-independence of Basuto people under their chiefs in the interests of other state — the Union Government, by turning our country into a British Colony. This political case, without your intervention will culminate in the successful accomplishment of this project achieved by means of enmeshing our members into criminal machinations of the worst type and the suppression of our innocent Association so that it may be easy for British Government to carry into effect her policy of importing vast armies of immigrants into our country to colonise it in violation of the treaty of our alliance with her. We pray you that you may do everything in your power to ask British Government not to do what Hitler was prevented by both British Government and other united nations combined from usurping the lands and political independence and freedom of other small nations for the aggrandisement of his country — Germany.

We regret that this Court may also try our chiefs who are at the present time promiscuously being arrested for murders. We petition this way because in these murders committed by these chiefs the British Government is an accomplice and accessory. It is an accomplice because ever since British Government deprived Basuto chiefs of their powers as hereditary chiefs over their people and appointed them with warrants wherein their powers were defined under proclamation No. 61 of 1938 which had been imposed upon them against their will as well as against the will of the people, the chiefs began to appear before the Courts of Law as accused implicated in crimes of murder. Now since in pursuance of proclamation No. 62 of 1938, section 34 the High Commissioner in 1945 deprived the chiefs of their Judicial powers, the chiefs more than ever before became implicated in murders. This was done in an attempt to regain their lost and usurped powers and rights by regaining favour to the Govenment through the application and use of certain medicines and perfumes made up with ingredients mixed with pieces of human flesh. Now today that these murders are of common occurrence the British Government has got the pretext of expelling them from the positions of appointed chiefs under warrants called certificate of appointment to make them ordinary men. This will be done in violation of the treaty agreement of 1884 which had resuscitated the proposals and conditions put forward by Moshesh before the British Government in 1862.

49.

'Britain is trying to enslave us. Basuto people complain to U.N.O.' *The Guardian*, 13 January 1949.

The British Government, through the dramatic ritual murder trials which have been taking place in Basutoland during the past two years, has declared war against a peaceful nation and, under the pretext of suppressing murders, is trying to deprive the Basuto people of their rights, says Lekhotla la Bafo, the national organisation of the Basuto people, in a special petition to the United Nations Organisation.

Lekhotla la Bafo has appealed to U.N.O., the British Foreign Office and the Secretary of State for the Dominions to intervene. 'Our chiefs have been enmeshed in heinous crimes', says their petition. They allege that the three major cases so far held have been 'based on fictitious evidence'.

Chiefs Involved

Involved in these trials on charges of arson and ritual murder are the reigning house of Moshesh (a large number of important chiefs and sub-chiefs are already under sentence of death) and Lekhotla la Bafo.

'It surprises us to find that in practically every murder case a chief is involved with ten or more of his subjects,' states the petition, 'all of whom are ultimately convicted in the High Court.'

'In view of the terrible punishment meted out for ritual murders it is absolutely incredible that so many people should not have learned a lesson.'

They then cite a number of cases in Basutoland courts. In one, all the accused were acquitted because the evidence of the accomplice was found to be false. In another the accused were acquitted because the Crown witnesses stated before the Court that they were instigated by the police to give false evidence.

'It is distressing to find that the police have not made any serious attempt to improve their methods of investigation even after they have discovered the prevalence of perjury in these cases,' says the petition to UNO.

Back to Life

Citing another nine cases, the petition refers to one involving the Paramount Chief on a charge of murder. Here the person alleged to have been murdered by the Paramount Chief appeared after three of the Paramount Chief's people had already been arrested and compelled to state that they knew where the supposed murdered person was hidden or buried.

Lekhotla la Bafo says that neither the government nor the chiefs (both interested parties) should be represented on the commission of inquiry, which should have both European and Non-European members.

The Paramount Chief of Basutoland has also appealed to Britain for a judicial commission to investigate the trials.

King's Evidence

Documents submitted to UNO in Support of Lekhotla la Bafo's petition show that in some cases important Crown witnesses admitted they were party to the murders, and that some of the Crown witnesses have given evidence in more than one of the trials.

No law of habeas corpus appears to be operating in Basutoland. Africans have been placed under arrest, kept in custody for months on end, and then appear in court to testify to statements made by them while in police custody.

'Another factor which shows that under the pretext of suppressing murders the British Government is at war with a peaceful nation,' says the petition, 'is that a new proclamation has been issued providing for the collective punishment of all people in a district where a person is murdered. The police quartered in the area in which a person is murdered are allowed by this proclamation to live at the expense of the people there.'

'This is no less than a declaration of war upon an innocent and peaceful people.'

People's War

The people of Basutoland have their own explanation for this spate of trials. The story has gone the rounds that the administration has recently asked that an area in the centre of Basutoland of 40 miles square be set aside for European settlers, and is building a new main road and planning hotels — all this preliminary to greater British settlement in the protectorate.

Others say that Britain is preparing to accede to Premier Malan's demand for the incorporation of the territory in South Africa but must first break down all opposition to this proposal among the

Basuto people themselves.

Whatever the explanation, the story of the trials holds some secret not yet brought to light.

Reports received in Johannesburg last week tell of more arrests at Butha-Buthe, at Matsieng in Central Basutoland, Teyateyaneng in the East. New ritual murder cases are likely to open. The unrest among the people deepens.

50.

E.T. Mofutsanyana, 'Release of Basuto Leaders', *Inkululeko*, September 1948.

On August 21st, 1948, the following men were released from Maseru prison, and the charge of arson and murder against them was withdrawn:

Josiel Lefela, Roma Neko, Rabase Sekike, Nephthali Mosuoane, Mokeka Monyamene and Razak Tayob Surtie. Advocate Franz Boshoff of Johannesburg appeared for them. At the same time Pakalitha Mokhetha, Menzal Konka and Kelebone Rametse were also released from Teyateyaneng prison where they were detained for the same charge. All of them were kept in gaol for weeks and involved in expenses for the lawyers.

Although these men have incurred legal expenses and suffered inconveniences, they are grateful to all those who assisted them in the struggle for their release. Elsewhere in the Sesuto columns of this paper Mr. Josiel Lefela thanks those organisations which he feels have done much to weaken the charge of which they knew they were innocent; and in particular he thanks the *Inkululeko* and the Rev. Michael Scott.

Lekhotla la Bafo Becomes Powerful

Two conclusions can be drawn from the arrest of these men: (a) that the growth and the influence of Lekhotla la Bafo is now being definitely felt by the Basutoland Government. It must be remembered that during the war Mr. Josiel Lefela for demanding that the Basuto soldiers be armed had to spend two years in the internment camp.

Already at that time the Government realised the influence this organisation had among the Basuto people; and (b) That in a country like Basutoland where almost every European civil servant is an officer, and the whole police force is composed of Africans who, in most cases, have to do their duty even if what they have to carry out is against their own national interests, it is not easy to maintain any form of secrecy. The leaders knew that they would be arrested and what their chance would be.

Sincere and Militant

The Lekhotla la Bafo, an organisation which not very long ago was an organisation of a handful of people, regarded as a voice in the desert, today is the talk of the day; it is on the lips of both chiefs and commoners alike. It gives the rulers sleepless nights. Because of its sincere, militant and uncompromising attitude when it comes to the defence of the interests of the Basuto as a nation, Lekhotla la Bafo has won the respect among the masses of the Basutos. Its readers are courageously overcoming the main enemy of mankind, fear. It is through fear that the world is what it is today — fear keeps all of us in bondage.

Its Weaknesses

Like all African political national movements the Lekhotla la Bafo has so far failed to organise the African intellectuals and the going chiefs. The majority of the intellectuals are still vacillating on its doorsteps, while the minority of the chiefs (the higher strata) are still hostile to the organisation. But that the Basutos are awakening there can be no doubt. In fact, the chiefs today have nothing to lose by becoming members of Lekhotla la Bafo. Many of them have been deprived of their chieftainship, their number has been reduced, even those who are still recognised by the Government as chiefs are no longer deciding any cases, they are merely paid civil servants.

Josiel Lefela and Lekhotla la Bafo were a significant influence on a younger generation of Basotho politicians who came to the fore in the post-war era. Some like Ntsu Mokhehle, one of the founders of the Basutoland African Congress in 1952, cut their political eye-teeth under the tutelage of Lefela, whom they regarded as the 'Moses of the

Basotho' who had laid the foundation for the struggle for freedom.[69] During the 1950s the two organizations remained distinct but they were inseparable on most issues, and at the meeting described in the following article, Lefela charged the Congress party with carrying on the battle for independence.

51.

'The 12th of March, 1957', *Mohlabani*, June 1957.

In Basutoland the 12th of March is, every year, observed as a public holiday in honour, as it is said, of King Moshoeshoe the wise. This year this day was spent in different ways by different groups of people in this country.

To some it was a day of sports; to some a day of picnics and merry-making; to some a day of race meetings; and yet to some it was a day of leisure spent quietly at home. On the playgrounds, throughout the country, school children (innocent little souls) played and sang and ate for all they are worth, without in any way understanding the significance of the day.

Amidst all these festivities only one, lonely group of men, women and children spent this day as we think it ought to be spent. This group was composed of members of the 'Lekhotla la Bafo'. To them this day has never been regarded as, or taken to be a day of worthless festivities and purposeless jubilations. To them it has always been a day of mixed emotions engendered by past, present, and possibly future historical and political events in this country. These men have always appreciated the fact that on this day in 1868 the English, while extending an outwardly protecting hand to the Basotho, did in fact lay down in their tricky proclamation the basis of their future political acrobatics to annex the land of the Basotho. These men and women have always been sharply aware that since that day subsequent British activities, seemingly intended to further the political aspirations of the Basotho, were in fact carrying out a political programme calculated to further their own colonial plans and imperialistic aspirations. To Josiel Lefela's group this day is of a double significance, and must be regarded with a mixture of joy and sorrow — joy because the Basotho and their land were saved from the marauding Boers; sorrow because a political time bomb was set to blow up, in time, the Nation and its aspirations into smithereens. So as a matter of political and spiritual routine the old women and the grey-bearded 'Bafo' laboured their weary, time-worn roads from different parts of the country to their sacred mountain, Thaba-Bosiu. Yes, Thaba-Bosiu, which is the matrix of the Basotho Nation as it is known today; which is to them a source of political inspiration, an emblem of Basotho nationhood, the only hope of spiritual and political resuscitation.

This year they had invited the Paramount Chief of Basutoland, the British Commissioners of Basutoland, as well as political organisations to be present at Thaba Bosiu, so that all of them might think out together their political interrelations. Of these invitees only the Basutoland African Congress turned up, represented by three of its National Executive Committee members. The three B.A.C. men came in three buses and a van filled with men and women who had accompanied their leaders. The British Commissioners sent their spies while they and the Chiefs decided to attend a two-hour gathering at Thota-ea-Moli, the old meeting place of the Basotho and their Chiefs.

The morning of March 12, 1957, was a busy morning. Many white people and many Basotho had followed their big bosses to Thota-ea-Moli. The Government, in order to entice people to attend their gathering, spent a lot of the Nation's meagre funds putting cars, lorries and buses on the roads to be used to convey all those who would otherwise not have gone to the gathering, either because of indifference or lack of interest. But with free transport many who had not intended to go were successfully baited. The European officers drew handsome travelling allowances for driving their families and friends to Thota-ea-Moli. The country's hungry treasury spent over two hundred pounds on meat, the supply of which was well advertised beforehand as a bait to catch the overtaxed, hungry Basotho folks. And what shall we be told later after all this extravagance? We shall be told, as we have often been told, that there is no money to increase salaries of African employees, to provide pensions for African teachers, and to do a thousand and one things that this country stands in dire need of. Shall we be persuaded to believe this tale? Only idiots will believe it.

The result of all this extravagance was an encouragement to the 'Bafo' and the Congressites, for they felt that theirs was a humble but genuine gathering, while its counterpart, albeit flashy and pompous, involved the extravagant use of the money of the Basotho (including that of the 'Bafo' and the Congressites) to further political interests basically inimical to the political interests of the Basotho. There it was; the whites having overcome our chiefs were using their privileged positions to use our own taxes against our own selves.

From the moral point of view 'Lekhotla la Bafo' was victorious, for those who attended their pitso did so on their own free will (except, of course, the detectives who would fain have gone to Thota-ea-Moli where pots were overflowing with fat and broth), and paid freely for their presence there. They believed in the righteousness of their course and correctness of their choice. They did not need to be compelled by threats, and certainly they did not need free transport and free meals as an inducement to Thaba-Bosiu. Those who went out to Thaba-Bosiu were out on a mission of prayer and dedication. They went out to honour their ancestors who had died in the fight against colonialism. They went out to think of the past and compare it with the present, and also threw their political eyes into the future.

Long before sunrise they had gathered on top of their sacred Mount, Thaba-Bosiu, singing and praying. At sunrise they all stood in prayer, facing the East to catch the first rays of the sun from that exact position of the horizon where some of their ancestors (including the Great Moshoeshoe of Blessed Memory), at whose tombs they stood, had also seen the first rays of the selfsame sun on that date, 89 years ago, when their request for British protection (though now twisted for political ends of the same British) was granted, and their country saved from the Boers, who, having been armed by the selfsame British who were then extending the benevolent hand of protection, were on the verge of destroying our fortress.

Soon after sunrise they moved down to the village of Chief Jobo Libenyane at the foot of the Sacred Mountain. Later they gathered on an open space below the mountain. Here the two Liberatory Flags — the White and Green of the Lekhotla la Bafo, and the Black, Red and Green of the Basutoland African Congress, which we hope will one day be merged into a National Flag of Basutoland with a picture of the Crocodile somewhere in the centre — flew side by side in the morning breeze. As they rose and fell amidst historical and political speeches, interrupted from time to time by the singing and the drumming of melancholy songs of liberation, it would have taken a heart of granite not to have melted and allowed tears of sorrow, at the political morass into which this fair land of Moshoeshoe is today steeped, to run down without any shame. To anyone who is thoughtful it seemed as if the aged White and Green Flag was handing over the struggle to the youthful, virile Black, Red and Green Flag. And we believe it was so.

52.

'Call for United Front in Basutoland. Lekhotla la Bafo Takes the Lead', *New Age*, 27 September 1962.

A call for the formation of a broad National Liberation Front which would unite all parties in a demand for the immediate restoration of Basutoland's independence and sovereignty has been issued by Mr. Josiel Lefela, leader of the organisation Lekhotla la Bafo.

Mr. Lefela is the grand old man of Basutoland politics. Since the foundation of Lekhotla la Bafo in 1918, this organisation under his leadership has carried on a consistently progressive struggle against imperialism.

Mr. Lefela has been jailed several times in the course of the struggle. He was detained throughout the second world war and was jailed for 9 months in 1955 for sedition. He rejected the Crown constitution as a fraud and boycotted the elections held under it.

'The people of Lesotho (Basutoland) stand face to face with a grave crisis,' he says in his statement.

'The British Government, which has broken all the pledges made to our father Moshoeshoe the Great, is preparing to foist another constitutional farce on our country. Once more the imperial government is acting in complete defiance of solemn agreements entered into with it by the founder of our nation — Moshoeshoe.

'The pretence is being carried on of regarding Lesotho as a colony which is developing towards self-government. Whereas in truth and in fact Lesotho is an independent state which sought and entered into an alliance with Great Britain under definite conditions which have been ignored.

'To make matters worse the Basotho have never been so divided. Petty political wrangling and strife has taken the place of serious political thought for the future of our small country. Ambitions for Cabinet positions in governments formed under the auspices of the British government have taken the place of a struggle for the restoration of an independence and sovereignty which has always been our right legally and morally.

'Whilst no one can deny the right of people at a certain stage in history forming numerous parties representing every shade of political opinion the emergency in which we are demands that a machinery for ensuring the maximum unity of the nation is vital.

'Such a unity can be achieved by the creation of a broad National Liberation Front. Such a Front should properly unite all parties and organisations, trade unions, all religious movements, chiefs and other prominent personalities, peasants and intellectuals, in a demand for immediate restoration of our independence and sovereignty.

'The Lekhotla la Bafo calls on the people of Lesotho who are aware of its consistent record of struggle to participate in all work designed to lead to the formation of a Front of National Liberation uniting the whole nation irrespective of ideology or position.'

Songs of
Lekhotla la Bafo

1.

Ke Bone Ke Bone Tsela (I Have Seen, I Have Seen the Way)[70]

(1) *Fats'e lena la Afrika*   This land of Africa
Fats'e la batho ba batsǒ   The land of black people
Ke fatsě leo re le neiloeng   It is the land naturally
Ke Molimo ka hloleho   Given by God

CHORUS: *MaAfrika*   Africans
Ikopanyeng   Unite
Le tsebiseng   Let it be known
Chaba tsohle   To all nations
Tse teng hohle   That exist everywhere
Lefatsěng   on earth
Kamoo le nketsoeng toka   How you have been
                                  deprived of justice

(2) *Moshe bula bula tsela*   Moses, lead the way
MaAfrika a itseke   The Africans must defend
                                  themselves
A tseke khotso ea Afrika   They must defend peace in
                                  Africa
Molimo o tla re thusa   God will help us

(3) *Borena bohle ba rona*   All our royalty
Bo nyefotsoe ba nyelisoa   Has been scorned and despised
Hore re khetheloe bo bong   So that another could be selected
                                  for us
Boo re sa kang ra bo tseba   One which was unknown to us

(4) *Bang re tsuile ka mahlomola* Some of us left in sadness
Ka hlokofatso tsa marena   Because of persecutions by chiefs
A qhalang chaba sa Moshoeshoe Who scatter the nation of
                                  Moshoeshoe
Se bokeletsoeng ka bothata   Which was difficult to build
Hopolang Lesotho   Remember Lesotho
Lesotho leo ke la Basotho   That Lesotho belongs to the
                                  Basotho
Basotho ba loanne   The Basotho have fought
Lintoa tsohle ba sa lefuoe   Many wars without pay

(5) *Empa marena a kajeno*   But today's chiefs
A rerile ho le rekisa   Have plotted to sell it
A qala ka ho tšoenya batho   They start by excruciating the
Basotho   people, the Basotho
Hore ba tle hle ba qhalane   So they can really be scattered
Phuthehang Basotho   Come together Basotho
A re rereng tsela tsa ho khutla Let's plan how to return

Khutlelang Lesotho	Go back to Lesotho
Fatše le shoetsoeng ke Basotho	The land which the Basotho died for

(6) A na le ka rekisoa ke mang — Who can sell you out
Ha rona Basotho re tseka — If we the Basotho are defending
Tokelo tsa rona ho bona — Our rights from them
Ha re sa ipitse bafalli — If we don't call ourselves migrants

Ha re eeng Basotho — Let us go Basotho
Lefatšeng la rona la tsoalo — To the land of our birth
A re eeng re tseke tokelo tsa rona — Let's go and fight for our rights
Tse seng li hapiloe — Which have been usurped

(7) Hoba ha re qhalane mona — Because when we are scattered like this

Re tšabile ho tseka toka — We have feared fighting for all our rights

Tsohle tsa rona tse hapuoeng — Which have been usurped
Re sa ka ra ba ra rerisoa — Without any consultation with us
Ha re khutleng bohle — Let us all return
Re lahleng ho ts'aba ho tseka — And reject being afraid to demand

A re eeng Lesotho — Let us go to Lesotho
Re e'o tseka tokelo tsa rōna — And fight for our rights

(8) Ruri ha re ka likalika — Surely if we hesitate
Merero ea ho koala tsela — Plans to block the way
Ho koalloa Basotho ba tsuileng — To block the Basotho who went out

E reroa ruri ka potlako — Plans are quickly laid out
Lona basali ba Lesotho — You, the women of Lesotho
Akofang kapele — Hurry up
Kopanelang morero ona — Come together on this plan
O teng mona 'Musong Kopanong — Which exists in this government

(9) Makhooa a buoa ka hore — The whites are saying
Basotho ba lelekoe mona — That the Basotho must be expelled from here

Ba busetsoe Sothong la bona — And be returned to their Lesotho
Se thopeng chelete — Do not favour money
E koneleng ka thata-thata — Guard it very carefully
A re eeng Lesotho — Let us go to Lesotho
Re e'o tseka Lesotho la rōna — And fight for our Lesotho
Basotho ba bang ba rera hore — Some Basotho plan that

(10) Bohle ba bokelle chelete — All must collect money

Ba reke Mapolasi mona	And buy farms here
Mona re tlile mosebetsing	We are here to work
A re sebetseng ka hlompho	Let us work respectfully
Le hoja re le har'a lira	Even though we are among enemies
Ra hlorisoa hore re fose	We are being tormented to make us do wrong
Sebetsang Basotho	Work Basotho
O, kokobetsang lihlorisang	Please ease the torture
Hlomphang bahiri	Respect the employers

2.

Motse Oo Re O Hlolohetsoeng
(The City That We Yearn For)

(1) *Rona Basotho ba qhalaneng* — We the Basotho who are scattered

Hole le Lesotho la rona	Far from our Lesotho
Phuthehang tlong le tle 'Musong	Gather, come to the government
Re tl'o nahana tsa Lesotho	Let us come to think about Lesotho
Phuthehang Basotho	Come together Basotho
Hopolang lefatše la lona	Remember your land
Phuthehang ka khotso	Assemble in peace
Mafatšeng hole le Lesotho	In countries far from Lesotho

(2) *Nahanang boteng ba Lesotho* — Think about the existence of Lesotho

Lefatše la rona Basotho	The land of us Basotho
Re se re ka balahluoa	We resemble the rejects
Ana re le hlatsitse joang na	By the way, how did we reject
Lesotho le letle	The beautiful Lesotho
Lefatse la rona Basotho	The country of us Basotho
Ke joang na re tsuileng	How did we leave it
A re nahantsaneng Basotho	Let us help each other think about the Basotho

(3) *Banna ba bitsoa ba hurileng* — The men are being called the vagabonds

Basali ho thoe Machuchutha	The women are said to be prostitutes
Empa Lesotho le sa le teng	But Lesotho remains
Fatse le shoetsoeng ke Basotho	The land which the Basotho died for

Basotho phuthehang   Basotho unite
Re rereng tsela tsa ho khutla   Let's plan our return
Basotho lokisang   Basotho prepare
Ka litsela tse tletseng khotso   Through means that are filled
                                 with peace

3.

Banna Ba Khotla La Bafo
(Men of the Council of Commoners)

(1) Hlomohelang marena   Pity the chiefs
    A hlokang ho hlokomela   Who are unable to realise
    Ha chaba se loanela   When the nation is fighting for
    Borena le lona   Chieftainship and
    Lefatše la Basotho   The land of the Basotho
    Hlomohang Basotho   Lament, Basotho
    Ke fofu ba marena   The blindness of the chiefs

(2) Marena a foufetse   The chiefs are blind
    A tšepile makhooa   They are relying on whites
    Ha a sa rata ho eletsoa   They no longer want to be
                              advised
    Ke chaba sa Basotho   By the Basotho nation
    Marena a tšoenya batho   The chiefs harass the people
    Sechaba sa Basotho   The Basotho nation
    Joale sechaba sena   Now this nation
    Se ferekane pelo   Is greatly disturbed

(3) Mahlomola a bofofu   The sadness of the blindness
    Ba marena a rona   Of our chiefs
    Ke hore ke ba thetsoang   Is that they are deceived
    Ba thetsoa ke makhooa   They are deceived by the whites
    Marena ka lithetso   The chiefs through deception
    A hlorisa Basotho   Torment the Basotho
    A tšepile thetso ea lira Trusting the lies of the enemy

(4) Makhooa a hlalefatse   The whites are clever
    Ho fapanya sechaba   At dividing the nation
    Le balisa ba se busang   And the shepherds who oversee it
    A lutse a lisitse   They sit and watch
    Ha phapang e hlaha   For conflict to emerge
    A iketsa metsoalle   They pretend to be friends

A eletsa batho	And advise the people
Le marena sephiring	And the chiefs in secret

(5) Keletsong tseo tsa makhooa   In this advice of the whites
Ke tse holisang phapang   There is that which increases conflict

Ka phapang e teng lichabeng   Through the friction that is already there amongst peoples

Tokelo tsa sechaba   The rights of the nation
Li tlosoa kalosong   Are removed from the true protection

Ea 'nete ea marena   Of the chiefs
Li nkeloa makhooa   And given to the whites
Li hloke ba li tsekang   With no-one to fight for them

(6) Basotho ba khotla la Bafo   The Basotho of the Council of Commoners

Banna ka basali   Men and women
Emang le hlole moleko   Stand up and defeat the temptation

Oa ho hloea marena   To hate the chiefs
Ka hloko tiisetsang   With deliberation persevere
Le loaneng ka bohlale   Fight intelligently
Molimo oa khotso   The God of peace
O ke o re hlolele   Be victorious for us

(7) Mohla re hlotseng   On the day of our victory
Tokelo li khutlile   When the rights have been restored

Re tla eletsa marena   We will advise the chiefs
Ho busa ka mohau   To rule with compassion
Kajeno tiisetsang   Today withstand
Lihloho tsa marena   The cruelty of the chiefs
Re tsekeng Lesotho   Let's fight for Lesotho
Le pholosoe ho lira   And be saved from the enemy

4.

Ha Re Hlahlobiseng (Let Us Examine)

(1) Ha re hlahlobiseng   Let us examine
'Nete ea baruti   The honesty of the missionaries

Ba likereke tsohle   Of all churches
Tse hlahang Europe   Originating from Europe

CHORUS: Na ke ka baka la'ng   Why is it that
          Hohle moo ba kenang   Wherever they've been
          Chaba li felile   Nations have been destroyed
          Le tokelo tsohle   And all their rights lost

(2)   Lichaba tsa marena   All the chiefs of the nations
      'Ohle a fetileng   Have been told
      Li boleletsoe phelo   The end was in view
      Ke baruti bana   By these missionaries

(3)   Moo baruti ba keneng   Wherever the missionaries have
                                                 been
      'Me ba amoheloa   And were welcomed
      Bohle beng ba linaha   All the rightful owners
      Ba li amohiloe   Have lost their countries

(4)   Morerong oa Phutheho   In the plan of the congregation
      Baruti ba teng   The missionaries are there
      Chabeng tse nkileng Jesu   In those nations that have
                                                 accepted Jesus
      Ho utsoitsoe naha   The land has been stolen

(5)   Chaba tse rutoang Jesu   The nations that are taught
                                                 about Jesus
      'Melo, Pelo, le Moea   The body, heart and spirit
      Motho o li tsentsoe   With which man has been
                                                 endowed
      Hape li hloke mona   Also they must not have jealousy
      Hore li pholohe   So as to be saved

(6)   Hape baruti ba re   The missionaries also say
      Ho se be mohono   There should be no coveting
      Nthong ea ngoan'a bo naha   Of that which belongs to the
                                                 child of the land
      Ho pholosa moea   To save the soul

(7)   Empa lichaba tsohle   But all the nations
      Tse seng li timetse   That are already extinguished
      Le ho utsoetsoa naha   And whose land has been stolen
      Baruti ba khotso   The preachers of peace

(8)   Baruti ha ba nyatse   The missionaries do not criticise
      Le ho khalemela   Nor do they reprimand
      Mebuso e utsuitseng   The governments that have
                                                 stolen
      Linaha tsa batho   The people's countries

(9)   Baruti le 'muso   The missionaries and the
                                                 government

Ea habo bona	Of their countries
Ba na le lekunutu	They have a secret
Ka thuto ea Jesu	Through the teachings of Jesus

(10) *Ke chaba sa Jappane* — It is the Japanese nation
    Se se nang le puso — That has no government
    Se neng se hane Jesu — Which refused to accept Jesus
    Le baruti bohle — And all the missionaries

(11) *Ithapelleng Molimo* — Just pray to God
    Se nyeliseng Jesu — Do not despise Jesus
    Hlokomelang mamena — Watch out for all the traps
    'Ohle a baruti — Of the missionaries

5.

Mamelang Khotla la Bafo
(Listen to the Council of Commoners)

(1) *Mamelang khotla la Bafo* — Listen to the Council of Commoners

    Le buoang ka Lipallo — That talks of the treaty
    Na a se tsa motlotsuoa — Isn't it of the annointed one
    Mohlomphehi Moshoeshoe — The honourable Moshoeshoe

CHORUS: *O sireletsa Lesotho* — He protects Lesotho
        O boloka sechaba — He saves the nation
        O buoa ka selekane — He speaks of the alliance
        Sa pallo tse sa feleng — Of a permanent agreement

(2) *Utloang bana ba Moshoeshoe* — Listen Children of Moshoeshoe
    Taba tsa ntat'a lona — To the news of your father
    O sireletsa Lesotho — He protects Lesotho
    Ka mantsoe a hloekileng — With immaculate words

(3) *Motho eo re mo kopileng* — The person we have requested
    Ho 'Me Mofumahali — From the Queen
    A tla ntsamaise a mthuse — Will guide and help me
    Ho boloka meeli — To safeguard the boundaries

(4) *Ha u ka busa ka 'na feela* — If you could govern through me alone

    Batho ba ka Basotho — My people, the Basotho
    Ho keke ha e-ba khathatso — There will be no problem
    E tla ba khotso feela — There will be peace only

(5) *Ke rata ho busa bana*   I want to rule the children
     Ka melao ea Basotho   By the laws of the Basotho
     Ke ba rute ho boloka   Teaching them to preserve
     Meetlo ea bo bona   Their customs

(6) *Motlotlehi Mohlomphehi*   His majesty, the honourable
     Motlotsuoa Moshoeshoe   The annointed Moshoeshoe
     Mopatariareka oa Khotso   The Patriach of Peace
     Mokhethoa oa Jehova   Jehova's chosen one

CHORUS: A sireletsa Lesotho   He protected Lesotho
         A boloka sechaba   He saved the nation
         A etsa le selekane   He also made an alliance
         Sa ho boloka Lesotho   To save Lesotho

(7) *'Muso oa Mofumahali*   The government of the Queen
     O koana Engelane   Which is over in England
     O amohetse selekane   Has accepted the treaty
     Sa kopo tsa Moshoeshoe   Requested by Moshoeshoe

CHORUS: *Ho sireletsa Lesotho*   To protect Lesotho
         Ho boloka Lipallo   To preserve the treaties
         Ka letsoho la monghali   Through the hand of
         Oa hae Tsetrick   The District Commissioner

6.

Re Hlompha Leqosa (We Respect the Commissioner)

(1) *Re hlompha leqosa*   We respect the Commissioner
     Le sirelelitseng   Who is protecting
     Batho le lefatse   The people of the land
     Lena la Basotho   Of the Basotho
     Lumela mosireletsi   Greetings to you, Protector
     Amohela hloenpho ena   Welcome this respect

(2) *Qosa le romeloe*   The Commissioner was sent
     Ho ema lipakeng   To stand in the middle
     Meeling ea Lesotho   At the borders of Lesotho
     Ho thiba Maburu   To stop the Boers
     Re hlompha ka sebele   We truly respect
     Boteng ba hao har'a rona   Your presence among us

(3) *Molisa oa khotso*   Guardian of peace

Khotso ea Lesotho	The peace of Lesotho
Se furalle khotso	Do not turn away from peace
Re thuse ka khotso	Help us with peace
Se fe makhooa Lesotho	Do not give Lesotho to the whites
Re itebatse lipallo	And make ourselves forget the treaty

(4) Se cheke lemena   Do not dig a trap

(4) Se cheke lemena	Do not dig a trap
Ka ho lahla Pallo	By abandoning the treaty
Ua fapanjoe makhooa	Allowing the whites
Ua kenya makhooa	To enter
Fatseng lena la Lesotho	This land of Lesotho
Le boloketsoeng Basotho	Which has been saved for the Basotho

(5) Re se fapanyetsoe	Let us not be tricked
Ka makhooa a thetsang	By the whites who deceive
Ba nka naha ea rona	And take away our land
Ea Morena Moshoeshoe	Of Chief Moshoeshoe

(6) Re bureletsoe bohle	We have all been oppressed
Tokelo tsa rona	Our rights
Tse neoang makhooa	That are given to whites
Ka makhooa afe	Which whites?
Ka hohlomelisa makhooa	Through the stampede
E kentseng makhooa mona	That brought the whites here

(7) Oho tšepahala	Please be trustworthy
Hlonepha Lipallo	Respect the treaty
Re buseletse hle	Return to us, please
Tšoanelo tsa rona	Our rights
Pelo li be ntle tsa rōna	Let our hearts be kind
Seli ntsoe fatše morena	The light, the word, the world, Lord

(8) Re hlompha melao	We obey the laws
Le ha ho le joalo	Nevertheless
Se nehe makhooa	Do not give the whites
Tokelo tsa rona	Our rights
Tlas'a qheka la melao	Under the pretext of the law
Empa e le ho tlatlapa	When it is oppression

(9) Busa ka marena	Rule through chiefs
E seng ka makhooa	Not through whites
Ke eona poloko	That is the security
E re thabisang hle	That makes us jubilant
Re mamele hle morena	Hear us, O Lord
Mosireletsi oa rona	Our protector

7.

Lekhotla la Bafo le Ntša Maqosa
(The Council of Commoners Is Sending Out Messengers)

(1) *Lekhotla la Bafo le ntša maqosa*
The Council of Commoners is sending out messengers

Ho ea phutha monamane o hohle
To go and gather the clan

Bahlanakana le baroetsana bohle
Every young man and woman

Ba tšerileng Lesotho ka tsele tsohle
Who left Lesotho in many ways

Ba khutle ba tl'o tseka nah'a bona
Must come back and fight for their country

Ba tsoe mose ho meeli ea Lesotho
They must return from beyond the borders of Lesotho

(2) *Lekhotla la Bafo le hlokometse*
The Council of Commoners has realised

Hore ho qhalana ha chaba sena
That this scattering of the clan

Se qhaloa ka puso tse hlomolanang
Is caused by a pathetic leadership

Hore monamane o tsoele kantle
So that the clan goes out

Ho sale bafihli hara Lesotho
And leaves foreigners in Lesotho. This is to surrender the land to enemies

(3) *Ha moname o se o qhaliloe*
When the natives have been dispersed

Makhooa a rerile ho rekisa
The whites have plotted to sell Lesotho

Lesotho ka ho qhekella marena
By cheating the chiefs

Ka ho a tšepisa licheletana
By promising them a little bit of money

Ho thoe lefatše lena ke la oona
They claim this land is theirs

Hobane monamane o so qhaliloe tsoetse kannete
Since the clan will be thoroughly dispersed

(4) *Joale Lekhotla la Bafo le hlaba*
Now the Council of Commoners is making a plea

Mokhosi Basothong ba qhalakaneng
To all the scattered Basotho

Le re phuthehang ka hohle Basotho
It is asking them to gather

Ipokelleng le hopole Lesotho
And be united in memory of Lesotho

Lefatše le loanetsoang ke Basotho
The land the Basotho fought for

Lefatše le rekiloeng ka mali hle
The land that was indeed bought with blood

(5) *Bafihli ba sitoa ho ka le tseka*
The foreigners cannot defend it

Phuthehang monamane tlong Lesotho
Natives, return to Lesotho

Le loaneleng ka matla a lona
And fight with your strength

Tsoarang liboka mafatšeng asele
Hold meetings in foreign lands

Rerang ho pholosa lefatse lena
Plan to liberate this country

Lona bahlankana le baroetsana
You young men and women

(6) *Talimang Thaba Bosiu Lesotho*
Turn towards Thaba Bosiu in Lesotho

Hlomohelang Moshoeshoe le Basotho
Sympathise with Moshoeshoe and the Basotho

Ba bopileng Lesotho ka bothata
Who moulded Lesotho with difficulty

Se ngaleng boeang lefatšeng la lona
Do not give up, come back to your land

Ha marena a ka hla le rekisa
If the chiefs actually sell it

Sechaba se tla le fuoa ke bo mang
Who will compensate the nation

(7) *Lesotho ke lefatse la Basotho*
Lesotho is the land of the Basotho

Marena kaofela ke balisana
All the chiefs are sheperds

Balisa ba se ba rekisa naha
The shepherds will not sell the land

Ho makhooa a kenang ka Lesotho
For the whites who enter Lesotho

Ba qhala Basotho ho a suthela
They expel the Basotho to make room for them

Phuthehang ka potlako monamane
Unite quickly, clansmen

8.

Lesotho Fatše la Bo-Ntata Rona
(Lesotho Land of our Fathers)

(1) *Raohang bahlankana ba Lesotho*   Stand up young men of Lesotho
Le loanele tsoanelo tsa Lesotho   And fight for the rights of Lesotho

Molimo o re thuse   God help us
O re hauhele   Have mercy on us
O re fe matla   And give us strength

(2) *Emang 'me le hlabe mokhosi hohle*   Stand up and call upon
Lichabeng tsohle tsohle tsa Lesotho   People everywhere who belong to Lesotho
'Me moea oa kutlo   And may the spirits of understanding

O be teng sechabeng   Reside in the nation
Le ho marena   And among the chiefs

(3) *Lipallo tsohle tsa khosi Moshoeshoe*   All the treaties of King Moshoeshoe
Tse ba li ballaneng le Vikitoria   That were signed with Victoria
Bakeng sa Lesotho   Concerning Lesotho
Le sechabeng sa hae   And his nation
Ba li lahlile   Have been thrown away

(4) *Kajeno marena a lahla sechaba*   Today the chiefs mislead the nation
A iketsetsa khotso le ba 'muso   They make peace with the government
'Me khotsong ea bona   Also in the peacemaking

Ba rera sechaba	They plot against the nation
Ka mahlomola	In an unfortunate manner

(5) 'Me ho khethiloe melao e bohloko — And harsh laws have been chosen

E hlokofatsang chaba sa Basotho — Which hurt the nation of the Basotho

Ba 'nileng ba busoa	Who were once ruled
Ka khotso Lesotho	With peace in Lesotho
Ho se bothata	Without any difficulty

(6)
'Me rona sechaba re tenehile	But we the nation have had it
Re lla re talimile ho Jehova	We cry looking up to Jehovah
Oho hle Molimo	O, please God
Hopola Basotho	Remember the Basotho
Ba be le tšepo	Let them have hope

9.

Binang Mohla Tsoalo (Sing of the Day of Birth)

(1)
Binang ka ho thaba	Sing with joy
Binang bahlankana	Sing young men
Ba Lesotho	Of Lesotho
Hlase e qhomileng	The spark that exploded
Khotleng le Sechaba	From the National Council
E qhometseng chabeng sa Lesotho	That shot towards the Nation of Lesotho

(2)
Khotleng la sechaba	In the National Council
Ho kile ho a e-ba teng	There was once
Mohlankana	A young man
Ea bitsoang Lefela	Who was called Lefela
Ea buoellang batho	A spokesman for the people
A lelekoa hang teng	He was immediately expelled from it
Ha thoe a tsoe	And asked to leave

(3)
A tsoa teng ka hlase	He left there with a spark
Ka Lekhotla la Bafo	With the Council of Commoners
Ho tla chesa	To go and kindle
Pelo ea sechaba	The heart of the nation
Hore se itseke	To defend itself with
Ka hlomphong se tseki	Dignity, fight
Se phehelle	And persist

(4) *Kajeno sechaba*   Today the nation
    Sa Lekhotla lena   Of this Council
    Se ka tseka   Can fight
    Tokelo tsa sona   For its rights
    'Musong le mareneng   From the government and the
                                 chiefs
    Ka lebaka lena   For this reason
    Ha re thabeng   Let us rejoice

(5) *Binang ka ho thabo*   Sing with joy
    Hlase e qhomileng   Of the spark that sprang
    Mane thoteng   Over the hill
    E fetohe khabo   And turns into flame
    E tuka ka hohle   And burns everywhere
    Lesotho le hohle   Lesotho and over
    Ho Afreka   In Africa

(6) *Banna ba Lesotho*   Men of Lesotho
    Lelallang holimo   Turn your eyes up
    Ho Jehova   To Jehovah
    Le roetse lifubeng   Wearing on your chests
    Tšoao le sa feleng   The eternal brand
    La Khotla la Bafo   Of the Council of Commoners
    La Lesotho   Of Lesotho

(7) *Ka tsoalo ea lona*   By its birth
    Re beiloe bana   We became the children
    Ba Moshoeshoe   Of Moshoeshoe
    Ho fele tsa joale   Let those of now end
    Ho sale tsa khale   Let those of old remain
    Tsa Selekane seo   Those of the alliance
    Sa Moshoeshoe   Of Moshoeshoe

(8) *Morena Motšoene*   Chief Motsoene
    A hla a bolela   Immediately said
    Ho marena   To the chiefs
    A re Josiele   That Josiel
    O kotsi sechabeng   Was dangerous to the nation
    O tla chesa hlaha   He would start
    E sa tingoeng   An inextinguishable fire

(9) *Molimo boloka*   God save that same
    Eena Josiele   Josiel
    Oa Lefela   Of Lefela
    A tšoare liboka   Let him hold meetings
    Lekhotleng la Bafo   In the Council of Commons
    Ho isa qetellong   Till the end
    Ea litaba   Of time

10.

Mokhosi Borotse (Attention the Barotse)

(1) *Mokhosi o ntse o hola Mapoteng* — The call is growing at Mapoteng
Oa ho tsosa Basotho bohle — It awakens every Mosotho
Hore ba tsohe ka hohle borokong — To wake up from sleep completely
Ba tseke tokelo tsa bona — And fight for their rights

CHORUS: *Kopanang Bafo bohle* — Unite Commoners one and all
Kopanang le thusane — Unite and help each other
Ke ka kopano le ka boeloang — It is through unity that
Ke tokelo tsa lona kaofela — You can regain all your rights

(2) *Esale Pitso ea Thota ea Meli* — Ever since the Pitso of Thota-ea-Meli
E felisoa re phela mpe — Was stopped
Litokelo tsa sechaba kaofela — All the rights of the nation
Li inkeloa se sa rerisoa — Are taken away without any consultation with us

(3) *Melao e behaloang chaba sena* — The laws that are passed for this nation
Se e rutoa ka literonko — Are introduced through jails
Ka baka leo mohoo oa hola — Therefore the cry grew
O reng Basotho ba itseke — Requesting the Basotho fight for their rights

(4) *Moshoeshoe le Balimo ba Basotho* — Moshoeshoe and the ancestors of the Basotho
Ba re rapelise Molimo — Help us pray to God
Tokelo tsena re li amohuoang — For these rights that were taken away from us
Ba li sebelitse ka thata — That they laboured for with difficulty

11.

Libatso

(1) *Jesu Kreste Mopholosi oa rōna*   Jesus Christ our Saviour
    Ak'u re thuse kopanong ena   Please help us in this gathering
    Re kopa khotla la Bafo   We are requesting the Council of
     Monghali   Commoners, Lord
    Mehlorong le lillong tsa rōna   In our misery and tears

CHORUS: *Tiisetsang tsoelang pele*   Persevere, continue on
      Ba kopang Khotla lena   Those who call on this
        Council

      Leha lefu le ka ema ka pele   Even in the face of death
      Jesu Kreste o tla thusa   Jesus Christ will help

(2) *Litsietsi tsa Basotho li ngata*   The Basotho have many
     problems

    'Me Bafo re entsoe limumu   And the commoners we have
     been made mute

    Re sitoa le ho eletsa balisa   We cannot advise the leaders
    'Me re hlorisoa ha bohloko   And we are heavily oppressed

(3) *Re qabangoa ka matsatsi*   We the Basotho are turned
     Basotho   against one another daily
    Mali a tšoloha ha ngata   There is constant bloodshed
    Balisa ba hloka hloko sechabeng   The leaders do not heed the
     nation

    Sechaba se phela ka thata   The nation leads a difficult life

(4) *Linyeoe ha li ahloloe Lesotho*   Offences are not being judged in
     Lesotho

    Batho ba har'a ho makala   The nation is amazed
    Nyeooe tse ling li tloheloa ka   Some cases are ignored
     boomo   deliberately
    Hore li tle li be le lijo   So they can make profit

(5) *Bahlolohali le likhutsana*   Widows and orphans
    Ba phela ka thata   Live in misery
    Ha bana molomo oa ha ba tseru   They have no spokesman
    Hobane Bafo ba entsoe limumu   Because the commoners have
     been made mute

(6) *Re etsetsoa melao ka keletso*   Laws are made for us through
     the advice

    Ea lira tsa rona Basotho   Of our enemies
    Re amohuoa tokelo tsa rona   We are deprived of our rights
    Ka melao eo re sa e tsebeng   By the laws we do not know

(7) *Ka khotla lena lehano la Basotho*   Through this Council, the mouth of the Basotho

    Le kopeng ka phehello e ntle   Request with great perseverance
    Mali le topo tsa bakopi bohle   The blood and corpses of all the petitioners

    Li be li rapalle Lesotho   Till they are lain in Lesotho

12.

Ha Le Mpotsa (If You Ask Me)

(1) *Le khetiloe ka boqosa*   You have been chosen as ambassadors

    Ba Khotla la Bafo   Of the Council of Commoners
    Tsoang le ee ka ho tšepeha   Go out and be true
    Joale ka masole   Like soldiers

BASS: *Le rongoa ho phutha*   You are sent to gather
    Sechaba tšotlehong   The nation that is in bondage

    Se ipatlele pholoho   So it can seek its freedom

(2) *Le rongoa ho loanela*   We are sent to fight for
    Pallo tsa Lesotho   The treaty of Lesotho
    Le borena ba Basotho   And the chieftainship of Lesotho
    Moo bo nepang Pallo   Where it abides by the treaty

(3) *Joale le tla tlangoa ka thomo*   Now you will be bound by the message

    Le eo buoa 'nete   Go and tell the truth
    E nyatsang bohle babusi   That denounces all the rulers
    Ba robileng Pallo   Who have broken the treaty

(4) *Tsebang hore ha le buoa*   Know that when you speak
    'Nete tsa Lekhotla   The truths of the Council
    Le nyatsa bohle babusi   Denouncing all the rulers
    Le tla hlouoa hohle   You will be hated everywhere

(5) *E, leha le hloiloe*   Yes, even when you are hated
    Ikhopotseng thomo   Remind yourselves of the message

    Le shoe joaleka masole   Die like soldiers
    Se furalleng kano   Do not forsake the oath

(6) *Tsebang le rongoa ho tsejoa*   Know you are sent knowing

Le tla ea sotleha
Ka hobane le tla nyatsa
Ba ratang tlhoriso

You will suffer
Because you will condemn
Those who love persecution

(7) Tsamaea hle le loanele
Pallo tsa Lesotho
Le loaneleng mafutsana
Tlas'a 'nete eohle

Please go and fight for
The treaties of Lesotho
Fight for the poor
Abiding by all the truth

13.

Jehova Molimo Ke Qosa (God Jehovah Is the Messenger)

(1) Lumelang Basotho
Ba utluileng mokhosi
Ha bo bitsoa bohle
Ho tla tla ithera
Banna le basali
Ke lerato la 'Mopi
Lumelisanang bohle

Greetings to you, the Basotho
Who heeded the call
When everyone was called
To come and plan
Men and women
In the love of the Creator
Greet one another at this meeting

(2) A se ka papali
Kapa ka bokhabane
Re memaneng ho tla mona

It is not in frivolity
Or for show
That we have invited one another
here

Re kopaneng
Litokelo tsohle
Le bona boiketlo
Re li furalatsoa
Ka melao-lao

That we are assembled
All the rights
And even comfort
We are being made to abandon
Through various laws

(3) Molimo oa khotso
O tletseng matla ohle
O le fe bohlale mererong ea lona

God of Peace
Almighty
Grant your wisdom in your
projects

Tabeng tse tla reroa

In all matters that will be
considered

Molimo o memuoe
O tl'o fane bohlale
Matla, kellello

Let God be invited
So he can grant wisdom
Strength, and intelligence

(4) Ho tse tla sebetsoa

In things that are under
deliberation

Molimo oa balimo

God of the ancestors

O li salise pula	Follow them with rain
Phoka morao	Dew
Li tle li pholose	So that they can rescue
Tokelo tsa Basotho	The rights of the Basotho
Lefatseng lena	In this land
La khosi Moshoeshoe	Of King Moshoeshoe

(5) Lumelang maqosa	Greetings, messengers
A ratang fatše lena	Who love this land
Esita le bona borena ba rona	Even our very chieftainship
Kopanong ea joale	In this assembly
Re tšepeng tšireletso	Let us trust the protection
Boipuso bona e'n'ebe	This self-government
E'ne e be ba rona	Should remain ours

14.

Jubile Ka Tsatsi La Kajeno (Today's Jubilee)

(1) Ke tsatsi le teboho	It is a day of thanksgiving
Ke tsatsi la Moshoeshoe	It is Moshoeshoe's day
Ke tsatsi la khopotso	It is the day to remember
Ea mahlomola 'ohle	All the miseries
Le matšoenyeho 'ohle	And all the hardships
A ho bokella batho	Which brought people together
Ba neng ba qhalakane	Who were scattered all over

(2) Chaba tsa puo tsohle	Peoples of all languages
Tse neng li le hlorehong	Who were in suffering
Ha li qhaloa ke lira	When they were thrown asunder by enemies
Moshoeshoe a li thusa	Moshoeshoe helped them
A iketsa lehaha	And made himself a cave
La bohle ba qhaliloeng	For all who were scattered
A fepa likhutsana	He fed the orphans

(3) Moshoeshoe ka mohau	Of all the scattered nations Moshoeshoe in his mercy
Le ka Lerato la hae	And his love
Lerato le sa khetheng	A love that did not discriminate
Mofuta kapa puo	According to nationality or language
Ha kena tsatsing le leng	One day there arrived

Maburu a tsoang Kapa	Boers from the Cape
A kena fatšeng la hae	They entered his land
A qhaliloe ke puso	Running away from authority

(4)
Ha nako li tsamaea	As time passed
Maburu a fetoha	The Boers changed
A ikukela naha	They took the country by force
Ea Moshoeshoe ea khale	That which used to be Moshoeshoe's
A tšepile liletsa	Trusting in the efficacy
Tsa lithunya tsa oona	Of their guns
Le kanono tse matla	And their powerful cannon
Tsa ho qhala lichaba	To scatter the nation

(5)
Baruti bas'o fihle	Before the missionaries came
Lemong tse kabang tharo	About three years
Tse neng li sa tsoa feta	Prior to the arrival
Ho fihlile Batho	Of the people
Baruti ba tsoang Fora	The missionaries who came from France
Ba eletsa Moshoeshoe	Advised Moshoeshoe
Ho kopa tšireletso	To seek protection
'Musong oa Engelane	From the English government

(6)
Moshoeshoe a bohlale	The wise Moshoeshoe
A latela keletso	Followed the advice
A kopa tšireletso	And asked for protection
Tlas'a Pallo tse ngotsoeng	Under a written treaty
Tse tla sitisang maburu	Which would hinder the Boers
A nyoretsoeng ho hapa	Who were eager to conquer
Lefatše la Basotho	The land of the Basotho
Ka tlasa mano ohle	Through all kinds of intrigues

(7)
Ka baka la maqheka	Because of the tricks
Le mano a maburu	And craftiness of the Boers
Pallo tsa lilekane	The treaties of friendship
Li'nile tsa Kuenesoa	Were reversed
Lintoa tse thata-thata	Bitter wars have made
Tse hlorisang Basotho	The Basotho to suffer
Ba neng ba amohetsoe	Who accepted
Ka baka la maburu	Because of the Boers

(8)
Lekane se teng sena	This alliance that exists
Bakeng sa tšireletso	For protection
Ha li ntse li kueneha	As decisions are reversed
Ke sa ka'moi'a ntoa	It is a recurrent battle
Ea lithunya e matla	Of the Gun War
Ke sa bohlano sena	This is a fifth alliance

Se ratoang ho felisa	That is threatening to end
Ka tsela tsa bohlale	Through intrigue

15.

O Ho Se Fele Pelo (O, Please Do Not Be Impatient)

(1) *Lichaba tsa ba batšo*	Black nations
Mose ho maoatle	Overseas
Le tse mose o koano	And this side of the oceans
Li tlas'a botubo	Are persecuted
CHORUS: *Kopang*	Ask [bass]
Le kopeng Molimo	Ask the Lord
Kopang	Ask [bass]
Chaba li kopane	Nations to unite
(2) *Boko sa litloholo*	The weeping of grandchildren
Bana ba makhoba	Children of the slaves
Se utloala ka hohle	Is heard everywhere
Se llela Afreka	The weeping for Africa
(3) *Hore lichaba tsena*	That these peoples
Tse nkiloeng Afreka	Uprooted from Africa
E be li tsoetse bana	Have born children
Fatšeng la kholeho	In the land of slavery
(4) *Koetsa ea MoAfreka*	The danger to the African
E neng e le khotsong	Which used to be in peace
Lichaba tsa Europa	The nations of Europe
Tsa patela metse	Raided the villages
(5) *Ba ba nkela likepeng*	They took them to the ships
Ba ba isa mose	They took them overseas
Ba beoa mapetlelong	They displayed them in markets
Ba rekisoa bohle	And sold them all
(6) *Chaba tse rekisitsoeng*	The nations that were sold
Le phetse bothateng	Have lived in misery
Le har'a mahlomola	And in hardship
Le linyotobetsong	And in degenerate conditions
(7) *Ba sebelitse bohle*	They have all toiled
Ka lilemo-lemo	Year after year

Mesebetsi kaofela	On every task
Ho se e ka patoang	With none that could be escaped

(8) Mohau oa Molimo   The mercy of God
     Ka mora' lilemo   After many years
     Oa kena ho makhooa   Entered the hearts of whites
     O loantšoa bakhoba   And they opposed slavery

(9) Kajeno ho lilemo   It is now years since
     A lokolohile   They were freed
     A tsoile ka mahlale   And they have come out with
                             skills

     Le litsebo tsohle   And all kinds of knowledge

16.

Lelala U Tsoele Pele (Lift Your Head and Proceed)

(1) Borena bona ba rona   This leadership of ours
     Borena ba Basotho   The chieftainship of the Basotho
     Borena ba ho alosa   The leadership that safeguards
     Tokelo tsa sechaba   The rights of the nation
     Bo qaliso ho Moshoeshoe   It originates from Moshoeshoe
     Ka ho lisa litokelo   Who, by guarding the rights
     Sechaba sa motšepa   Was respected by the nation

(2) Ha sechaba se motšepa   Once the nation trusted him
     Tokelo tsa sechaba   All the rights of the nation
     Tsohle tsa bitsoa ka eena Were laid through him
     Tokelo tsa bolisa   The rights of leadership
     A re ke tsa sechaba   He said belonged to the nation
     Sechaba se re ke tsa hae The nation called them his
     E le ka ho tšepana   Through mututal trust
     Tokelo tsa sechaba   The rights of the nation
     Moshoeshoe ke molisa   Moshoeshoe is the overseer

(3) Tokelo ke tsa Basotho   The rights belong to the Basotho
     Moshoeshoe ke mohlanka   Moshoeshoe is the servant
     A phetha thato ea sechaba   He does the will of the nation
     Ka botšepehi bohle   In complete honesty
     Hona tšepahalong ena   In this honesty
     Tokelo tsa sechaba   The rights of the nation
     Tsa nka bitso la Moshoeshoe Took on the name of
                                   Moshoeshoe

     Ka baka la ho tšeptjoa   Because of the trust

(4) *Ho boloka botšepehi*   The trustworthiness
     Ha morena a tšepala   When the king is honest
     Ea tla beleha morena   He who will give birth to a king

17.

Jesu O Ntsa Mpokela (Jesus's Spirit Is Visiting Me)

(1) *Basotho ba fihletsoe*   The Basotho are experiencing
     Ke nako tse bohloko   A painful time
     Poloko ea sechaba   National security
     Ke mapolesa   Is in the hands of the police

CHORUS: Eba marena kae   Where are the chiefs
         Joale ha ho reroa   When the planning
         Poloko ea sechaba   Of national security
         E ba lipapaling   Is a game

(2) *Lipallo tsa Moshoeshoe*   The treaties of Moshoeshoe
     Polokong ea Basotho   For the protection of the
                                   Basotho
     Li fetohile lefu   Has turned into death
     Ho chaba sa Basotho   For the Basotho nation

(3) *Haeba chaba se bina*   If the nation sings
     Pina tsa ho hlomola   Songs of sorrow
     Ke puso ea Khatello   It is due to the rule of
                                   oppression
     E phuthoang ke marena   Which is practised by chiefs

(4) *Marena ka tlotliso*   The chiefs in honourable
     Khotatsong tsa March   At the sermons of March
     E ba a ka menyakong   Are towards the doors

(5) *Bafo ha ba bitsane*   When the commoners have
                                   summoned one another
     Ho tla tseka marena   To fight for the chiefs
     Ha a tlositsoe sechabeng Who have been removed from
                                   the nation
     Pitsong Thoteng-ea-meli   At Thota-ea-meli

(6) *Ba fetoloa mahlanya*   They are branded lunatics
     A hlokang motsebetsi   Who are without work

Ha ba tseka melao	When they fight laws
E hlorisang sechaba	That oppress the nation

(7) Marena a kholisitsoe — The chiefs are satisfied
Ke hoba mapolesa — Because the police
A leshoang ka chelete — Who are paid with cash
A lahlile sechaba — Have misled the nation

(8) Tokelo Basotho — The rights of the Basotho
Tse nkiloeng ke makhooa — That have been taken by the whites

Ha chaba se li batla — When the nation demands them
Ha ho reroa hammoho — It is necessary to plan together

(9) Ka tsatsi la Moshoeshoe — On Moshoeshoe's day
Ka tsatsi la khopotso — On the day of commemoration
Ha chaba se b-kane — When the nation is gathered
Mane Thaba Bosiu — Over at Thaba Bosiu

(10) Tloholo tsa Moshoeshoe — Moshoeshoe's descendants
Letsatsing la khopotso — On the day of commemoration
E ba li lireisising — Are at horse races
Le thabong ea litantsi — And the fun of dances

(11) Moo bara ba Moshoeshoe — Where are the sons of Moshoeshoe

Ba rerang le sechaba — Plan with the nation
Ha ho reroa tsa puso — When the government is planned
Hleka le bakeng sefe — Where in fact are you?

(12) Sechaba sa Moshoeshoe — The nation of Moshoeshoe
Binang ka mohlomola — Sing with sorrow
Le batleng ho pholoho — Seek to be free
Melaong ea khatello — From the laws of oppression

(13) Topollo ha e batla — If freedom means
Batho ba literonkong — People in jail
Le bophelo ba batho — And costs people's lives
E neheng tse e li hlokang — Give it what it needs

(14) Ha chaba se ka hloloa — If the nation fails
Ho boloka Lipallo — To maintain the treaty
Tsa 'Muso le Basotho — Between the government and the Basotho

Ho buse ba Moshoeshoe — Let those of Moshoeshoe rule

18.

A Keng La Hlalobeng Kotsi E Lieang Lesotho
(Please Investigate the Danger That Is Lesotho's Downfall)

(1) *Bahlankana*   Young men
    Baroetsana   Young women
    A keng le hlahlobeng   Please investigate
    Kotsi e lieang Lesotho   The danger that is Lesotho's
                                       downfall

    Hoba e tsoetsoe ke'ng   What is its origin?

(2) *Ka lithuto*   In the education of the schools
    Tsa likolo
    Le ka likerekeng   And inside the churches
    Ho patiloe 'nete tsohle   Are hidden all the truths
    Bakeng sa Lesotho   From Lesotho

(3) *Moshoeshoe oa hlonepheha*   Moshoeshoe is honourable
    O kentse Lesotho   He has put Lesotho
    Tsireletsong   Under the protection
    Ka lipallo   With agreements
    Tse sa rutoeng bana   That are not taught the children

(4) *Baruti ba li patile*   The missionaries have hidden
                                       them
    Pallo tsa Basotho   The agreements of the Basotho
    Ho lokisetsa   To prepare for
    Makhooa   The whites
    Kukong ea Lesotho   Takeover of Lesotho

(5) *Baruti ba teng Lesotho*   Missionaries who reside in
                                       Lesotho
      Ba basoeu bana   These white ones
      Khothatsong tsohle   In all their counsel
      Tsa bona   They have instilled cowardice
      Ba kentse bokoala

19.

Mano Ho Pepesoa (The Intrigue Is Exposed)

(1) *Mona ho pepesoa mano* The intrigues are exposed
   A lohuoeng khale koo Which have been woven a long
                                  time ago

   Ha chaba tse ling tse matla When some of the powerful
                                  nations

   Li ea utsoa mafatše Were going to steal lands

CHORUS: *Kolobetso ka hlapantšo*   Through baptism by oath
        Ba qhekella lichaba   They intrigued nations

(2) *Chaba tsa ea amohuoa* Nations that were going to be
                                  deprived

   Mafatše le lipuso Of lands and governments
   Li romeloa Lipijone There were sent spies
   Pieone tsa baruti The spies of missionaries

(3) *Lipijone ke baruti* The spies are the missionaries
   Hohle moo ba fihland teng Wherever they arrived
   Ba pata thoma ea 'Muso They concealed the message of
                                  the government

   Ba bolele ea Jesu And spoke of that of Jesus

(4) *Ba re chaba li lumele* They ask nations to believe
   Ho Jesu oa Morena In Jesus the King
   Morena Mor'a Molimo The King, son of God
   Mong'a motse o holimo The Lord of the city on high

(5) *Ba re Jesu o boletse* They say Jesus has told
   Motse oo o holimo Of that city on high
   O kenoang ke baiteli Which is entered by the
                                  dedicated

   Batho ba tela tsohle People who sacrifice everything

(6) *Ba re batho ba tele Satane* People must denounce Satan
   Le libe le lefatše And the sins of the earth
   Le menate eohle ea lefatše And the pleasures of the earth
   Ba nt'o ka kolobetsoa Before they are baptised

(7) *Ha ba hlapantšitsoe* After they have been sworn
   Kapele ho lipaki In front of witnesses
   Ba tšepisoa leholimo They are promised heaven
   Ba tla putsoa ke Jesu They will be rewarded by Jesus

(8) *'Me ba tla jesoa selallo* And then they will partake of the
                                  bread and wine

Se bitsoang se khopotso	Which are said to be in remembrance
Ha ba ipoletse libe	After they have confessed their sins
Tsa ho lahla lefatše	And abandoned their country

(9) *Chaba li lahlisoa tsele* — Nations are misled
Ho rapela Molimo — To pray God
Li lahlisoa le Balimo — They are made to denounce their ancestors
Li neoe basele — And offered different ones

(10) *Lichaba tsa thuto ena* — The peoples of this new teaching
Ba Jesu le Bibele — Those of Jesus and the Bible
Ea Ntate Mora le Moea — Of Father, Son and Spirit
Deutronomo oa basupa — Deutoronomy Seven

(11) *Baruti ke lipijone* — The missionaries are spies
Mafetšeng a ea haptjoa — Lands are annexed
Tlasa hore ke Molimo — Under the pretext that it is God
Oo o ba fileng naha — Who gave them the country

(12) *Joale ha re ithutile* — Now that we have learned
Ha re batleng likhoro — Let us seek the means
Tsa ho ea batla pholoho — Of demanding freedom
Lekhotleng la lichaba — In the Council of Nations

CHORUS: *Kukang 'Muso oa Russia* — Let the government of Russia

Ore kenye ka U.N.O. — Introduce us at the U.N.

1. Lekhotla la Bafo is incorrect in stating that Thota-ea-Moli was the site where Moshoeshoe and his successors held their national pitsos. The national pitsos held there were for consultations between Basotho chiefs and colonial administrators beginning in the 1870s.
2. Before the National Council was established in 1903, a consultative council of chiefs and headmen had been proposed by the Resident Commissioner, Marshall Clarke, in the 1880s. However his recommendation was not acted on by Letsie who feared that allowing rival chiefs to have an institutionalised voice in decisions would diminish his own authority. In 1889, Letsie changed his mind and, along with nearly three hundred other chiefs, supported Clarke's proposal, but the idea foundered again when it was realised that one of the functions of the council was to settle land disputes between chiefs.
3. Gabriele Winai Strom, *Development and Dependence in Lesotho the Enclave of South Africa* (Stockholm, 1978), p.64. She bases her reading of the constitution on Gordon Haliburton's 'Politics and Religion' (paper for the Conference on the History of Southern Africa, Gaborone, 1973). Haliburton repeats his error in 'Walter Matitta and Josiel Lefela: a prophet and a politician in Lesotho', *Journal of Religion in Africa*, VII, 2 (1975), p.126.
4. As it turned out members of Lekhotla la Bafo supported the organisation not only with dues, but with contributions in kind: small animals (especially chickens), bags of mealies, and crops.
5. In 1928, the Resident Commissioner introduced two draft Proclamations to the National Council defining the powers of chiefs and reorganising the chiefs' courts. They were debated at length in the Council in 1928 and 1929 and met with such opposition that they were shelved for almost another decade.
6. Abimael S. Tlale was the son of Sefonea Tlale, who established two presses after the Anglo-Boer War — one at Mafeteng which printed *Mochochonono* and the other at Maseru which printed *Naledi*. Abimael was educated at Morija Institution and became a teacher before serving the colonial administration as a policeman and later as a court interpreter. After retiring from the colonial service in 1908, he devoted his time to editing *Naledi*. He was a member and president at one time of the Progressive Association. He also served in the National Council and as a councillor to the Paramount Chief. He died on 19 August 1938 (*Basutoland News*, 20 September 1938; *Mochochonono*, 27 August 1938).
7. For a listing of the few extant issues of *Naledi*, see Les and Donna Switzer, eds., *The Black Press in South Africa and Lesotho* (Boston, 1979), p.54.
8. Edwin Ntsie Tlale was born in 1884 and was educated at Morija and Lovedale. Before the First World War he served a stint as editor of *Naledi* until 1916, when he joined the South African Native Labour

Contingent serving in France. He returned to edit *Naledi*. Later he became a teacher at an Anglican school at Mafeteng as well as a small businessman. He was a founder of the Basotho Traders' Association and was its representative in the National Council. He died on 25 April 1955 (*Mohlabani*, July 1955, pp.15-16).

9. LNA, S 3/5/8/3.

10. E. Tlale to Resident Commissioner, 1 November 1920, LNA, S 3/5/8/3.

11. *Ibid*. For a similarly voiced protest in Lefela's defence, see *Umteteli wa Bantu*, 8 January 1921, p.9.

12. Garraway to High Commissioner, 2 December 1921, PRO, CO 417/655.

13. Lefela is probably referring to the movement to build hostels for African female domestic servants working around Johannesburg. Although he is incorrect in asserting that the hostels were for breeding whores, he is close to the mark when he discusses their control functions for employers and missionaries. For an excellent discussion of the women's hostel movement, see Deborah Gaitskell, 'Christian compounds for girls: church hostels for African women in Johannesburg, 1907-1970', *Journal of Southern African Studies*, VI, 1 (1979), pp.70-92.

14. A governor of the Cape Colony, George Napier signed a peace treaty with Moshoeshoe at Thaba Bosiu in December 1843. Moshoeshoe agreed 'to be a faithful friend and ally of the colony' while preserving peace in his jurisdiction. In return the British were to give him £75 annually in money or arms and ammunition. The treaty also set boundaries for Moshoeshoe's kingdom, resulting in his losing land that he laid claim to.

15. Interview, Abdul Razak Surtie, May 1980; Gani Surtie, May 1980; *Inkululeko*, May 1945. The small Indian community (in 1918 there were 153 male adults) was concentrated in the Leribe and Mohales Hoek districts. Most earned their living as traders. Their principal grievances against the colonial administration in Lesotho were that they were not represented in the Chamber of Commerce; that they had difficulty in bringing in their families and hiring clerks and shop assistants of Indian extraction; that they could not transfer a European trading licence to themselves; and that they were not able to get hawkers' licences to peddle in the mountains.

16. The Punjab massacre refers to the killings at Amritsar, India, in 1919, in which British troops fired on a peaceful political gathering killing almost four hundred people and wounding over twelve hundred others. The massacre had been preceded by the Rowlett bills which were designed to quell nationalist movements.

17. Garraway to High Commissioner, 2 December 1921, LNA S 3/5/1/4. Garraway confirmed that Lefela was the author of the above letter.

18. See also his other articles: 'Advice to the National Council', 'The people complain against the National Council', 'Chief Leloko Lerotholi ill-treats us representatives of the Council of Commons' (all found in LNA S 3/5/8/3) and 'Council of Commons — ill spoken of by white traders', LNA S 7/4/14.

19. See Note 5.
20. Robert Henry Dyke (1850-1912) was born at Thaba Bosiu, the son of the head of the Paris Evangelical Mission Society's normal school for teacher's training. He had first trained in England for a business career, but then studied for the ministry and returned in 1877 as a PEMS missionary.
21. Theal's collection of documents was published as the *Basutoland Records*, covering the period 1833-1868. Another three volumes for the years 1868-1872 have yet to be published.
22. Godfrey Lagden was Resident Commissioner of Basutoland from 1894 to 1900 when he was appointed Chief Native Commissioner for Transvaal.
23. Part of the text of the letter in the Bloemfontein *Friend* (2 December 1921) entitled 'Native Court System in Basutoland' read: 'Believe me . . . the chiefs have turned the Basutos into a nation of slaves by making them plough and hoe patches of lands belonging to the chiefs' many wives without food or payment. While at work those in charge of them even refuse to allow them to go for a drink of water'. 'Mosotho' also pointed out that the courts administered by chiefs were being misused. Chiefs kept people waiting for months before rendering decisions causing considerable aggravation. Moreover, it was difficult to lodge appeals to the Resident Commissioner's Court since a chief had to write a letter on behalf of the appellant. 'Mosotho's' accusations caused a stir when they were published, but it took several more decades before the colonial administration took concrete steps to curb the abuses.
24. The Paris Evangelical Mission Society was the first mission society to begin work among the Basotho in 1833. Moroka (c.1795-1880) was chief of the Seleka Barolong centred at Thaba 'Nchu. Although he was given shelter by Moshoeshoe, Moroka became a rival to him and sided with the Boers in the disputes with the Basotho nation. Nevertheless the Boers took away most of his land.
25. In 1862 Governor Philip Wodehouse sent J.M. Orpen and J. Burnet to meet with Moshoeshoe and ascertain his views on his relationship with the British Crown. Moshoeshoe asked for a British agent to come and reside with him, although it is clear that he had no intention of allowing the agent to have any say in the internal affairs of his kingdom. Rather he wanted the agent to strengthen his hand in staving off the pressures by Boers and internal dissidents. Moshoeshoe's proposal was put to Wodehouse, who shelved it after objections by the Free State. His reticence to act sealed the fate of the Basotho kingdom. For more details, see Peter Sanders, *Moshoeshoe Chief of the Sotho* (London, 1975), pp.253-56.
26. Patrick Duncan had been Colonial Secretary in the Transvaal (1903-1907) and held several cabinet positions as a member of the Union House of Assembly (1911-1924). Later he was to serve as Governor-General of the Union of South Africa (1936-1943).
27. At its first meeting in 1903, the National Council adopted a code, the laws of Lerotholi, which brought together Basotho customary law on a

number of key issues, such as chiefly succession, the authority of chiefs, the chiefs' control over land allocation, *matsema* labour, and the right to a fair trial.

28. Report of a Proceeding of a Meeting of Lekhotla la Bafo, Hlotse, 5 August 1930.

29. Notes taken at the meeting of Lekhotla la Bafo, Hlotse, 2-4 August 1930.

30. Report of a Proceeding.

31. *Ibid.*

32. Meeting at Matsieng, 21-22 June 1929.

33. Meeting at Thaba Bosiu, 12-14 March 1930.

34. Meeting at Matsieng, 21-22 June 1929.

35. Meeting at Kennon Khethisa's, Leribe, 26-27 December 1931.

36. Report of a Meeting at Motlatsi Ramahimane's Village, Leribe, 7 December 1930.

37. *Ibid.*

38. *Ibid.*

39. *Ibid.*

40. *Ibid.*

41. *Ibid.*

42. Report on the Meeting of Lekhotla la Bafo at Thaba Bosiu, 6 March 1929.

43. *Ibid.*

44. *Ibid.*

45. *Ibid.*

46. *Ibid.*

47. *Ibid.*

48. *Ibid.*

49. *Ibid.*

50. *Ibid.*

51. *Ibid.*

52. *Ibid.*

53. *Ibid.*

54. Meeting at Kennon Khethisa's, Leribe, 26-27 December 1931.

55. *Meeting at Hlotse, 22 February 1931.*

56. *Ibid.*

57. Report of a Proceeding.

58. Speech by Josiel Lefela, Matsieng, 26 December 1928.

59. For example, *Basutoland News*, 3 March 1931, which observed that Lekhotla la Bafo was '. . . a small body . . . of mad-brained Natives with revolutionary ideas . . . . It is a marvellous association of half-educated revolutionaries whose main object it would seem, is to do away with all European influence in the territory and to have their own Magistrates, High Commissioner, and so on. What a glorious mess they would make of their country in five minutes'.

60. Eugene Casalis, *The Basutos: or Twenty Three Years in South Africa* (London, 1861).

61. Police Report of Lekhotla la Bafo Meeting, 11 May 1931, LNA S

3/22/2/6. One of Matitta's lieutenants, Raymond M. Mohono (1885-1968) remained closely associated with Lefela till his death. Educated at Morija, he taught in Dutch Reformed Church schools in the Orange Free State and became a court interpreter in Kestell where he met Matitta in 1916. He joined Matitta's church and came to Lesotho in 1927 to look after congregations. He was stationed until his death. (Interview, Samuel Mohono, April 1986).

62. Presidential Address, Mapoteng, 2 August 1930, LNA S 3/22/2/4.

63. Ronald Hyam, *The Failure of South African Expansion, 1908-1948* (London, 1972), pp.77-82.

64. In 1907 Lord Selbourne, the High Commissioner, issued the Partition Proclamation which divided Swaziland into Crown land, a European area, and a Swazi nation area. Over 56 per cent of the land was set aside for white occupation, while only 40 per cent was given to the Swazi. In 1913, a ruling gave white farmers the right to evict Swazis living on white land if they did not enter into contracts with the farm owner. In 1922-23, Allister M. Miller, who had been Resident Adviser to the Swazi nation at the time of the late nineteenth century land concessions, began evicting Swazis from his farm, and this in part prompted the law suit. For details, see Hilda Kuper, *Sobhuza II Ngwenyana and King of Swaziland* (London, 1978), esp. pp.75-96.

65. Tshekedi Khama was regent for the Ngwato after the death of Khama III in 1923.

66. A discussion of the annexation is found in A. Sillery, *Founding a Protectorate: History of Bechuanaland, 1885-1895* (The Hague, 1965).

67. *Ibid*.

68. 'Mote is referring to the investigation conducted by William Ballinger and Margaret Hodgson and published as *Indirect Rule in South Africa: Basutoland* (Lovedale Press, 1931).

69. *Mohlabani*, V, 4/5 (July 1959), p.6. See also *Mohlabani*, IV, 6 (July 1958), pp.12, 15, and V, 11/12 (December 1959), p.5.

70. These songs are selected from a songbook compiled by Hlakane Mokhithi and translated with the assistance of Maleboheng Mohale, Edwin Mofutsanyana, Nana Mahomo, and Motsumi Moja.

Index

Aaron, Emma 125
Abantu-Batho 22
Aborigines Protection Society 21, 55, 164
Africa 90, 95-96, 99-101, 127, 142-143, 163-164, 192, 211, 224, 231
African Auxiliary Pioneer Corps (see also Second World War) 30, 47-48
African Federal Church Council (see also independent churches) 17, 142-145
African Methodist Episcopal Church (see also missions) 17
African National Congress 22, 90, 116
African National Congress Youth League 38
Afro-Americans 17, 71, 124, 129, 145-146, 163-164, 231
agriculture 134, 140
ancestor worship 16, 123
Anglican Church (see also missions) 80, 116
Anglo-Boer War 4, 46, 238
Arden-Clarke, C.N. 50
Arthur Frederick, Prince 56, 92
Athlone, Earl of 45, 160
Australia 97

Ballinger, William 168, 242
Bantu Social Agency 171
Barolong, Seleka 240
Basotho Farmers and Wool Growers Association 15
Basotho Traders Association 239
Basutoland 3, 20, 60, 65, 80-81, 92-95, 98, 100-101, 105-114, 118, 124-126, 129-130, 134-135, 139-145, 148, 150, 152-153, 162, 165-169, 171
Basutoland African Congress (BAC) 37, 202-205

Basutoland Association to Oversee the Abroad Basuto Invalids 7
Basutoland Chamber of Commerce 239
Basutoland Congress Party (BCP) 39
Basutoland National Council (BNC) -
    and District Councils 180-183
    criticisms of by Basotho 14, 119-120, 122, 125-126, 129, 169-171
    criticisms of by J. Lefela 7-10, 33, 37, 40, 177, 223-224
    criticisms of by Lekhotla la Bafo 24-25, 57-59, 61-62, 65-66, 80, 89, 100-101, 132, 135, 165
    functions 4-5, 238, 240
    post-war developments 32-34
Basutoland Progressive Association (see Progressive Association)
Basutoland Records 103, 240
Bataung 6
Bathoeng, Chief 159
Batlokoa 81, 98
Bechuanaland (see also High Commission territories) 21, 29, 121, 136, 156, 158-159, 161-162, 186, 190
Bevin, E. 184, 192
Bloemfontein 82, 171
Bloemfontein Friend 86, 157, 240
Blyth, Captain 83
Board of Education 133
Board of Licenses 134
Boers 18, 21, 71-72, 98-100, 103, 121-122, 126, 128, 151, 197, 240
bohali 16, 69, 77-79, 81
Boshoane, Chief 26, 127
Boshoff, Franz 201
Botha, Louis 92-94
Bunting, S.P. 23
Burnet, John 104, 240

Maseru 8, 19, 26, 33, 120, 125, 128, 146, 170, 175, 181, 201, 238
Masupha 27
Masupha, E.L.D. 15, 26-27, 157, 163-164
Masupha, Gabashane 35, 37
Matabele 99
Matasane, Thaba 122
matsema labour 10-11, 24, 35, 137-138, 170, 182
Matsepe 195
Matitta, Walter 17, 27, 242
Matsieng 8, 26-27, 29, 34, 48, 79, 86, 100, 112, 154, 201
Metapanyane, Alice 125
Miller, Allister 157, 160-162
Milner, Alfred 106-108, 166, 190
mine labour 5-6, 87-88, 127-128, 171-172, 180
missionaries -
  and education 145-147, 168-169
  and independent churches 142-145
  attacked by Lekhotla la Bafo 16, 65, 68-70, 75-80, 89-92, 97-98, 109-110, 114, 116, 122, 124-127, 131, 133, 149
  in Lekhotla la Bafo songs 230, 235-237
  support by Lekhotla la Toka 27
missions (see Anglicans, PEMS, Roman Catholics)
Mochochonono 157, 238
Mofutsanyana, Edwin 23, 50, 177, 201-202
Mohai, Paulus 169
Mohales Hoek 239
Mohlabani 38
'Mohlokalebitso' 86
Mohoanyane, Samuel 124
Mohono, Raymond 17, 142, 145, 242
Mokema, Treaty of 124
Mokhehle, Ntsu 37-39, 202
Mokhethea, Pakalitha 36, 196-197, 201
Mokhithi, Hlakane 31-32, 242
Mokhotlong 180
Mokoaleli, Nyepe 125
Mokunutlung 6
Molapo, Jonathan 8, 81, 119
Molelekoa, Mikael 120
Moltoli, R.S. 145
Monathi, C. 121, 126
Monne, Solomon 67
Monyamane, Mokeka 36, 96, 194, 201
Moore Commission 38
Morija Institution 238, 242

Moroka, Chief 99, 240
Moshoeshoe I 112, 113, 119, 120, 125, 203, 205 -
  black unity 117-118
  Boers 121
  British Government 14, 39, 56, 58, 65, 67, 71-72, 81-83, 91, 98-100, 103-106, 110, 122, 124, 131, 141, 149, 154, 166, 177, 184, 186, 188, 198, 206, 239-240
  circumcision 114
  dagga 127
  education 145
  in Lekhotla la Bafo songs 217-219, 221-222, 224-225, 229-230, 232-235
  law of trade 139
  Lekhotla la Bafo 12-14, 18, 90
  matsema labour 10
  missionaries 16, 69-70, 82-83, 117, 142-143
  pitso 56-57, 61, 164-165, 238
  sons of Moshoeshoe 25, 27, 126, 169, 199
  Thaba Bosiu 112, 171, 205
Moshoeshoe, Halefetsane 124
Moshoeshoe, Sentle 124
'Mosotho' 86, 108, 240
Mosuane, Nephtaly 196, 201
'Mote, Keable 44, 168, 242
Motsoene, Chief 8-9, 26, 224
Motsoene, Joel 135
Motsoene, Letsie 135
Mulumba, Semaluka 173
Mzilikazi (Moselekatsi) 99

Naledi ea Lesotho 9, 46, 67, 92, 97, 238-239
Napier, George 71-72, 239
Natal 99, 108
National Council (see Basutoland National Council)
National Pitso 4, 56-57, 61, 66, 83, 100, 32, 238
National Treasury 34-35, 182-183
Native Courts 34
Nchee, Mr 180
'Neko, Joseph 126
'Neko, Roma 36, 122, 196-197, 201
Netherlands 176
Nigeria 185, 192
Non-European Federation of Trade Unions 23